Abby Stoddard

Necessary Risks

Professional Humanitarianism and Violence against Aid Workers

palgrave
macmillan

Abby Stoddard
Humanitarian Outcomes
New York, NY, USA

ISBN 978-3-030-26410-9 ISBN 978-3-030-26411-6 (eBook)
https://doi.org/10.1007/978-3-030-26411-6

This Palgrave Macmillan imprint is published by the registered company Springer Nature Switzerland AG.
The registered company address is: Gewerbestrasse 11, 6330 Cham, Switzerland

For my parents

Acknowledgments

Of all the people whose experience and expertise I have exploited in the writing of this book, I owe the biggest thanks to Adele Harmer, my research partner for 15 years, without whom Humanitarian Outcomes and its program on aid worker security would not have existed. Despite being a co-parent to the Aid Worker Security Database and equally responsible for every research finding and published product that sprang from it, Adele had both the good sense to decline to co-author this book and the good grace to give it her full blessing—as well as her invaluable input on drafts. The writing in these pages was also improved by my other Humanitarian Outcomes partner, Paul Harvey, who generously gave his time to review and comment on early drafts, and my wonderful editor, Dan Crissman. Sabrina Fondren, my dear friend and long-time graphic designer, provided the data visualizations.

The Aid Worker Security Database, which provides the evidence base for much of the analysis used in this book, was established with funding from the governments of Canada, Ireland, and the United States, and receives continued support from the Office of U.S. Foreign Disaster Assistance (OFDA/USAID), making our ongoing research program possible. I would especially like to thank Elissa Golberg and Shawn Bardwell for being early champions of the database initiative within their donor agencies. My former colleague Katherine Haver was an important contributor to our early aid worker security studies and played a critical role in producing our first published research on the subject, *Providing Aid in Insecure Environments: Trends in Policy and Operations,* as well as co-authoring several subsequent reports. The initial research program would not have come into being without the institutional support of the Overseas Development Institute's Humanitarian Policy Group and New York University's Center on International Cooperation. I am also grateful to Monica Czwarno for her attentive care and feeding of the database for the past three years as well as her sharp analysis.

Finally, to the current and former humanitarian practitioners who agreed to speak to me about their experiences and allowed me to share their stories and insights in this book: Elizabeth Jones,[1] Nitin Madhav, Milet Mendoza, Michael O'Neill, Robert Painter, Craig Spencer, Jen Taylor,[1] Jake Trees, and Mustafa Haj Yousef, I am overwhelmed by your generosity and grateful beyond words.

[1] Pseudonyms.

Contents

List of Figures

Prologue

When the phone rang before dawn on 19 January 1997, I had only been asleep for a few hours. Having spent a late Saturday night out with friends, I was in a poor state to field an urgent call from my boss's boss, the board president of the US chapter of Médecins du Monde ("Doctors of the World"), an international aid organization. Still groggy, I struggled to take in the sketchy information she had been given about an attack a few hours earlier on our medical team in Rwanda. There had been a raid and a shooting at the field office in Ruhengeri, and three of our four team members were dead. The fourth was gravely injured.

As we learned by increments in the hours and days that followed, a group of armed men had stormed the house that served as the team's office and living quarters early that evening. The four were already huddled in silence in a back room when the raid began, having earlier heard some gunfire from down the road. The group included the medical director, a seasoned international volunteer doctor named Manuel Madrazo Osuna, 42, and two other Spanish team members, Flors Sirera Fortuny, a nurse, and Luis Valtueña Gallego, a logistician, both in their early 30s. The youngest, and the sole American on the team, was a 28-year-old project administrator named Nitin Madhav, whom I had personally recruited for the project and deployed to the Rwanda field office just weeks earlier. Nitin was at the start of his career in international humanitarian work but already had some experience with volatile environments, such as in post-civil war Tajikistan. At Nitin's behest, the group had just been sitting down to discuss formal emergency evacuation procedures when they heard the shots.

From the dark of the back room, they heard the noise of people entering the house. Evidently, the unarmed guards at the gate had been scared off and the invaders had entered the compound easily. Figuring they were soon to be discovered, Luis went into the living room to confront the men. When the others followed a few seconds later, they saw four or five Hutu men dressed in fatigues and heavily armed. The apparent leader—wearing a purple t-shirt atop his camouflage pants and, even more incongruously, a hot pink beret—was pointing a pistol at Luis. He ordered all of the team members to sit, and, speaking in French, asked them questions about who they were and what they were doing in Rwanda. They explained that they were aid workers from Spain and America, working in Ruhengeri to support local health facilities with much-needed medicine and equipment. As he sat listening, the man in the beret slowly ran his finger around the muzzle of his gun, while his comrades went from room to room loading up black garbage bags with computers and any other valuables they could find. Having filled their bags and taken the passports of each team member, the men left the house.

For a minute, the four team members stood in the living room, absorbing the fact that they had just been robbed at gunpoint. They were beginning to settle their nerves and assess the losses when suddenly the man in the pink beret came back through the door, this time carrying an AK-47, and opened fire. Manuel was killed where he stood. Luis and Flores tried to run, but Flores was hit and crumpled to the floor at the end of the hallway. Luis made it to the kitchen before he was shot down, inches from the open back door.

Nitin had been standing near Manuel when the gunman returned, and as the shooting started, he dove to the floor. Manuel's body fell partially across Nitin's and Nitin saw his colleague's head explode. The sweep of bullets mercifully missed Nitin's head and vital organs but pulverized his left leg. He shut his eyes and waited for the next round of fire, expecting to die. Instead, the shooting stopped.

Left for dead in the house with his murdered colleagues, Nitin crawled across the room to radio for help, feeling a flash of rage when he was unable to figure out how to operate the Codan. Luis hadn't taught him yet; it was supposed to be a part of that day's emergency preparations meeting. As he tried to stand, Nitin looked down and saw that his left foot was still lying on the other side of the room. He grabbed for the nearest thing he could find—an orange decorative cloth from the wall—and tied it around his thigh as a tourniquet. Nitin's next thought, as he would later tell me, was to use the regular telephone to call me on my emergency number in New York, which he had memorized. The line was dead.

Eventually, one of the compound guards returned to the house. The man was distraught. Nitin remembers him repeating "I'm so sorry" and "You came to help us and look what happened" as he carried Nitin to the Land Rover. It was late and very dark as the guard drove him to the rural health center, struggling to pilot the unfamiliar vehicle through the winding dirt roads, while Nitin tried to instruct him on how to use the stick shift, every bump in the road causing agony. At the health center, a bare-bones facility supported and staffed by another international aid organization, Nitin was left to wait alone on a stainless steel exam table while someone went to fetch the nearest doctor. He knew just by looking at his leg that there was no saving it; most of it would need to be amputated. But he also knew that he risked bleeding out before a doctor could reach him. Nitin had some basic medical training, so he found some sterile gauze and began to pack it around his wounds to staunch the bleeding. Just before passing out, he took a bag of Ringer's lactate and started his own IV line. A short time later, he was awakened by a kind Cambodian volunteer doctor who had come to take his leg.

The Ruhengeri raid was the first armed attack on aid workers in Rwanda since agencies began pouring into the country to meet the much larger flood of Rwandan refugees returning from across the border of what was then Zaire (present-day Democratic Republic of Congo). Two years earlier, close to two million Rwandans, mostly of the majority Hutu ethnicity, had fled the country after the genocide of the Tutsi minority, fearing reprisals from Tutsi forces that had stopped the slaughter and taken control of the government. Now the refugees were returning, en masse and on foot, at the insistence of the Zairean authorities who had forcibly emptied the camps.

The mass return was rushed and chaotic, and there were reports of many *Interahamwe* fighters—the perpetrators of the genocide—slipping back into the country among the throngs of returnees. Nonetheless, international aid groups had not considered it to be an especially dangerous place for international organizations to work, even during the frenzied days at the height of the genocide when 800,000 Rwandans were slaughtered by their fellow countrymen. This was a conflict between Hutu and Tutsi; the international aid community was effectively irrelevant to the bloodshed.

A few weeks before the raid on our office, I had visited the country as part of the preparatory team sent to set up the project. Staff security was not expected to be an issue. The project we designed was supporting the already under-equipped health clinics in the Ruhengeri province to meet the increased demands occasioned by the mass return. My colleagues and I were under what was, in hindsight, the fatally misguided impression that the main challenge we would face in this project was the occasional over-bearing and uncooperative local official.

About 24 hours after the attack, I boarded a plane to Nairobi with Nitin's quietly composed but deeply shaken father and a supply of anti-retro-viral medications. Nitin had needed an emergency transfusion during the amputation in Rwanda, and there was a not insignificant chance that he was exposed to HIV from contaminated blood, so the drugs had hurriedly been procured for me to bring as prophylactic treatment. The US Embassy had arranged for Nitin's evacuation to Nairobi Hospital, which offered the best medical care in the region, but anti-HIV drugs were still hard to come by at the time. For the entire flight, I tried to suppress the appalling thought of my colleague surviving a massacre only to be infected by a deadly disease.

After we arrived in Nairobi, we spent a week at Nitin's bedside while doctors worked to ensure he was stable enough to travel back to the States. Nitin's attempts to cheer all of us up with his gallows humor were interspersed with moments of excruciating physical pain and grief for his lost coworkers. A tortuous flight home in a small medevac plane (a journey which he nevertheless managed to render funny in the recounting) delivered Nitin back home to Pittsburgh, where he began the hard work of recuperation and adapting to life with a prosthesis. Two decades later, Nitin continues to work in the international aid sector, most recently as Acting Deputy Assistant Administrator for Afghanistan Affairs at the United States Agency for International Development (USAID). He has traveled the world many times over, for both work and pleasure, taking award-worthy photographs from the remotest of places.[1]

The wound to Médecins du Monde was slower to heal; the Ruhengeri raid was a seismic shock that reverberates in the organization to this day. Although it was by no means the first time that aid workers were attacked, in the mid-1990s, such occurrences were still rare. Among most humanitarian non-governmental organizations (NGOs), an act of major violence

[1] Examples of Nitin Madhav's photography can be seen at https://nitinmadhav.com/

affecting staff members was treated almost as a freak occurrence, residing in the same mental category as traffic accidents or office fires. By the early 2000s, however, the attitudes of humanitarian practitioners toward security risk had shifted palpably, propelled by a spate of violent incidents where humanitarians were deliberately targeted—including the execution-style murder of six Red Cross workers in Chechnya in 1996, shot in their beds in the dormitory of a hospital under the universally known emblem signifying their neutrality. Many prominent voices in the field declared that the once-respected "humanitarian space" amid war was shrinking, and aid workers were being targeted like never before. A smaller group of contrarians dismissed the notion that anything had changed at all. Humanitarian aid work has always been dangerous, they argued, because wars and disasters are dangerous. In their view, the biggest difference was that aid organizations had become more risk-averse and timid, to the detriment of their mission.

The problem with both claims was that neither was based on real evidence. No one had a clear idea of how real or how large the aid worker insecurity problem was, or how much things had changed, because no one had ever measured it. When measurable evidence is lacking, cognitive biases can skew our perception. For example, availability bias makes our brains seize on the most recent and most vivid and frightening events, causing us to overestimate the risk and perceive new trends where they may not exist. Similarly, confirmation bias leads people to "see what they believe," cherry-picking the facts that fit with their preconceived notions, while underplaying or discounting new evidence to the contrary. Without a clear set of agreed-upon data to refer to, the debate was essentially meaningless.

It was in this ambiguous state of discourse that my colleague, Adele Harmer, and I began our research on aid worker security. Like many others in the sector at the time, we were interested in the seemingly growing overlap between military and humanitarian action in the post-9/11 landscape. On the one hand, the US military and its coalition allies were wading into aid activities as an element of counter-insurgency strategy, using "quick impact" aid projects designed to foster good will and win over local populations. At the same time, the mounting number of aid workers being killed in the field was beginning to resemble a military level of casualties. Up to that point, our research on humanitarian action at our respective institutions (mine at New York University and hers at the London-based Overseas Development Institute) was primarily qualitative, based on observing operations and interviewing policymakers and practitioners, from which we derived policy recommendations. But we recognized that before we could say anything sensible on the subject of aid worker attacks, we needed a clearer understanding of what was going on with the numbers.

As we began our research, we found only one prior attempt to quantify violence against aid workers worldwide. Dennis King, a United Nations consultant who would later move to the US Department of State, had compiled a list of every reported incident of violence that had affected humanitarian workers from 1997 to 2001, culled from news media and aid agency reports on the UN-sponsored humanitarian website "ReliefWeb." Using King's list as a starting point, we began building a database to record major attacks on civilian humanitarian operations by date, location, type of organization and staff affected, means of violence used, and the outcomes for victims. Because in those days aid organizations were so inconsistent in tracking their security incidents, we limited our entries to "major attacks," meaning only those in which an aid worker was killed, kidnapped, or seriously wounded (i.e., requiring medical attention). We reasoned that these more serious attacks were likelier to be reported by the aid agencies or picked up by the media, and thus we'd be able to capture them more comprehensively in our data search. We used our contacts in the sector to establish direct information channels with NGOs and UN agencies that could confirm or correct the information we found and provide us with additional reports that had not been made public. At the time, aid groups rarely shared their security incident reports, even with other organizations working in the same field locations. This was because there was no established means to do so and also because such events did not reflect well on the organizations affected; they feared it would harm their funding and recruitment prospects. To encourage information sharing, we assured our contacts that we would not publicize the names of victims or their agencies, whether or not these details had been publicly reported.

Our first piece of published research using these data was a 2006 report entitled *Providing Aid in Insecure Environments.*[2] We found that the absolute numbers of major attacks on aid workers worldwide had almost doubled between 1997 and 2005; the violence was indeed picking up. However, the number of aid workers in the field around the world had

[2] Stoddard, A., Harmer, A., & Haver, K. (2006). *Providing Aid in Insecure Environments: Trends in policy and operations.* London: Overseas Development Institute.

also risen, as aid agencies grew and proliferated with increased foreign aid contributions from governments. So, while the *absolute* numbers of violent incidents had soared, the *rate* of casualties per aid worker in the field had risen more modestly (a 22 percent increase).[3] We also found that most of the aid worker victims were deliberately targeted, as opposed to being caught up in the violence as collateral damage, and that nearly 80 percent of them were national staff as opposed to the international aid worker victims who tended to grab most of the headlines. The numbers allowed us to more clearly define the outlines of the problem.

This book is an attempt to distill the key findings and observations from over 15 years of applied research on the overlapping subjects of humanitarian action in war and operational security for aid workers. As someone who spends most of my time down in the weeds of quantitative analysis, writing this has been an opportunity to zoom out and reflect on the larger landscape of evidence to see the broader political and institutional dynamics at work. Specifically, I wanted to explore the questions of how and why aid workers are targeted in current conflicts, what implications this violence has for the civilians trapped in those conflicts, and what the international community can do about it.

The rising number and intensity of attacks against (unarmed, independent) humanitarian actors mirror the surges of civil conflict in a small number of countries. In addition to plundering their resources, non-state armed groups use aid organizations as proxy targets for the order they seek to overturn—whether it be their own country's government or the entirety of the Western-dominated nation-state system. The international legal instruments that were designed to protect a neutral humanitarian aid presence amid war are maladapted to many of the civil conflict settings where humanitarian aid workers operate today. The fact that aid workers (both local and international) are often conflated with the "enemy," combined with their relative softness and availability as targets, has resulted in casualty rates that seem more appropriate to uniformed armed forces than charitable organizations. More than a just a side effect of the proliferating and fragmenting civil conflicts of the past decade, attacks on civilian aid operations are themselves a symptom of state fragility and failure, directly related to instability and weak governance. Aid worker attacks, I have argued, can be as reliable an indicator of a downward spiraling government as any now

[3] Ibid.

used by economists and political scientists.[4] Additionally, the long-term upward trend in violence is also a function of the growth of the international humanitarian sector. Steeply increasing budgets since 2000, driven by governments' humanitarian contributions, have meant more aid operations in more dangerous places than in the past decades. Many agencies now face a growth-induced identity crisis, struggling to square their management responsibilities with the ethical demands of their mission to reach those most in need. As the evidence makes clear, success is scant on both counts: devastating attacks on aid workers continue, while critical needs of people in crisis go unmet.

How to establish and maintain secure access to provide aid to people in need in dangerous places is perhaps the most important question facing the global humanitarian sector today. The answer, I argue, is not to be found in some fictional past heyday of intrepid aid workers motivated purely by the "humanitarian spirit" and their own wits, free of institutional constraints like risk management protocols. Nor is it to further bunkerize, bureaucratize, and shrink from risk. In reality, the choice of "passion" versus "professionalism" in humanitarian action is a false one. The notion springs from an ethical divide in the international humanitarian sector in which both sides wrongly focus on the interests of the providers rather than the receivers of aid. Rejecting this flawed premise, I propose a reframed ethos of humanitarian professionalism, de-linked from organizational or political interests, emphasizing evidence-based standards and best practices. It is an ethical framework centered on the goal of achieving the best outcomes for the affected populations as opposed to the personal motivations of humanitarians or the corporate interests of the organizations that employ them.

The goal of this book is not to simply recapitulate the statistical analyses or summarize the literature on humanitarian operational security practice.[5] Rather, I attempt a broader examination of the underlying features of risk and incentives for humanitarians, institutions, and political actors that affect the ability of people in crisis to obtain vital assistance. Chapter 1 begins by sketching the outlines of the aid worker insecurity problem with

[4] Stoddard, A., Harmer, A., & Hughes, M. (2012). *Aid Worker Security Report 2012: Host states and their impact on security for humanitarian operations.* Humanitarian Outcomes.

[5] Various authors (2010). *Operational Security Management in Violent Environments (Revised Edition).* London: Humanitarian Practice Network, Overseas Development Institute.

the data evidence from the past two decades. Then, in the chapters that follow, I divide the discussion of causes and consequences of aid worker attacks into three main aspects of the phenomenon: environments, individuals, and institutions. Chapter 2 examines modern non-international conflicts and weakly governed spaces where the humanitarian sector increasingly finds itself working. Chapters 3 and 4 look at the interests and motives of the attackers, and the rational basis upon which they target humanitarians for violence, as well as the key points amid the shifting conflict dynamics where they are most likely to strike. In Chap. 5, I discuss how the institutions of humanitarian aid, in particular the large international non-governmental organizations (NGOs) have evolved in their perception and management of security risk. Woven throughout these chapters are the themes and subject areas in humanitarian operational security that my colleagues and I have researched in some depth, such as the surge in aid worker kidnappings, the complicated roles played by host governments (often parties to the conflict), the specific challenges facing national organizations and staff, and the new attitudes and practices of risk management in the sector. Chapter 6 concludes with an argument for the cultivation of a new ethics of professionalism in the sector that would more effectively meet needs of people in crisis while minimizing risks to those trying to help them. The book also includes personal stories and details of attacks that are absent from most research reports on the topic. It can be too easy to forget that every data point cited has a human being behind it—and often a personal tragedy—so I wanted this book to honor their sacrifice.

Though it was never a conscious decision, the attack on my organization in Rwanda back in 1997 undeniably had some influence over the subject I chose to spend the better part of my career researching. Over the years, I have repeatedly revisited my role in that aborted Ruhengeri health project trying to find mistakes—of omission or commission, of naiveté or carelessness—that may have facilitated the tragedy or the missed warning signs that could have averted it. With all the additional knowledge and technical expertise that the humanitarian sector has developed over the ensuing years on the principles of risk assessment, site security, and threat mapping, I like to believe that a similar attack would not have had such deadly results if we were setting up the project today. There is an element of randomness to violence, of course, and every successful attack is by definition a surprise to its victims. But understanding that there will always be variables beyond our control does not mean that we shouldn't attempt to control those that we can. And to the extent that there are facts to be known, we should endeavor to know them.

Notes on Definitions, Sources, and Methods

Most of the security incident data used in this book comes from the Aid Worker Security Database (AWSD), which is available online at www.aidworkersecurity.com, with some additional data on humanitarian presence and coverage from other research streams run by Humanitarian Outcomes, such as our 2013–2015 study on Secure Access in Volatile Environments (www.saveresearch.net), and our Global Database of Humanitarian Organizations (GDHO). As mentioned, the AWSD has a strict policy of anonymity for the published incident data, keeping agency and victim names confidential even if they have been widely reported in the media. The assurance of confidentiality has allowed us to build and maintain the trust of the agencies we rely on to provide information and verification of security incidents. For this book, however, I use specific cases to illustrate themes and issues, and for those I have obtained permission from the individuals and organizations named and have conducted additional interviews to ensure accuracy. I have also drawn from the notes of hundreds of interviews conducted over the course of my research. When found to be relevant for citing directly in the book, I returned to the source for permission and additional information or elaboration.

I have tried to avoid the jargon of my field and to minimize the use of acronyms wherever I could (a quixotic endeavor in the humanitarian sector). This required some choices in terms and definitions. For example, academics and journalists use many different terms for the organized groups that have taken up arms to advance political aims and that in many cases have been behind the violence against humanitarians. These groups are variously referred to as "non-state actors" (NSAs), "non-state armed groups" (NSAGs), "armed opposition groups" (AOGs), "militants," "rebel forces," and so on. Although in our past published research my colleagues and I have favored the acronym NSAGs,[6] in this book I mostly use "insurgents" as the catch-all term. To my view, the word insurgent conveys the fighter's non-state status and oppositional/revolutionary

[6] Stoddard, A., Harmer, A., & Czwarno, M. (2017). *Aid Worker Security Report 2017. Behind the Attacks: A look at the perpetrators of violence against aid workers.* Humanitarian Outcomes.

objectives in a more precise and value-neutral way than do words like "militant," "rebel," or "terrorist." As a general term, it is sufficiently broad to cover all types of conflict actors that seek to overturn an established order, from international jihadist organizations down to small local armed groups. Merriam Webster's definition of "insurgent" includes "a rebel not recognized as a belligerent," meaning not "belonging to or recognized as an organized military power protected by and subject to the laws of war." And this, I argue, is the salient point in understanding the threat they pose to the notion of neutral and protected humanitarian action.

When I refer to "humanitarian aid workers," "aid workers," or simply "humanitarians," I am referring to the personnel and volunteers of organized groups, organizations, and agencies that provide assistance to people in humanitarian crisis contexts. The assistance can be material (food, medicine, clean water) or technical (training, expertise), but it serves to meet people's basic needs. This is the same definition we use for inclusion in the Aid Worker Security Database, and it means that certain other types of voluntary agencies and personnel are excluded. For instance, the definition does not apply to human rights monitors, political advocacy groups, peacekeepers, or members of organizations with primarily religious missions.

Finally, I would like to add the caveat that this book is written from a particular perspective: that of the personnel and institutions of organized humanitarian assistance. By focusing specifically on violence against humanitarian operations within the broader conflict environment, I am conscious that the book may produce the erroneous impression that the attacks on aid workers are somehow worse or more numerous than the violence and atrocities suffered by the civilians they are trying to help. Of course, nothing could be further from the truth. I approach the topic with a similar view as it seems was held by Red Cross founder Henry Dunant. It begins by acknowledging that the larger problem of war is one that has always been with us and is not within the power of humanitarians to solve. Still, while we entreat and await political leaders to resolve the root causes of conflicts, we can be justly concerned with the security of those who work amid the fighting to reduce the amount of suffering and death that result.

References

Stoddard, A., Harmer, A., & Haver, K. (2006). *Providing Aid in Insecure Environments: Trends in Policy and Operations.* London: Overseas Development Institute.

Stoddard, A., Harmer, A., & Hughes, M. (2012). *Aid Worker Security Report 2012: Host States and Their Impact on Security for Humanitarian Operations.* Humanitarian Outcomes.

Stoddard, A., Harmer, A., & Czwarno, M. (2017). *Aid Worker Security Report 2017. Behind the Attacks: A Look at the Perpetrators of Violence Against Aid Workers.* Humanitarian Outcomes.

Various Authors. (2010). *Operational Security Management in Violent Environments* (Revised Edition). London: Humanitarian Practice Network, Overseas Development Institute.

CHAPTER 1

Tracking the Toll: Measuring Violence Against Aid Workers

Several years ago, I spoke to an official at the Office of US Foreign Disaster Assistance in Washington, DC, who mentioned he had two sons, both working in war zones overseas. One was a US Marine on a tour of duty in Iraq, and the other was a humanitarian aid worker posted in Darfur, Sudan. I asked him which one of his kids he was more worried about.

"The aid worker. No question," he answered.

For someone with no direct experience of humanitarian aid work, his answer may have come as a surprise. But his reasoning was sound: Even though his Marine Corps son would be in the thick of the hostilities as part of a fighting force, the military puts a high priority on "force protection" as part of their mission, making itself a much harder target. In contrast, the aid workers employed by non-governmental organizations (NGOs) working in conflict settings are not only unarmed, but also much more exposed, extended, and in smaller numbers, making them much more vulnerable to violence.

The concept of a "humanitarian aid worker" evokes certain images—young perhaps, idealistic, willing to live and work in rough conditions—but does not fall within most people's mental category of especially dangerous professions. Then again, there is a lot that the aid worker stereotype gets wrong. For example, contrary to media portrayals in the West, most people who work for international aid organizations never leave their home country. National staff members make up over 90 percent of the field personnel of the world's largest international agencies in

A. Stoddard, *Necessary Risks*,
https://doi.org/10.1007/978-3-030-26411-6_1

scores of crisis-affected countries. Moreover, for every international humanitarian agency responding to a crisis, there are many more national and local organizations that are working across the country to provide relief aid. Though smaller and often dependent on the international organizations for sub-grant funding, these national and local organizations are usually the first and frontline responders, and the lynchpins of the overall relief response. In 2017, the global humanitarian aid sector comprised an estimated 569,700 aid workers in the field. Of those, 529,000 were nationals of the country in which they worked.[1]

What may be more surprising than the size or makeup of this workforce, though, is the risk of violent injury and death as compared to other jobs we tend to consider more dangerous. Going by the available statistics on workplace deaths and injuries, there are two main categories that define society's most dangerous occupations. First, there are the jobs that run a high risk of serious accidents, such as high-altitude construction workers, deep-sea fishers, and long-haul truckers. According to the US Bureau of Labor Statistics data (2011–2017),[2] the most hazardous of these jobs is logging; loggers have the highest rate of fatal accidents of all at 136 job-related deaths per 100,000 workers. The second type of high-risk occupation includes people who engage directly with violence and deadly force, such as combat soldiers and law enforcement officers. The job-related fatality rates for these uniformed services are lower than those of loggers, fishers, and truck drivers, but still in the double digits. In 2017, the rate of US law enforcement officers killed by deliberate violence was 46, or a rate of about 6 officers killed per 100,000.[3] (When including job-related accidents, the fatality rate climbs to 14.6.[4]) In that same year, a total of 33 US military forces were killed in action, which amounted to a fatality rate of roughly 20 per 100,000 soldiers deployed in combat operations worldwide. In comparison, the global rate of humanitarian aid workers killed in

[1] Knox-Clarke, P. (2018). *The State of the Humanitarian System, 2018 Edition*. London: ALNAP/ODI, p. 17.

[2] US Department of Labor, Bureau of Labor Statistics, "Census of Fatal Occupational Injuries (CFOI) – Current and Revised Data." US Department of Labor, Bureau of Labor Statistics, 2018. Retrieved from: https://www.bls.gov/iif/oshcfoi1.htm#rates

[3] Data from FBI, "Law Enforcement Officers Killed and Assaulted, 2017" https://ucr.fbi.gov/leoka/2017/tables/table-1.xls, and Statista, "Number of full-time law enforcement officers in the United States from 2004 to 2017" (https://www.statista.com/statistics/191694/number-of-law-enforcement-officers-in-the-us/).

[4] Ibid.

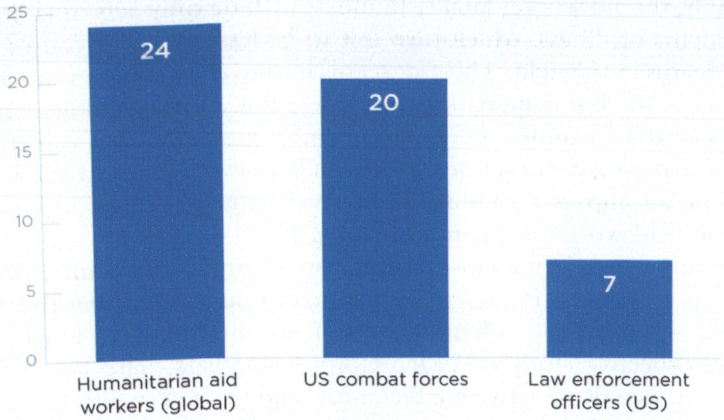

Fig. 1.1 Fatality rates (per 100,000) 2017. (Source: Aid Worker Security Database, www.aidworkersecurity.org; US Department of Defense, https://dod.defense.gov/News/Casualty-Status/; FBI, https://ucr.fbi.gov/leoka/2017/tables/table-1.xls, and Statista, https://www.statista.com/statistics/191694/number-of-law-enforcement-officers-in-the-us/)

deliberate attacks in 2017 was about 26 per 100,000. In other words, humanitarian aid workers, despite their civilian status, had a violent fatality rate exceeding that of uniformed police and active duty soldiers (Fig. 1.1).

In 2017, the Aid Worker Security Database (AWSD) recorded 139 humanitarian aid workers killed in deliberate attacks out of an estimated global population of 569,700 workers.[5] Compared to past years, 139 aid worker fatalities are somewhat higher than usual, but not the highest on record. In fact, in every year since 2013, the number of aid workers killed in deliberate attacks has exceeded 100. According to the AWSD, the years 2013–2018 saw an average of 127 aid workers killed, 120 wounded, and 104 kidnapped (not counting the kidnapping victims who were killed by their captors).

[5] The aid worker population estimate is calculated by compiling the staffing figures of the principal international and national humanitarian organizations, including national and international NGOs, the International Red Cross/Crescent Movement entities, and the United Nations humanitarian agencies. Missing data is systematically imputed by a formula for conditional mean imputation using average budget-staffing ratios.

Notably, the aid worker fatality numbers include only acts of violence—not accidents or illness, which turn out to be less prevalent causes of aid worker deaths in the field. This fact seems intuitively wrong, even to many who work in the humanitarian sector, where it is a longstanding article of faith, invoked in countless safety and security trainings, that vehicle accidents cause most aid worker deaths. If you have ever been in a 4 × 4 going too fast on an unpaved, muddy, or icy road (which is to say, if you have ever done field work for any international NGO), you will naturally find this easy to believe. Upon closer inspection, though, this claim cannot be substantiated. Attempting to trace its source, I discovered that the "most aid workers die in car accidents" assertion seems to have originated in a 1985 retrospective study of Peace Corps volunteers. The Peace Corps tends not to deploy to active conflict areas, and has a very different model of field work and living arrangements for its volunteers, who, in fact, do not meet the standard definition of humanitarian aid worker counted by the AWSD.[6] Furthermore, at least during the period covered by the study, the volunteers evidently relied on motorcycles, notoriously dangerous vehicles, as their primary means of local transportation.[7] A later, more relevant study published in the *British Medical Journal* found that most aid worker deaths from 1985 to 1998 "were due to intentional violence (guns or other weapons), many associated with banditry"[8] as opposed to car crashes. What makes the vehicle accident myth especially sticky is the frequency with which vehicle accidents happen. Nevertheless, although they may represent the majority of injuries and insurance claims for many organizations, they are not the cause of most aid worker deaths.

[6] From AWSD, "About the Data," https://aidworkersecurity.org/about: "'Aid workers' are defined as the employees and associated personnel of not-for-profit aid agencies (both national and international) that provide material and technical assistance in humanitarian relief contexts. This includes both emergency relief and multi-mandated (relief and development) organizations: NGOs, the International Movement of the Red Cross/Red Crescent, donor agencies and the UN agencies belonging to the Inter-Agency Standing Committee on Humanitarian Affairs (FAO, OCHA, UNDP, UNFPA, UNHCR, UNICEF, UN-Habitat, WFP and WHO) plus IOM and UNRWA. The aid worker definition includes various locally contracted staff (e.g., drivers, security guards, etc.), and does not include UN peacekeeping personnel, human rights workers, election monitors or purely political, religious, or advocacy organizations."

[7] Hargarten, S. (1985). Fatalities in the Peace Corps. JAMA, 254(10), 1326. doi:https://doi.org/10.1001/jama.1985.03360100076017

[8] Sheik, M. (2000). Deaths among humanitarian workers. BMJ, 321(7254), 166–168. doi:https://doi.org/10.1136/bmj.321.7254.166

What this means is that if you are a humanitarian aid worker in a field posting today, you are more likely to die from deliberate violence than any other job-related cause. Partly this is because you are also more likely to be working in a place where armed conflict is occurring. Unlike natural disasters, where the acute emergency phase is over in a matter of weeks and the recovery phase typically lasts 6–12 months, the humanitarian crises that are caused or exacerbated by ongoing civil conflict can drag on for many years. Some countries, such as Sudan, Afghanistan, and the Democratic Republic of the Congo, have hosted continuing international humanitarian response programs for more than a decade and a half. So, while natural disasters come and go, these oxymoronically termed "chronic emergencies" accrete in the international caseload year by year, and the result is an increasingly higher proportion of financial and human resources of the humanitarian sector being deployed to meet the needs of these highly vulnerable, long-suffering populations. The security risk to aid workers will naturally be higher in these environments, even if the fighting is low-level or sporadic, because they are exposed to ambient violence and potential targeting by insurgents.

Shootings

According to 20 years of data from the AWSD, most aid workers killed in the course of their work have died from gunshot wounds. It stands to reason that this means of violence would be the most common, given that in many contexts where aid programs operate small arms are abundant. Even in areas where there is no active armed conflict, the combination of the ubiquity of firearms and the attractive targets presented by aid workers and their resources can lead to armed robberies with sometimes fatal results. Aid workers have been fatally shot during carjackings and ambushes; in "drive-along" shootings, where gunmen on motorbikes pull alongside the victims' vehicles; in the course of armed robberies and raids; and in public places, assassination-style. In total, over all the years for which we have data, small arms fire accounted for half of all fatal incidents where the means of violence is known.

Aerial Bombardment

After shootings, the second most lethal means of violence affecting workers was aerial bombardment. This type of attack accounts for 16 percent of reported aid worker fatalities, and in many cases, is coded as "incidental" in the motive category, meaning that the aid worker victims were collateral damage and not intentionally targeted by the bombers. In a surprising number of these attacks, however (we estimate 49 percent from AWSD data), we cannot say the aid workers were injured or killed by accident. In Syria, where aerial bombing strikes cause the majority of aid worker casualties, aid workers are often targeted in "double tap" strikes, where the bombers return to shell the rescue teams trying to help injured civilians. Aid workers have also died when bombs were dropped on health facilities and aid convoys, despite their humanitarian status having been clearly marked and communicated to the warring parties.

Explosives

As is the case with aerial bombardment, the aid workers who died as a result of explosives were mostly working in places where there was active armed conflict. Thirteen percent of aid worker deaths were the result of bombs and improvised explosive devices (IEDs), including stationary, body-borne, and vehicle-borne explosives. Attacks against aid workers that involved explosives occurred in relatively smaller numbers compared to shootings or kidnappings (the database records nearly 200 during 1997–2018), but the high lethality of these types of weapons makes them the third largest contributor to the fatality numbers. In a separate category, landmine detonations affecting aid workers occur less frequently than they once did, but over the years have caused 4 percent of aid worker deaths.

Fatal Kidnappings

Kidnapping is the second most common means of violence used against aid workers, after shootings, but the majority of kidnapping incidents (86 percent according to AWSD data) are nonfatal, with the victims typically released after some period of negotiation. However, a small percentage of kidnapped victims do not survive, and these cases accounted for eight percent of aid worker fatalities between 1997 and 2018. They included incidents where the victim was killed in a kidnapping attempt, executed by the kidnappers after a period of captivity, and, in a very small number of cases, inadvertently killed during a rescue attempt.

Bodily Assault

Aid workers have also died as a result of attackers using non-firearm weapons, such as knives, machetes, or clubs, or no weapons at all. This category of violence is more often the cause of injury than of death, but it is still responsible for 5 percent of fatalities overall. Bodily assaults are seen most often in the contexts of street crime, detention by local authorities or armed groups, and in cases where fear or resentment among local community members and aid recipients provokes attacks against the aid providers. Such assaults have occurred during mob violence in refugee and internally displaced persons camps and, in recent years, against health workers in rural areas affected by Ebola.

Complex Attacks

A small number of aid worker deaths (4 percent) occurred as a result of complex attacks, so-called because the attackers use a combination of suicide bombers, vehicles, and teams of armed raiders to penetrate a compound or building and inflict maximum casualties. These are relatively sophisticated operations, requiring a considerable amount of planning and funding, as well as fighters willing to sacrifice themselves as suicide bombers. Complex attacks have occurred mainly in regions and conflicts involving jihadist elements, such as Afghanistan, Pakistan, and Somalia.

Rape and Violent Sexual Assault

Sexual violence is the most challenging category to capture and reflect accurately in the global data. In keeping with its being the most commonly underreported crime worldwide according to global statistics, incidents of rape and other sexual assault also appear artificially low in our dataset. At the time of this writing, the AWSD shows only 19 reports of attacks that have involved rape and other violent sexual assault, involving 29 victims, all reported as female. At the same time, we have anecdotal information of many other such incidents that have gone unreported, either because the victims decline to report it to their organizations, or because the organizations choose not to enter a report at the victim's request. The UN humanitarian agencies and some international NGOs have a policy not to report this type of attack (even if fully anonymized) unless given express permission by the victim. Additionally, some rapes can

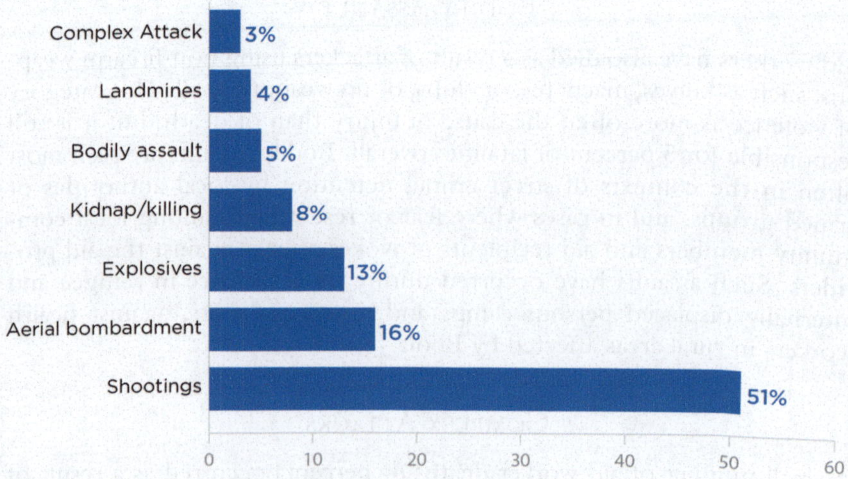

Fig. 1.2 Percent fatalities by means of violence, 1997–2018. (Source: Aid Worker Security Database, www.aidworkersecurity.org)

be obscured in the data when they are committed within the context of another attack. For instance, as we wrote in our 2019 report on the subject,

> It is not uncommon for female kidnap victims to experience repeated rape during their captivity, or for attackers to rape the residents of a compound in the course of a raid. Rapes also sometimes occur when aid workers are detained and removed from their vehicles at checkpoints. Often these additional assaults do not show up in the official incident reports.

The number of reports specifying sexual violence has risen over the past two decades, largely, we think, as a function of reporting and reporting systems in general improving (Fig. 1.2). Nevertheless, most humanitarian security experts I interviewed for that report seemed to agree that, in all likelihood, "More sexual assaults are unreported than reported."

Nonfatal Kidnappings

Kidnappings, the second most common form of violence affecting aid workers globally, can also take place within a broader context of attack, such as an ambush or a raid. Alternatively, they can occur as a specific, targeted abduction from the victim's home or in public. More than one aid worker has been snatched in the briefest window of opportunity, such as in the few short steps between their vehicle and the compound gate. Kidnappings warrant particular attention as a general category of attack and will be discussed at greater length at various points in this book, because of the outsized impact they have on an organization and its operations. While a kidnapping is ongoing, it is almost as if the entire organization is held hostage while staffers worry about and work to secure the safe release of their colleague. Our research for a 2012 study found that international staff members are more likely to be held for longer durations than national staff members, "illustrating the often steeper terms of ransoms or concessions demanded and the complexity of negotiations." A review of kidnapping reports going back to 1997 found further that "the average duration of international staffers' captivity was 53 days, as compared to 12 days for national staffers." Anecdotally, a prolonged kidnapping tends also to be the type of incident most feared by many aid workers, and when it occurs, it can have a pronounced chilling effect on the entire community of organizations working in that area.

Tactics/Contexts of Attacks

In terms of the contexts and locations of attacks, a few things come through clearly in the data that speak to the main operational hazards facing humanitarian personnel. Most notably, no matter the country or the type of conflict or crime conditions that prevail, the most dangerous place for aid workers is unquestionably on the road. The more than 1800 aid workers who were attacked while on the road make up the largest group of victims between 1997 and 2018, for whom the details are known—more than all other attack categories combined. The perpetrators will often use makeshift roadblocks or phony checkpoints to ambush and rob, kill, kidnap, or carjack humanitarians. Other tactics include remote control IED detonations and shootings from roadside or from other moving vehicles. Road attacks are a favored tactic by bandits and armed insurgent groups alike, as they can be executed without the need for heavy weaponry, complex planning, or significant manpower. In response, training in defensive driving techniques, blast-proof floor mats, and even fully armored ("thick skin") vehicles have become more common among humanitarian organizations working in high-risk areas, but these inputs are costly (with prices of just one armored vehicle running between

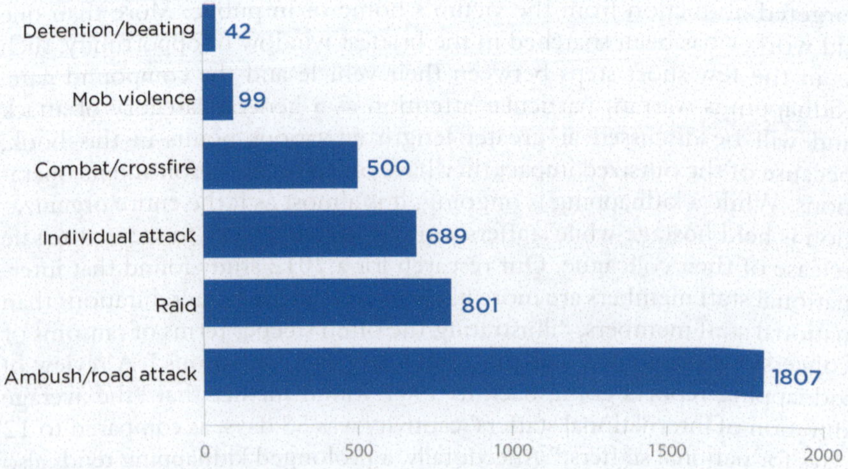

Fig. 1.3 Number of victims by tactic/context, 1997–2018. (Source: Aid Worker Security Database, www.aidworkersecurity.org)

$70,000 and $100,000) and mostly unaffordable for all but the largest international agencies (Fig. 1.3).

Types of Organizations and Staff Affected

The different types of humanitarian organizations have different operational profiles and risk thresholds. In our dataset, we define humanitarian aid workers as the employees of the United Nations humanitarian agencies, the International Red Cross and Red Crescent Movement, and local and international NGOs that provide assistance to people in humanitarian emergencies. The UN agencies are unique among these humanitarian actors in that they have a mandated responsibility to respond to humanitarian emergencies wherever they may occur throughout the world. However, they also tend not to be as "operational" as the other humanitarian actors, performing coordinating roles more often than direct provision of aid. NGOs, on the other hand, come in a wide range of sizes and capacities and necessarily pick and choose where they want to operate. Within the International Red Cross/Crescent Movement, the International Committee of the Red Cross (ICRC) is the international entity charged with responding in situations of armed conflict, whereas the International Federation of Red Cross and Red Crescent Societies (IFRC) is more often present in natural disasters, supporting the work of the national society staff and volunteers. The National Red Cross and Red Crescent Societies generally respond (in varying degrees, depending on the country in question) to whatever emergencies occur within their borders, natural and man-made, and most of them have a mixed portfolio of both crisis response and longer-term development (anti-poverty) programming. Of the over half a million humanitarian aid workers in the field, most of them are attached to NGOs. There are hundreds of such organizations, but only two dozen or so typically respond to conflict-related emergencies. Those organizations that are more present in extreme conflict environments unsurprisingly tend to have the highest attack rates.

In addition to types of organizations, the AWSD tracks the different types of humanitarian staff affected, recording their gender and whether they were international (expatriate) or national staff. Since the first year of recorded incident data, national staff members have constituted, on average, roughly 85 percent of aid worker victims, reflecting their far larger numbers in the field. Until recently, however, the data showed that internationals suffered higher rates of attack. As recently as 2015, the attack rate for internationals was 68 per 100,000 and for nationals it was 63.[9] There are a couple of possible explanations for this. One is that internationals have a higher value as targets for certain perpetrators such as armed insurgent groups, and the fact that they are often readily identified as foreigners makes them visible targets for common criminals as well. Another possibility is that major attacks on national staff are less likely to be formally reported and recorded or picked up by media sources in a way they could be captured in the data. It is likely that both explanations are at work here to some degree.

In 2018, however, the attack rates reached 71 per 100,000 for both nationals and internationals. In addition, fatality rates for national aid workers (24 per 100,000) have been and remain higher than those for internationals (7 per 100,000).[10] Climbing rates of violence for national aid workers is a reflection of intensifying violence meeting a shrinking international aid presence in hard-to-access areas in places like South Sudan and Syria. The trend points to something that many in the sector have long observed anecdotally, but which international organizations

[9] Stoddard, A., Harvey, P., Czwarno, M., & Breckenridge, M. (2019). Aid Worker Security Report 2019, Speakable: Addressing sexual violence and gender-based risk in humanitarian aid. *Humanitarian Outcomes*, June, p. 6.

[10] Ibid., p. 7.

were loath to admit: As operational environments become more insecure, international aid groups tighten their security and constrict their operational presence in ways that mainly benefit their international staff members, while potentially transferring the risk to national staff and national partner organizations.

High-Risk Contexts

In 15 years of analyzing incident data, one constant has been that the numbers of attacks each year have been concentrated in a small number (typically five or six) of countries that are experiencing active armed conflict. Whenever we saw sharp increases in the global incidence of violence, they were invariably driven by the handful of most violent contexts, which typically represent more than 60 percent of global incidents. Some of the countries within this top group have changed over the years, and some seem to rotate on and off, but Afghanistan and Somalia have been among them almost every year since the first year of recorded data. Syria has been on it since the beginning of its civil war. In 2018, the top five were South Sudan, Syria, the Democratic Republic of the Congo, Afghanistan, and the Central African Republic. Others that have spent time in this unfortunate club have included Iraq, Pakistan, Chad, and Yemen (Fig. 1.4).

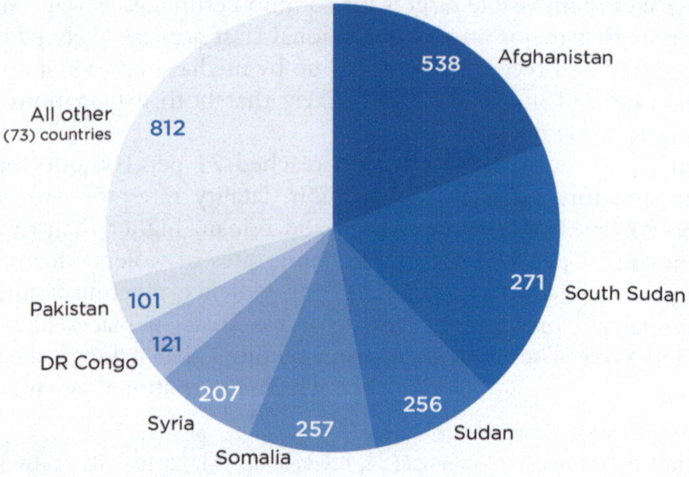

Fig. 1.4 Attacks by country, 1997–2018. (Source: Aid Worker Security Database, www.aidworkersecurity.org)

Over the years, my colleagues and I have repeatedly underscored this clustering of attacks in a minority of countries representing the most violent emergency environments. Violence against aid workers is not a global phenomenon, and aid workers everywhere are not equally imperiled. To the contrary, when we omit these extreme cases and look at data from all the other emergency contexts, we do not see the same upward trend in violence. Instead, the trend line is essentially flat, or in some years sloping downward, which we attribute to improved security awareness and management among humanitarian actors.

On the Uses and Misuses of Data

It is fair to ask what use the preceding figures have to humanitarian practitioners attempting to do their work and stay safe in dangerous environments. Does knowing these global totals, patterns, and trends offer them anything of practical value? The answer is no, at least not in terms of it translating into actionable information to guide their daily decisions at the field level. More useful data are increasingly being gathered by field-level security platforms established by NGO consortia and by offices of the UN Department of Safety and Security, which cooperate and share information and analysis with NGO humanitarian entities. These platforms are locally based and highly context-specific, which is what is needed for real-time decision-making. The information that they track necessarily goes beyond the major incidents of violence to include things like cases of threats and harassment against aid workers, local political events, military developments, and other potential indicators of changing security conditions. The information and analysis they share help the participating organizations to flesh-out their own situational analysis and better assess their risks.

While global numbers may not be helpful for day-to-day security management decisions, they enable international humanitarian organizations to compare the operational security needs of different contexts, which can help inform the allocation of scarce resources. In addition, a 50,000-foot view of the situation can afford some interesting perspectives on the interaction of aid worker violence with broader political trends and events. For instance, looking back over the years of AWSD data, we can say with certainty that the number and sophistication of attacks against aid workers in the Middle East and Central Africa increased after the US invasions of Afghanistan and Iraq and the doctrine of the "global war on terror." The data can also turn

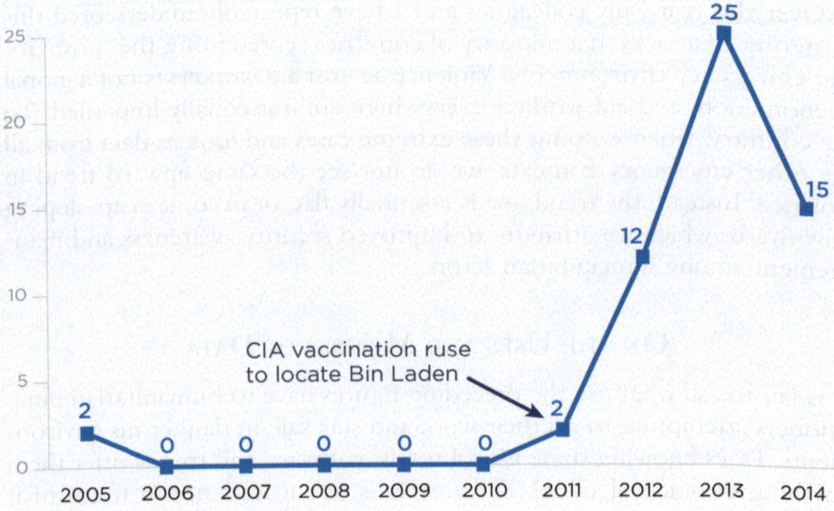

Fig. 1.5 Vaccinators attacked, 2002–14. (Source: Aid Worker Security Database, www.aidworkersecurity.org)

up evidence of specific cases where politics and military strategy have impacted humanitarians, such as the dramatic spike in attacks on vaccination teams and medical volunteers after the CIA used a vaccination campaign as a cover to locate and kill Osama Bin Laden in Pakistan (Fig. 1.5).

Some data can be more useful than others, but thoughtful analysis of relevant data should inform policymaking. This might seem to go without saying, but it is not a view shared by everyone. I once heard a fellow humanitarian researcher quip at a conference, in his characteristically politically incorrect manner, "Statistics are like bikinis. What they reveal is suggestive, what they hide is essential." Women's swimwear aside, it is natural and healthy for there to be some pushback to the "big data revolution" and its over-promises of predictive ability. In truth, all forms of data have the potential for misinterpretation or misuse. Nate Silver, in his book *The Signal and the Noise,* points out that, "The numbers have no way of speaking for themselves. We speak for them. We imbue them with meaning [and] may construe them in self-serving ways that are detached from their objective reality."[11] One such error is when we imagine that the data

[11] Silver, N. (2012). *The Signal and the Noise: Why So Many Predictions Fail-but Some Don't* (p. 9). Penguin Publishing Group, p. 9.

reveal something that isn't there. In other words, Silver writes, quoting MIT neuroscientist Tomaso Poggio, "finding patterns in random noise."[12] A popular website called *Spurious Correlations* illustrates this phenomenon with several graphs that show strikingly close correlations between random trends, such as "per capita cheese consumption" and the "number of people who died by becoming tangled in their bedsheets" (correlation: 94.71 percent ($r = 0.947091$)).[13]

If data can be wrongly interpreted, it can also create problems in certain circumstances if it is presented with no interpretation at all. The fire hose of information that confronts all of us today can have the paradoxical effect of diminishing our understanding of certain subjects and causing us to cling more tightly to our biases. Unable to absorb all available pieces of information, we rely on mental shortcuts and heuristics—what behavioral economists like Daniel Kahneman call "System 1" or "fast" thinking—and will either preferentially focus on that which validates our preexisting beliefs or latch on to the latest or most memorable piece of information we received. The latter phenomenon, known as availability bias, can be particularly deranging when it comes to considering risk. A common example is people's tendency to inflate the risk of airplane crashes and terrorist strikes in their perception to a degree far exceeding their probability of actually encountering them. My colleagues and I found ourselves falling prey to availability bias more than once in our qualitative research. When discussing an issue that we were in the midst of researching, each of us found ourselves giving more weight and credence to the last interview we had conducted or the last document we reviewed. Because what is latest tends to be loudest, by virtue of it being more prominent in our memory we had unconsciously decided that this piece of information was more telling, or that view more representative of the whole than it likely warranted. It was only after we went through a process of systemically reviewing and comparing the entirety of interview notes and other evidence that we were able to properly weight them in the analysis.

Availability bias effects can occur in the reading of security incident reports as well. This is one reason why my colleagues and I decided not to publish more frequent updates from the Aid Worker Security Database.

[12] Silver, N. (2012). *The Signal and the Noise: Why So Many Predictions Fail-but Some.* Penguin Publishing Group, p. 12.

[13] 15 Insane Things That Correlate With Each Other. (2019). Tylervigen.com. Retrieved 21 January 2019, from http://tylervigen.com/spurious-correlations

The data are available to the public for search and download in real time, but we only update our global trends overview once a year. Publicizing running tallies of security incidents can actually be a disservice to security analysis and decision-making. When we first began compiling incidents, we noticed that some UN security offices in the field would disseminate regular reports listing all manner of security incidents in a given area that had occurred over the past week or month, organized only by date and location. There was little or nothing in the way of analysis about what it all might signify or what the organizations operating in the area were supposed to do with the information. While the underlying intention was good, for it is critically important for humanitarian actors working in the same area to share incident information with each other, this type of reporting without an analytical framework of the context could easily distort perceptions of the security situation.

Some uses of data can also be actively harmful. In her book *Weapons of Math Destruction: How Big Data Increases Inequality and Threatens Democracy,* data scientist Cathy O'Neil gives multiple examples of how some mathematical models and computer algorithms "encoded human prejudice, misunderstanding, and bias into software systems that increasingly managed our lives."[14] The bias-infected models that came to pervade the insurance, financial, and educational sectors reinforced discrimination, reduced people's chances of escaping poverty, and exacerbated divisions in society. While warning us about the downsides and pitfalls of data and modeling, experts like Silver and O'Neil are certainly not suggesting dispensing with them altogether for the good of society. The way forward, according to Silver, is to adopt an attitude of "healthy skepticism" regarding what numbers can and cannot tell us, to be alert to spurious correlations and false patterns, and to become more comfortable with the notion of ranges of probability rather than binary predictions. O'Neil has called for data scientists to recognize their creations' potential for harm, and to adopt a kind of Hippocratic Oath to mitigate it. One key to this is making algorithms more transparent to allow for positive feedback loops to improve their accuracy and fairness.

It makes sense for humanitarians to adopt a do-no-harm approach to the gathering and use of data, and to heed the warnings not to over-interpret them or expect them to solve most problems. For example, using

[14] O'Neill, C. (2016). *Weapons of Math Destruction: How Big Data Increases Inequality and Threatens Democracy*. Crown.

data to gain a better understanding of past and present situations is one thing; using it to try to predict future events or to generalize "laws" on how things work is quite another. A large dose of humility is essential, especially when dealing with issues in social science where any one observed variable inevitably affects, and is affected by, countless other variables, both seen and unseen. In matters as layered and complex as armed conflict, it is hubris to expect that a dataset of this type could potentially determine causality or reveal anything more than a clearer picture of one element of the situation. At best, such observational data will be indicative of trends and potentially useful for generating hypotheses.

Understanding these limitations, however, it is important we do not succumb to quantophobia, a strain of which can be found in the humanitarian sector. When noted thinkers in the sector like Mark Duffield argue that data "is antagonistic to knowledge,"[15] or Fabrice Weissman warns that quantitative analyses can do little more than "produce ignorance,"[16] they are not discrediting the importance of empirical evidence so much as they are giving voice to a gathering fear that data and digital technology are ultimately and inexorably dehumanizing.[17] In Duffield's view, they are paving the way to a dystopian future dominated by artificial intelligence and increasingly precluding human agency. While I wholeheartedly agree that the answers to humanitarianism's biggest problems will not be found in numbers or lines of code, I would submit that such pessimistic predictions are unfounded. There is a necessary place in our sector for both quantitative and qualitative analysis, just as there is a place, in science and in human reasoning, for both inductive and deductive approaches. Statisticians have a saying, "All models are wrong, but some are useful."[18] The key idea here is that statistics and data models are *tools* that human beings can use to augment our limited capacity to retain and process infor-

[15] Duffield, M. (2019). *Post-Humanitarianism: Governing Precarity in the Digital World.* Wiley, p. 9.

[16] Neuman, M. and Weissman, F. (Eds.) (2016.) *Saving Lives and Staying Alive. Humanitarian Security in the Age of Risk Management. London:* Hurst, 2016.

[17] In an interview with the LA Times about his book, Mark Duffield observed "What's new—or late in the case of this stage of capitalism—is that the digital world no longer requires the direct intellectual mastery, management, or even the skilled labor it once relied upon. Humans are out of the loop, as it were." From Evans, B. (2019) "*The Death of Humanitarianism.*" *Los Angeles Review of Books.* Retrieved 21 March 2019, from https://lareviewofbooks.org/article/the-death-of-humanitarianism/#!

[18] Attributed to the statistician George E.P. Box, whose writings included various versions of the aphorism, beginning in 1976.

mation. It makes little sense to think in terms of a binary, either-or choice of knowledge versus data, instincts versus algorithms, or individual experience versus organizational systems. Optimal understanding and decision-making result when both sides are well developed. Blaming data for its misuses is like blaming the hammer for a carpenter's shoddy work and then insisting that he do the job without it.

As should be obvious, I would place myself among the more data-optimistic contingent of the humanitarian sector, where many practitioners and researchers are now endeavoring to make their work more evidence-based and data-driven, by bucking the remnants of a culture that at times has seemed to glorify an intrepid, seat-of-the-pants approach. It is the nature of emergencies, of course, that the time for planning and reflection is in short supply, and "quick-and-dirty" measurements are often necessary. Notwithstanding the exigencies and limitations of relief work, though, the importance of evidence and the need for better measurement for quality and accountability[19] have increasingly gained traction in a sector that in too many ways is data-poor. Typifying this new attitude, the president of the International Rescue Committee, David Miliband, has pledged that by 2020 his organization "will make all of its programs evidence-based or evidence-generating."[20]

A quote attributed to Galileo Galilei advises those engaged in scientific inquiry to "measure what is measurable and make measurable what is not so." Violence against aid workers is a measurable phenomenon, and reducing it is an important enough objective to bring all empirical resources to bear. Data are simply information. Information, when used appropriately, decreases uncertainty—and this can decrease risk.

References

Duffield, M. (2019). *Post-Humanitarianism: Governing Precarity in the Digital World*. Oxford: Wiley.

Emergency Capacity Building Project. (2007). *Good Enough Guide: Impact Measurement and Accountability in Emergencies*. Oxford: Oxfam GB.

[19] Examples include the Sphere Standards, a multi-agency collaboration to codify measurable performance standards, and tools such as the Emergency Capacity Building Project's *Good Enough Guide: Impact Measurement and Accountability in Emergencies*.

[20] Miliband, D. @DMiliband (2016, May 27) [Twitter post]. Retrieved from https://twitter.com/dmiliband/status/736251885359894529

Evans, B. (2019). "*The Death of Humanitarianism.*" *Los Angeles Review of Books.* Retrieved March 21, 2019, from https://lareviewofbooks.org/article/the-death-of-humanitarianism/#

Hargarten, S. (1985). Fatalities in the Peace Corps. *JAMA, 254*(10), 1326. https://doi.org/10.1001/jama.1985.03360100076017.

Humanitarian Outcomes, Aid Worker Security Database. *About the Data.* Retrieved from https://aidworkersecurity.org/about

Humanitarian Standards Partnership. sphere.org. Retrieved from https://www.spherestandards.org/humanitarian-standards/standards-partnership/

Knox-Clarke, P. (2018). *The State of the Humanitarian System* (2018th ed., p. 17). London: ALNAP/ODI.

Neuman, M., & Weissman, F. (Eds.). (2016). *Saving Lives and Staying Alive. Humanitarian Security in the Age of Risk Management.* London: Hurst.

O'Neill, C. (2016). *Weapons of Math Destruction: How Big Data Increases Inequality and Threatens Democracy.* New York: Crown.

Sheik, M. (2000). Deaths among Humanitarian Workers. *BMJ, 321*(7254), 166–168. https://doi.org/10.1136/bmj.321.7254.166.

Silver, N. (2012). *The Signal and the Noise: Why So Many Predictions Fail – But Some Don't.* New York: Penguin Publishing Group.

Statista. *Number of Full-Time Law Enforcement Officers in the United States from 2004 to 2017.* Retrieved from https://www.statista.com/statistics/191694/number-of-law-enforcement-officers-in-the-us/

Stoddard, A., Harvey, P., Czwarno, M., & Breckenridge, M. (2019). Aid Worker Security Report 2019, Speakable: Addressing Sexual Violence and Gender-Based Risk in Humanitarian Aid. *Humanitarian Outcomes*, June.

Tylervigen.com. (2019). *15 Insane Things That Correlate With Each Other.* Retrieved from http://tylervigen.com/spurious-correlations

U.S. Department of Labor, Bureau of Labor Statistics. *Census of Fatal Occupational Injuries (CFOI) – Current and Revised Data.* US Department of Labor, Bureau of Labor Statistics, 2018. Retrieved from https://www.bls.gov/iif/oshcfoi1.htm#rates

U.S. Federal Bureau of Investigation. *Law Enforcement Officers Killed and Assaulted, 2017.* Retrieved from https://ucr.fbi.gov/leoka/2017/tables/table-1.xls

CHAPTER 2

Today's Wars and the Challenge to Humanitarian Neutrality

A Bombing in Baghdad

On the morning of 19 August 2003, Robert Painter left the Canal Hotel, where he was stationed as the Baghdad Area Coordinator for the United Nations' humanitarian mission in Iraq, to attend some meetings in the nearby Green Zone. By the time he returned that afternoon, the first steps of a plan were already in motion that would culminate in the deadliest attack ever perpetrated against UN civilian personnel.

Bearing the tight haircut and self-contained demeanor of a 1950s TV detective, Painter was by then a 20-year veteran of humanitarian field operations. He hadn't originally set out to make his career in the UN. He and his wife signed up for a Peace Corps assignment in Ghana in the late 1980s, looking for a bit of adventure before settling down back in the United States. But the work clearly suited him. From Ghana, the UN recruited Painter for a humanitarian post in Sudan just as the southern part of the country was erupting in civil war. There he worked on Operation Lifeline Sudan (OLS), a precarious but successful collaboration of UN and non-governmental humanitarian agencies to deliver food and relief materials to the South. Among Painter's responsibilities was developing a training program for all OLS participants to contend with threats and hazards in the environment, an experience that launched him on a UN career track involving a string of challenging field missions in insecure settings. As he once quipped, his higher-ups at the UN had obviously worked out that "this frog is used to boiling water." After Sudan, Painter

A. Stoddard, *Necessary Risks*,
https://doi.org/10.1007/978-3-030-26411-6_2

was tapped for postings in conflict hotspots throughout the 1990s, including Sierra Leone, Tajikistan, and Yugoslavia. Along the way, he negotiated several hostage releases (including his own) and took a bullet escaping a rebel ambush in Sierra Leone that killed the driver of his vehicle, John Reignat,[1] at which point Painter took the wheel.

In the spring of 2003, the latest swerve of Painter's career track found him crossing the desert in a convoy that was transporting the first wave of UN humanitarian staff into Iraq in the wake of the US invasion. There was no doubt that Baghdad was a threat environment as extreme as any the UN had faced in the past. While never putting its stamp of approval on the US-led invasion, the UN nevertheless followed hot on the heels of the coalition forces and worked closely with them in the recovery and state-building efforts. The UN's association with the occupiers only intensified the enmity that many Iraqis felt toward the global organization, the resentment building over the years of the UN-run Oil for Food Program—the most visible element of the longstanding international sanctions regime against Iraq. The hostility was palpable from the beginning. On his first morning in Baghdad, Painter watched from the roof of the Canal Hotel as the soldiers guarding the perimeter collected the bodies of men they had killed during the night in thwarted attacks. The security situation worsened as summer arrived, with 15 attempted attacks on UN facilities in Baghdad, Mosul, and elsewhere, including incidents of small arms fire and rocket-propelled grenades.

UN security protocols for the heightened risk level in post-invasion Iraq required that the total number of staff deployed in the country be capped at no more than 200 "essential" personnel, but this limit proved difficult to enforce. The senior UN official Ramiro Lopes da Silva was nominally in charge of security as the "designated official" (or DO) and faced a great deal of pressure from the heads of the UN humanitarian agencies to increase their maximum staff allotments to meet the anticipated humanitarian needs in the wake of the invasion. Quite a few "non-essential" staff members made it in through the net this way, and once an exception was made for one agency, it became politically difficult for the DO to refuse the request of another. As a result, by August the number of UN staffers inside Iraq exceeded the personnel ceiling by at least 150

[1] The quick reaction and expertly executed defensive driving techniques of John Reignat are credited with saving the lives of others in the vehicle that day.

people.[2] A large proportion of them were based in Baghdad at the temporary UN headquarters in the Canal Hotel. Adding to the population inside the hotel by day were the staff of international humanitarian non-governmental organizations (NGOs) that had returned to the country to run their own humanitarian aid programs and who visited the hotel frequently, using it as a central meeting point and information hub.

When Painter returned to the hotel from the Green Zone on the afternoon of August 19, he noticed immediately that something was off. The usual perimeter security team of Iraqi uniformed guards tasked with stopping and searching all incoming construction vehicles for explosives, was absent. Their checkpoint was unmanned, leaving the left-side access road to the hotel wide open to traffic. Even more noticeable, a large US military rocket launcher that had been standing at the front left side of the hotel in front of the service access road had also disappeared. The presence of that rocket launcher and its crew at the front of the hotel had been a point of contention among the UN's senior management team for some time. The humanitarian agency heads hated the optics it created, and wanted it removed. Keenly aware of the negative political feelings toward the UN already held by many Iraqis, they were trying desperately to carve out some perceptual distance between their humanitarian mission to provide neutral and impartial aid to civilians, and the military-backed political project that was the occupation and rebuilding of the Iraqi state. The official reports that would later be published on the events that day did not identify the source of the decision to remove the rocket launcher, but in Robert Painter's mind there is no doubt that its presence would have deterred the shattering violence that transpired soon after.

Once he reached the hotel, Painter hastened to the office of the UN international security officer in charge of the inspection team to report the missing men. He was surprised by the officer's lack of urgency in his response, which was something to the effect of "I'll look into that once I finish my tea." Painter promptly went over the fellow's head to inform the senior UN Security Officer of the situation. The senior officer picked up his phone, called the other officer, and instructed him to rectify the situation immediately. Satisfied that his concerns had been addressed, Painter walked away.

[2] Ahtisaari, M. et al. (2003). *Report of the Independent Panel on the Safety and Security of UN Personnel in Iraq*. United Nations.

An hour or so later Painter was in his office, located on the left side of the hotel's ground floor, with a new situation to worry about. A field team that was expected to return from an exploratory mission to Anbar had lost radio contact with HQ earlier that day and now was worryingly late getting back. At 4:20 pm, to his relief, the team suddenly appeared at his office door, safe and in good spirits. The men explained that their radio had died, but that it had been a highly productive mission. They were eager to brief him, they said, but they were hungry, and asked if he wouldn't mind meeting in the hotel cafeteria instead. Painter agreed to meet them there as soon as he finished up a bit of work in his office. A little while later, he made his way across the lobby to the cafeteria and, spotted the table where his team was sitting. At that moment, the building was rocked by a tremendous blast.

Even for someone like Painter who had firsthand experience with explosions, the massive truck bomb that detonated just outside the hotel was unlike anything he had ever witnessed. Cobbled together from 1000 kg of explosives raided from old Iraqi munitions, the colossal IED demolished the left front corner of the building, leaving a crater 11 feet wide and 5 feet deep. Shrapnel radiated from the blast with such force that it penetrated walls and perforated furniture and computer monitors. The 10-foot window panes in the cafeteria shot out of their frames, each in one undulating piece, with blast film holding the shards together in massive blankets of glass that flew into the room and enveloped the people sitting at adjacent tables. The shock wave pushed a jumble of trays and tables and chairs and people to the opposite end of the room. Ears ringing, and barely able to see through the dust cloud, the first instinct of Painter and his colleagues was to herd people into the kitchen and barricade the door. They feared a follow-up attack. In so-called "complex attacks," a suicide bombing outside the building is often phase one, to blast through the perimeter and gain entry for a team of gunmen to conduct an armed assault on survivors inside the building. Subsequent years would see such complex attacks launched against humanitarian facilities in Afghanistan, Pakistan, and elsewhere, but it was not the case in the Canal Hotel that day. The bomb had done its full work.

The aftermath was predictably horrific. Emerging into the daylight of the parking lot, Painter saw on the ground the severed head of a Canadian colleague, the Programme Coordinator for UNICEF in Iraq, who had just finished parking his car when the bomb was detonated. An Iraqi UN employee was walking aimlessly about and talking to himself, a piece of rebar jutting from his forehead. As surviving staff members gradually began to assemble at their pre-assigned emergency muster points, each person's trauma manifested in starkly different ways.

"You had some people just silent, stone-faced, frozen. You couldn't get them to talk," Painter told me in an interview. "With others, it was like they were having a seizure; their bodies shaking uncontrollably, falling on the ground."

US military personnel arrived on the scene quickly and began to triage the wounded. Painter, who was bleeding heavily from his leg, was tagged to go with the first group to get medical treatment, and he used the opportunity to contact his family in the States, who had been watching, horrified, as scenes of the bomb site started appearing on cable TV news. As soon as the medics had patched him up, he returned to join in the search for wounded colleagues. He and a young Polish UN humanitarian officer, Wojtek Wilk, were among the first to talk to Special Representative Sergio Vieira de Mello, the head of the UN mission, as he lay buried in the rubble where the building had collapsed upon him. Vieira de Mello, 55, a handsome and charismatic career diplomat, was a rising star in the UN and considered a strong candidate to be the next Secretary-General. Described by Samantha Power as "a cross between James Bond and Bobby Kennedy,"[3] Vieira de Mello had already completed a succession of difficult diplomatic missions for the UN in war zones, including helping to negotiate East Timorese independence from Indonesia. Having initially declined the Iraq mission role, he reportedly changed his mind after being lobbied personally not only by Secretary-General Kofi Annan, but also by US President George W. Bush and his National Security Adviser, Condoleeza Rice.[4]

Vieira de Mello's office had been on the front left side of the hotel, one floor above the access road where the truck bomber pulled up. A large portion of those killed in the bombing were members of his staff, along with others working in that section of the building. As US soldiers worked to extricate him, Vieira de Mello called up to Painter and Wilk, telling them to leave him and go help others. It was hours before he died, still encaged in concrete. His last words were reported to be, "Don't let them pull the mission out."

[3] Power, S. (2008). The Envoy: The United Nations' doomed mission to Iraq. *The New Yorker*, January 27, 2008.

[4] Traub, J. (2006). *The best intentions: Kofi Annan and the UN in the era of American world power* (1st ed.). New York: Farrar, Straus and Giroux.

In all, 22 UN and NGO workers died that day and over 150 were wounded, many severely, in what remains the most lethal attack on the global organization. That night, when Robert Painter finally arrived back at his new lodgings, he went to the bathroom and filled the tub with water. He climbed in and immediately fell asleep, waking up there the next day.

In the months that followed, the UN Secretary-General convened an independent panel to review the facts surrounding the attack and propose recommendations for "preventing further such tragedies in high-risk missions, or at least limiting their effects."[5] The panel, led by former Finnish President Martti Ahtisaari, found that "the UN security management system failed,"[6] highlighting examples of "sloppy" implementation of regulations and poor compliance with rules. "Adequate security arrangements may not have been able to prevent the attack against the Canal Hotel perimeter," it concluded, "but would certainly have minimized the vulnerability of the staff and premises and reduced the number of casualties caused by the attack."[7]

By emphasizing the management and procedural aspects of security, the Ahtisaari report paved the way for a badly needed restructuring of UN security management, which had grown into an incoherent jumble of separate and independent services operating at UN facilities around the world and within each agency. The UN Security Coordination Office (UNSECOORD), where Painter worked before coming to Baghdad, had been an earlier attempt to bring some semblance of coherence to the system across the organization, but with a staff of only a half-dozen officers, it could barely keep up with the information flow coming in from the field, let alone provide organization-wide analysis and direction. Before the bombing, there had been other evaluations of the problem by external teams of security experts, and their recommendations were consistent with those the Ahtisaari report would later put forward.

But windows of opportunity for change can sometimes only be forced open by major crises. The bombing of the Canal Hotel, now commemorated every August 19 as World Humanitarian Day, sparked major institutional change at the UN in terms of securing staff, and in particular for humanitarian missions, which typically require exposure to risky conditions.

[5] Ahtisaari, M. et al. (2003). *Report of the Independent Panel on the Safety and Security of UN Personnel in Iraq*. United Nations, p. 3.

[6] Ibid.

[7] Ibid.

Later that year, the UN Secretariat established a new Department of Safety and Security (UNDSS), replacing UNSECOORD and the separate security services, under the leadership of a newly created Under-Secretary-General position. The institutional changes ushered in a new way of thinking about managing risks to humanitarian programming and a more professional approach to security, which had also begun to take root among several of the larger humanitarian NGOs.

With its practical, mitigation-focused recommendations, the Ahtisaari report did not spend a lot of time considering the larger political issues of why the UN was targeted and what may have made its humanitarian mission in Iraq especially perilous. In fairness, it wasn't tasked to. As shocking and tragic events often do, the Canal Hotel bombing spurred a demand for *actionable* proposals to address concrete, understandable problems, and thus restore a collective sense of control. And in that sense, readers of the report's recommendations could be forgiven for concluding that the crux of the problem lay with things like disorganized staff lists, inadequate application of blast film on windows, and lax compliance with security regulations. While all these things may have been true—and assuredly contributed to the casualty count—they are relatively tiny pieces of the risk equation. Considering the larger picture, three factors stand out as having put the UN humanitarian mission in particular danger at that place and time:

1. The civil conflict environment, in which the non-state armed groups fighting the government and the occupying forces equates the humanitarian mission with its enemies
2. The strategic calculus of the attackers, which has a great deal to do with the proximity and accessibility of the target as well as the potency and visibility of the message they will send by attacking it
3. A tipping point moment in the course of the conflict when the dynamics are in sudden flux

In terms of the first factor, for many Iraqis in the growing and fracturing insurgency, the UN was so closely linked to the Western occupying powers and the state-building project in Iraq they may as well have been one and the same mission. Not fully grasping this fact led some in the UN to over-rely on the protective power of the UN flag and their agencies' formal mandates as humanitarian actors. The associative risk factor is especially salient for the UN humanitarian agencies, but, as we will see, also affects NGOs and even the Red Cross Movement in modern conflicts. Indeed, the conflict in Iraq was emblematic of a particular type of modern warfare, a protracted civil conflict involving the intervention of external states and non-state actors, which has proven to be the backdrop of more than 80 percent of violence committed against humanitarians. These internationalized internal conflicts are very different from the type of war for which international humanitarian law and humanitarian action were originally conceived.

The second major contributor to the risk the UN mission faced at that time was the softness of the target that the UN headquarters presented in the context of its environment. Compared with the much heavier security protection that surrounded the other nearby targets (including the Green Zone and other U.S. military assets), the relatively lightly defended hotel headquarters offered the accessibility, vulnerability, and potential impact that meet the main targeting criteria of a force engaged in asymmetric warfare. In a chaotic environment awash with unsecured weaponry and explosives, the attackers—later revealed as Al-Qaeda in Iraq, a precursor to today's Islamic State—were afforded both the opportunity and the necessary resources to pull it off.

Finally, the attack took place in a particularly hazardous moment in the post-invasion political environment. In all conflicts, there are peaks and valleys of intensity, periods of stasis, and periods of flux in the power dynamics. During stasis periods, humanitarian actors can learn the lay of the land and develop relationships with the main players, which add to their security. Volatility begets unpredictability, which begets insecurity. Therefore, the risk is highest at the flux points, when power is contested and the current order is being challenged or overturned, and also when humanitarian actors are newly arrived on the scene.

Our research has found that these same three factors apply to a great many of the attacks on humanitarian entities over the past two decades. In the following chapters, we will explore these other contributors to violence against humanitarians, but first we must look back on how the modern humanitarian sector came to be, in what was then a very different context of war.

The Decentralization of Warfare and the Problem of "Neutrality"

When one takes the (very) long view, the world has become progressively less warlike and more humane throughout history. In his book *The Better Angels of Our Nature,* Steven Pinker presents data evidence that wars (and violence in general) have dramatically diminished since the time of the earliest known human societies.[8] But of course, it is the nature of long-term trends that they span many peaks and valleys, and today, in the current snapshot of time since the end of the Cold War, we find ourselves on the sharp end of a spike in violent civil conflicts. What's more, these types of conflicts pose particular challenges and dangers for humanitarian aid workers who find themselves appealing to normative protections from a century-and-a-half ago, designed for an entirely different kind of warfare.

Wars between nation-states are now rare, but civil conflicts and organized violence occurring *within* sovereign nations have increased, as non-state armed groups have increasingly proliferated, fragmented, and armed up. According to a comprehensive global database maintained by the Uppsala Conflict Data Program (UCDP), in the period immediately following World War II there were slightly more than two interstate wars, on average, occurring or ongoing per year. Today that average has fallen to 0.7.[9] However, during the same stretch of time, major internal conflicts (civil wars and smaller-scale violent conflicts), including those marked by international intervention, have increased by 40 percent, reaching an average of 39 such conflicts waged per year. The especially fractured nature of these internal conflicts stood out in a 2018 report by the ICRC, which noted that almost half of the conflicts occurring today are being fought by more than two parties and 22 percent of them involve as many as ten or more distinct fighting forces (Fig. 2.1).[10]

Armed conflicts worthy of the name (UCDP sets the threshold at "25 battle-related deaths per year"),[11] all have separate and distinct causes and characters, but at a very basic level we can divide them into two broad categories throughout history: wars of equilibrium and wars of entropy. The first category includes conflicts fought between generally equivalent

[8] Pinker, S. (2011). *The better angels of our nature: Why violence has declined.* New York: Viking.

[9] Allansson, Marie, Erik Melander & Lotta Themnér (2017) Organized violence, 1989–2016. Journal of Peace Research 54(4); Gleditsch, Nils Petter, Peter Wallensteen, Mikael Eriksson, Margareta Sollenberg, and Håvard Strand (2002) Armed Conflict 1946–2001: A New Dataset. Journal of Peace Research 39(5). (Website: www.ucdp.uu.se).

[10] Terry, F. and B. McQuinn (2018). The Roots of Restraint in War. Geneva, International Committee of the Red Cross.

[11] UCDP/PRIO Armed Conflict Dataset Codebook, Version 17.2, Uppsala Conflict Data Program (UCDP), www.ucdp.uu.se, International Peace Research Institute, Oslo (PRIO), www.prio.no.

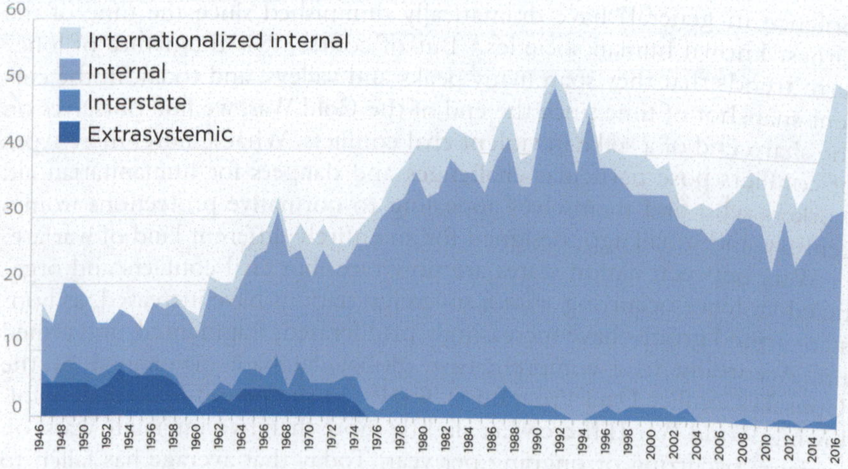

Fig. 2.1 Conflict types, post-World War II. (Source: UCDP/PRIO Armed Conflict Dataset https://www.prio.org/Data/Armed-Conflict/UCDP-PRIO/)

entities (such as empires, nations, city-states, and so on) over status, territory, or treasure. Such wars are prosecuted within a commonly understood context and parameters, and they result in a rebalancing of power positions within the system, rather than a complete systemic disruption. Examples include the Hundred Years War, the Napoleonic wars, World Wars I and II, and the US-Soviet rivalry with its proxy wars during the Cold War era.

Wars of entropy, on the other hand, are fought between non-equivalent entities, resulting either from a breakdown of an old global order or from an internal challenge to the current political system. Revolutions, civil wars, and the fractious conflicts that took place after the fall of the Roman and Ottoman Empires come under this category, as does the ethnic strife that erupted amid the dissolution of the Soviet bloc and the global jihadist movements of Al Qaeda and the so-called Islamic State (IS). Such conflicts preoccupy state actors and drain their coffers, while subjecting civilians to years of insecurity and deprivation. This is the predominant character of warfare at the beginning of the twenty-first century: Conflicts in Afghanistan, the Democratic Republic of Congo, Iraq, and Somalia ushered in the new century, and the list has since expanded to include South Sudan, Syria, and Yemen.

Perhaps the biggest contributor to the current surge of entropic wars has been the democratization of war-fighting ability. Just as computer and information technology, once the exclusive realm of governments is now in the hands of common individuals, the capacity for major organized violence has also decentralized. The illicit trade of small arms, ammunition, and light weapons across the world represents a "multi-billion-dollar business"[12] and helps fuel hundreds of armed conflicts each year. Non-state armed actors enjoy ready access to arms and explosives, as well as near total impunity across many areas outside the control of state governments. These things combined with the advancements in telecommunications and social media have enabled even small groups to pose a meaningful threat to fragile states and to regional stability. For example, Boko Haram, a violent jihadist insurgency operating in northern Nigeria and adjacent countries, has only around 6000 fighters, yet it has stymied the Nigerian armed forces, one of the largest militaries on the continent, while carrying out a campaign of massacres, mass kidnappings, and other major attacks that have destabilized the country socially and economically.[13] In the tribal areas of the Pakistan-Afghanistan border, a widespread cottage industry of explosives manufacturing operated largely unimpeded for years, supplying bombs to militant groups such as the Afghanistan Taliban, the Haqqani Network, and the Tarik-e-Taliban (Pakistani Taliban). Even the Lord's Resistance Army, a bizarre Christian terrorist personality cult of just a few hundred fighters at last estimate, remains a non-trivial security concern to the Ugandan government and the African Union.[14]

In addition to being democratized, civil war-fighting has gone global. Non-state actors like IS and Al Qaeda have effectively taken guerrilla insurgency to scale, waging and fomenting jihadist uprisings with a transnational operational presence and worldwide propaganda and recruitment campaigns. These groups nurture ambitions of overturning the current nation-state system and replacing it with a worldwide Islamic caliphate; it

[12] United Nations, Meetings Coverage and Press Releases, Human *Cost of Illicit Flow of Small Arms, Light Weapons Stressed in Security Council Debate,* 13 May 2015. https://www.un.org/press/en/2015/sc11889.doc.htm

[13] CIA Factbook, Retrieved from https://www.cia.gov/library/publications/the-world-factbook/geos/ni.html (November 2018).

[14] UN envoy Abou Moussa is quoted as saying "…no matter how little the LRA may be, it still constitutes a danger [as] they continue to attack and create havoc." Urquhart, C. (2012) Joseph Kony: African Union brigade to hunt down LRA leader, *The Guardian*. guardian.co.uk, 24 March 2012.

is not hyperbole for some analysts to describe their version of jihad as a "global insurgency."[15] It is not their ability to mount terrorist attacks on domestic targets in Western countries that distinguishes these international terrorist groups from others throughout history, such as the nineteenth century anarchists. By the measure of death and destruction they cause, such attacks pose a relatively insignificant threat. Rather, it is the capacity of these groups to deploy foreign fighters to civil conflicts in multiple countries that marks the essential difference from asymmetric conflicts of the past. For while there is nothing new about insurgencies, non-state armed groups, or criminal organizations that operate within and across borders, what *is* new is the extent of harm they can inflict on local populations and the stability of the global order by waging multifront warfare across fragile states.[16]

What implications does the current spate of entropic wars have for the Dunantist vision of neutral and inviolate humanitarian aid providers operating in war zones? It is plain, though rarely acknowledged, that the international legal instruments stipulating a protected status for humanitarian action amid war ("*inter-arma caritas*") are an uneasy fit to the sort of conflicts now riddling the globe.

The body of international humanitarian law (IHL) enshrined in the Geneva Conventions was born of nineteenth century European interstate warfare and thus applies primarily to cases of sovereign state entities fighting each other. That is not to say that non-international conflicts are completely ignored in IHL. When humanitarian advocates argue that warring parties are obliged to allow for and protect humanitarian action in *all* conflicts, they will generally invoke the Geneva Conventions' Common Article 3 and the 1977 Additional Protocol II, both of which attempt to grapple with the civil conflict phenomenon. Common Article 3 (i.e., common across all four of the 1949 Geneva Conventions) defines non-international conflicts as "occurring in the territory of one of the High

[15] Kilcullen, D. (2009). *The Accidental Guerilla: Fighting Small Wars in the Midst of a Big One*. Oxford University Press.

[16] "Whether the bulldozers and social media savvy of ISIL, the missiles and electronic warfare of Hezbollah, or the high-altitude air defense of the Ukrainian rebels, all these forces have deployed capabilities traditionally associated with nation-states. The hybrid warriors have merged these capabilities with traditional insurgent tactics in their fight against nation-state forces." Ollivant, D. (2016). "The rise of the Hybrid Warriors: From Ukraine to the Middle East." warontherocks.com. Retrieved from https://warontherocks.com/2016/03/the-rise-of-the-hybrid-warriors-from-ukraine-to-the-middle-east/

Contracting parties" (states) and stipulates that the belligerents are bound to refrain from the same violations against humanity that are proscribed in international wars, including torture, summary executions, and hostage-taking. It also stipulates that "the wounded and sick shall be collected and cared for." The language is weaker on the obligation of warring parties to allow and protect an organized humanitarian response, saying only that "An impartial humanitarian body, such as the International Committee of the Red Cross, may offer its services to the Parties to the conflict." In 1977, states adopted Additional Protocol II as an amendment to the Geneva Conventions, stipulating that medical personnel and facilities are to be protected and obliging the warring parties to allow the activities of relief organizations "such as Red Cross."[17] However, the protocol also contains language that provides state parties with a yawning loophole to this obligation: "Nothing in this Protocol shall be invoked for the purpose of affecting the sovereignty of a State or the responsibility of the government, by all legitimate means, to maintain or re-establish law and order in the State or to defend the national unity and territorial integrity of the State [or] as a justification for intervening…in the armed conflict."[18] Thus, when a war occurs between a state and a non-state armed group within its borders, it is fundamentally up to the state to decide whether and where to allow humanitarian groups to operate, and even whether to call their dealings with the non-state group an "armed conflict," in the legal sense, at all.

Our basic moral intuition that the rules of humanity should apply equally to non-international conflicts as they do to international ones often obscures this weakness in international humanitarian law.[19] The belligerent state in question has little incentive to treat the non-state opposition force as a co-equal entity, not to mention that the non-state group may have no intention of honoring the Geneva Conventions. To shore up this shaky foundation of treaty law, the ICRC and other humanitarian actors have argued that protected humanitarian access in non-international conflicts is also enshrined in international customary law that is founded upon widespread and repeated state practices, statements, and behaviors

[17] International Committee of the Red Cross (ICRC), *Protocol Additional to the Geneva Conventions of 12 August 1949, and relating to the Protection of Victims of Non-International Armed Conflicts (Protocol II)*, 8 June 1977. Commentary 4872.

[18] Ibid, Preamble.

[19] Harmer, A., Stoddard, A. Sarazen, A. (2018). *Humanitarian access in armed conflict: A need for new principles?* Humanitarian Outcomes, December.

that invoke the spirit of the legal principle in question. Many governments include provisions for allowing the free passage of relief supplies in their own military manuals, for example, and have voiced this principle in numerous public statements. On this basis, the ICRC has codified a rule of customary international law it calls "Rule 55: Access for Humanitarian Relief to Civilians in Need," which states that: "The parties to the conflict must allow and facilitate rapid and unimpeded passage of humanitarian relief for civilians in need, which is impartial in character and conducted without any adverse distinction, subject to their right of control."[20] Note that the last clause, "subject to their right of control," effectively negates the intent of the rule in many non-international conflicts. It means that a government engaged in a civil war could refuse to allow humanitarian relief to be provided in parts of its country that are controlled by opposition forces. Just such a situation in Syria prompted the UN Security Council to pass a series of exceptional resolutions beginning in 2014 to grant explicit permission for humanitarian groups to run cross-border humanitarian relief operations into Syria from their bases in neighboring countries.

In most of today's conflicts, therefore, international humanitarian law on the protection and facilitation of humanitarian aid is "neither definitive in doctrine nor compelling in practice."[21] And in truth, most humanitarians attempting to negotiate with armed groups for secure access will spend very little time on the letter of the law. Said one, "IHL (international humanitarian law) is usually only the first two minutes of the conversation," before getting down to the quid pro quo. Of course, these negotiations are made all the more challenging by the fact that in non-international conflicts one must secure the cooperation of non-state armed actors (sometimes multiple groups within a single conflict), which can range from fairly disciplined forces that possess a clear agenda under a unified command structure to shambolic, quasi-criminal enterprises. Some can be so erratic in their behavior that even after arrangements have been carefully and explicitly negotiated, terms can break down immediately, resulting in aid being blocked or stolen and aid providers attacked. The ICRC itself has come to acknowledge this conundrum and how it challenges the

[20] ICRC. (2015). "Rule 55: Access for Humanitarian Relief to Civilians in Need." International Committee of the Red Cross (ICRC).

[21] Harmer, A., Stoddard, A. & Sarazen, A. (2018). *Humanitarian access in armed conflict: A need for new principles?* Humanitarian Outcomes, December, p. 5.

humanitarian mandate. Its 2018 report called *The Roots of Restraint in War* puzzles with how to promote adherence to international law when the majority of war-fighting forces involved in today's conflicts are decentralized entities, driven by wholly different values and incentives than are states.

The truth, of course, is that even in international wars, there was never any golden age of respect for and adherence to these principles; warring parties had occasion to violate the Geneva Conventions just as soon as they were ratified. But breaking the law is not the same as overturning it, and violations of a norm within a stable context do not negate that norm. (They may in fact work to strengthen it if the violator receives sufficient opprobrium and is shamed into changing the behavior.) In the absence of an overriding means of enforcement, international laws in some sense function more like societal norms, which is to say they set a "standard of appropriate behavior"[22] that carries with it an air of morality and legitimacy that is in the interest of a state to cultivate among peers. Norms are much more seriously undercut when the original social framework in which they emerged has dissolved or is dissolving. Actors who seek to destroy the old order will disregard or redefine its norms as their *raison d'être*—they intend to establish new ones. They are playing a different game.

Humanitarians define neutrality as an "instrumental" principle, meaning it is not valued for its own sake (as it is never moral to be neutral in cases of oppression or genocide, for example), but rather as a means to gain the trust and tolerance of the warring parties in order to get in and do their work.[23] Asymmetric conflicts confound this concept. Humanitarian neutrality, the cornerstone of Dunant's vision for enabling and protecting a humanitarian presence in war, loses all potency as a tool in non-international, asymmetric conflicts because it ceases to be of equal benefit to both sides. Aid operations, by providing for people's basic needs and creating a degree of stability amid the conflict, are de facto supporting the status quo that the weaker side is seeking to overturn. As humanitarian researcher-practitioner Fiona Terry wrote, "Neutrality ratifies the law of

[22] Finnemore, M. & Sikkink, K. (1998). "International norm dynamics and political change." 52(4): 887–917.

[23] Slim, H. (2015). *Humanitarian Ethics: A guide to the morality of aid in war and disaster.*

the strongest."[24] Even if the armed opposition groups do not believe (which they often do) that the humanitarians are directly colluding with the current government or occupying force, they may still see their aid operations as helping to stabilize and shore up the current order, thus performing a valuable service to their enemies. They have no incentive to treat them as "neutral and inviolate" actors.

The same dynamic applies to armed groups that are waging asymmetric wars at the global level, or what is typically thought of as international terrorism.[25] The institutions of international humanitarian assistance are a creature of the modern global order and so cannot avoid association with the system and its power structure. More specifically, the international humanitarian sector is unable to shed its identity as a predominantly *Western* project, funded and implicitly steered by its largest funders: the United States, the European Union, the United Kingdom, and a handful of other Western governments.[26] The fact that so much of the humanitarian sector is underwritten by Western donors undermines a second core humanitarian principle: independence. When these same donor governments are also the occupying powers in a conflict zone, the delineation of a neutral, protected space for humanitarian action becomes inherently harder to draw. Jan Egeland, the former UN Emergency Relief Coordinator and now Secretary General of the Norwegian Refugee Council, has written that "humanitarianism, a universal imperative and shared intercultural system of principles, has become so Westernized in its funding, staffing, organizational structure, and political profile that it risks long-term adversity in many non-Western settings."[27]

Projecting neutrality and independence has proven especially difficult for the United Nations humanitarian agencies, who have labored long and largely unsuccessfully to draw clear lines between their humanitarian work and the UN's political and peacekeeping roles. The resulting efforts have sometimes been almost laughably superficial, such as when UN agencies in the field try to underscore the difference between the "blue UN," refer-

[24] Terry, F. (2002). *Condemned to Repeat? The paradox of humanitarian action*. Ithaca: Cornell University Press.

[25] Pfanner, T. (2005). "Asymmetrical warfare from the perspective of humanitarian law and humanitarian action." *International Review of the Red Cross* 87(857): 149–174.

[26] UN OCHA. (2018, July 10). *Financial Tracking Service*. Retrieved from Financial Tracking Service: https://fts.unocha.org/

[27] From the foreword to Barnett, M. & Weiss, T. (2011). *Humanitarianism Contested: Where Angels Fear to Tread*. Routledge.

ring to the blue lettering on the vehicles of the humanitarian agencies like UNICEF and the World Food Program, and the "black UN" used for the other, political UN entities. In many country programs, moreover, the UN's broader and long-range political priorities will generally override humanitarians' operational concerns of projecting independence and political neutrality. In many post-conflict transitional contexts, once the acute crisis has abated, the UN will exert intense pressure on all international actors "to operate within a single, unified peace-building strategy."[28] In such cases, humanitarian organizations sacrifice not only their perceived neutrality and political independence, but their field-level operational independence as well.

In August 2003, the post-invasion state-building project in Iraq had scarcely begun, and the UN's mission was still focused on humanitarian aid rather than peace-building or other political functions. Yet as a humanitarian mission, the UN found its relationship to the occupying forces an impossible needle to thread, as it required both independence and protection from those forces. As the Ahtisaari report noted:

> The relationship between the United Nations and the Coalition Forces regarding the security of UN staff and premises remained ambiguous. Although there were clear needs for security arrangements and Coalition Forces/CPA was formally responsible for the security UN staff in Iraq, members of UN senior management in Baghdad felt uncomfortable because of the visible presence of Coalition Forces elements in and around the UN Canal Hotel compound. On several occasions, they asked the Coalition Forces to remove protective positions and equipment around the perimeter of the Canal Hotel without requesting alternative security arrangements.[29]

Recalling the heated discussions at the UN Baghdad headquarters over removing the US military's rocket launcher from the front of the Canal Hotel, Robert Painter has little patience for his UN colleagues' misplaced faith in what he refers to as "emblematic protection"—the notion that personnel operating under a blue UN flag (or a red cross) will be shielded from attacks. "I mean, come on," Painter told me. "The United Nations

[28] Stoddard, A., & Harmer, A. (2006). Little room to maneuver: The challenges to humanitarian action in the new global security environment. *Journal of Human Development, 7*(1), 23–41.

[29] United Nations (2003). Report of the Independent Panel on the Safety and Security of UN Personnel in Iraq. New York: United Nations.

is the world's biggest political organization. You think that by sending that gun away you're going to change the impression that people have of you?" Even so, he and others worried that the UN's connection to the occupation was in other ways made more prominent than it needed to be, particularly when Sergio Viera de Mello began appearing on television with the American head of the Coalition Provisional Authority, Paul Bremer. Vieira de Mello also had a needle he was trying to thread. Writing in *The New Yorker* about Vieira de Mello's ill-fated mission in Iraq, the US diplomat Samantha Power writes, "He knew that his two goals—earning the trust of the Iraqis and developing a strong working relationship with the Coalition—might be seen as contradictory by Iraqis hostile to American rule."[30] According to UN staffers in Baghdad at the time, it seemed at first like the UN mission chief was keeping a "healthy distance" from the Coalition Provision Authority, but when it appeared that the CPA was gaining traction in the early days of that summer, Vieira de Mello may have flown too close to the occupation, making a few joint TV appearances shortly before the attack.

In light of what is now known about the slow-motion disaster that was the early US occupation of Iraq, it does indeed seem as if the Ahtisaari report on the Canal Hotel bombing is overly focused on the smaller details of security procedure and inputs while ignoring the elephant in the room: militants perceived the UN simply as an arm of the US-led occupation, and hence an enemy target. The lack of sufficient blast film and incomplete staff lists were examples of weak compliance to regulations. The security officer more concerned with his tea than his missing guards could be deemed negligence. The removal of the rocket launcher (whoever may have ordered it) was a naïve miscalculation. But the larger political problem was exemplified by the missing Iraqi guards, who had been bribed or coerced to abandon their posts at the front of the access road on that specific day by insurgents who saw an opportunity to take out a high-profile target. This would not be the last time insurgents took aim at humanitarian workers in Iraq, nor would the UN be the only organization affected. Just two months later, the Baghdad headquarters of the International Committee of the Red Cross was attacked by a suicide bomber driving a white truck emblazoned with a red cross.

[30] Power, S. (2008). The Envoy: The United Nations' doomed mission to Iraq. *The New Yorker*. January 27, 2008.

When humanitarian organizations become political targets, their operational security becomes more complicated to ensure. It is no longer a matter of simply taking standard precautions and adhering to procedures, as it would be to prevent opportunistic crime or accidents. Rather, aid agencies must think in more strategic terms about other actors in the environment who seek to do them harm and when and why they may be targeted. For this reason, the degree to which attacks on aid groups are driven by political motives as opposed to purely criminal ones (such as the theft of vehicles, cash, or equipment) is critical to understanding the threat environment and calculating risk. In the data we have collected on aid worker attacks since 1997, we have attempted, where possible, to categorize the motives of the attackers to distinguish between straightforward economic crime (robbery, banditry) from those that target aid workers at least in part *because* of their status as aid workers and the political gain afforded by striking them. By its very nature, this is the fuzziest and least objective of our data categories, entailing the most judgment calls and greatest percentage of "unknowns." Still, we persist in recording it because it can be an important descriptor and bellwether. For example, as the Taliban regrouped and gradually gained strength in the years after the US forces invaded in 2001, the proportion of attacks attributed to political as opposed to purely criminal motives incrementally grew from a minority to a majority proportion.[31] The switch occurred in 2008—the same year the US increased its troop strength in Afghanistan and suffered peak military losses.[32]

Some armed groups do make distinctions between different aid organizations at a local level, but the general linking of the international humanitarian sector with Western power and stabilization agendas should not be understated as the default view of these fighting forces. Interviews with members of the Taliban, Haqqani Network, and Al Shabab on this topic show them to be extremely firm in their belief that aid organizations were not simply aligned with the broader objectives of the government and Western powers but working directly for them as either spies or implementing agents.

Unfortunately, it does not follow that where international aid organizations are suspect, the national and local humanitarian organizations will

[31] Stoddard, A., Harmer, A., DiDomenico, V. (2009). Providing Aid in Insecure Environments: 2009 Update. London, ODI.

[32] "US deaths in Afghanistan makes 2008 deadliest year", *Washington Times.*

necessarily be trusted and tolerated. In many cases, the local humanitarians are viewed as coopted by and in league with the international entities (not least because they often work as partners and sub-contractors for the international agencies and/or their host governments). And even if armed groups do not associate the local aid groups with the international system, they often link them with one or the other of the conflict parties, meaning that local or national status for a humanitarian organization does not automatically confer protection. As one Taliban soldier from the Khost province in Afghanistan declared, "None of the [the aid groups] are performing activities that can benefit our people and country. Because I know about their activities. They say that they are working for promoting people's rights, but in reality, they are spying for foreigners or the government."

The normative and legal framework for protection of humanitarians in war, thin to begin with, is only diluted further when there are undeniable political and military associations between the humanitarian responders and one side of the conflict. Non-state armed groups have used these connections to justify attacks, even on schools and hospitals, as morally justified and legitimate military targeting. After all, these facilities were paid for and used for strategic purposes by the enemy side, they reason, so they cannot be regarded as truly neutral. When the purpose of a warring party is to disrupt or overturn the current order and to counter the Western agenda by sowing instability, humanitarian operations that aid civilians not only become legitimate targets, but, as we will see, highly expedient and attractive ones as well.

"Neutral and Inviolate"

The origins of the modern humanitarian movement can be traced to a young Swiss banker, Jean-Henri (Henry) Dunant, who accidentally bore witness to the grisly aftermath of a major battle in the Franco-Austrian War. On a sweltering day in June 1859, Dunant was traveling in Italy near Solferino, a typical northern Italian village of red-tiled roofs surrounded by green fields and low hills, where the opposing armies were marshaling their forces. The Battle of Solferino came at the end of an era when heads of state were still often present on the battlefield, personally commanding their armies. Napoleon III led the French forces, which, joined by Sardinian allies, confronted the Austrian troops commanded by the 29-year old Emperor Franz Joseph I. Combined, their ranks totaled roughly 300,000 fighters amassed outside the town. It was not yet dawn on June 24 when the first bugles sounded to commence fighting, and the combat grew increasingly intense as the day went on, churning through wave after wave of clashing bodies. Dunant's memoir *A Memory of Solferino* described the scene:

> During the torrid midday heat, the fighting that rages on all sides grows more and more furious. Compact columns of men throw themselves upon each other…Whole divisions threw off their knapsacks in order to be able to charge the enemy more freely with their fixed bayonets. As one battalion is repulsed, another immediately replaces it. Every mound, every height, every rocky crag, is the scene of a fight to the death; bodies lie in heaps on the hills and in the valleys.

By nightfall, there were over 5000 dead and four times as many wounded and soon to die. The little town and its surrounding fields and woods were blanketed with victims in unimaginable numbers: at least 20,000 men that had been shot, bayoneted, or crushed under wagon wheels and horses' hooves. In anguished prose, Dunant described the young soldiers' wails and pleas for water, for medical care, for any sort of relief. For the vast majority of them, help never came. "[T]hough the army, in its retreat, picked up all the wounded men it could carry in military wagons and requisitioned carts, how many unfortunate men were left behind, lying helpless on the naked ground in their own blood!"[33]

Witnessing the enormity of such suffering packed into a few square miles of fields and woods was transformative to Dunant, who harbored a religious bent and a penchant for international causes. Together with the local inhabitants of Solferino and adjacent towns, he joined in makeshift volunteer efforts to collect and care for the wounded as best as possible, a task that vastly overwhelmed the resources of the region. As Dunant wrote:

> Wounds were infected by the heat and dust, by the shortage of water and lack of proper care, and grew more and more painful. Foul exhalations contaminated the air, in spite of the praiseworthy attempts of the authorities to keep hospital areas in a sanitary condition. The convoys brought a fresh contingent of wounded men into Castiglione every quarter of an hour, and the shortage of assistants, orderlies and helpers was cruelly felt.[34]

[33] Dunant, H. (1939). *A Memory of Solferino*. Geneva: International Committee of the Red Cross, p. 38.

[34] Dunant, H. (1939). *A Memory of Solferino*. Geneva: International Committee of the Red Cross, p. 60.

The insufficiency of these relief efforts impressed upon Dunant the need to conceive of a far larger, more organized aid response that would be prepared in the event of mass casualties. He used his written account of the experience to promulgate his idea for a new international movement and rules for warfare so that in future wars it would at least be possible to abate the scope and scale of misery left in their wake.

The battle had also left its mark on the European monarchs and political elites. It had been the largest, bloodiest clash since the Napoleonic wars of earlier decades, and even Emperor Napoleon III seemed chastened by the human toll. In 1863, a year after Dunant published his memoir, representatives from 16 countries met in Geneva to take forward his proposal for establishing voluntary societies in each country that would mobilize to provide relief aid to war-wounded, when and if warfare should take place on their soil. The signees agreed also that the warring parties would hold these humanitarian actors as "neutral, i.e. inviolate,"[35] and "that similar protection be extended to army medical staff, voluntary helpers and the wounded themselves."[36] They chose the emblem of a red cross against a white background, an inversion of the Swiss flag, to be the distinctive marker to signal neutrality and protected status. Thus, the International Committee of the Red Cross (ICRC) was founded. The next year saw the signing of the first "Geneva Convention for the Amelioration of the Condition of the Wounded in Armies in the Field," which took forward the 1863 conference recommendations and "stated the principle—crucial for the whole undertaking—that wounded and sick soldiers must be taken in and cared for without distinction of nationality."[37]

Dunant's ideas had fallen on fertile soil. The notion of an inviolate space for humanitarian action enshrined in the Geneva Conventions was a recognition by political powers that medics and relief aid providers benefit all sides and bring a modicum of civilization and humanity to the bloody business of war. The aid-providers would be governed by the core principles of ***humanity***, ***impartiality***, ***neutrality***, and ***independence*** to assure the warring parties that their sole purpose was humane, and their work constituted no threat. While rooted in compassion and altruism, the idea was at the same time profoundly pragmatic. There was no question of eliminat-

[35] Dunant, H. (1939). *A Memory of Solferino*. Geneva: International Committee of the Red Cross, (ICRC afterword), p. 33.

[36] Ibid.

[37] Ibid.

ing war itself; the continual power struggle of empires and nations through warfare was accepted as an immutable fact of life. Wars may be inevitable, reasoned Dunant, but it was possible to reach a gentlemen's agreement about how to limit their barbarity by laying down some rules and establishing some mechanisms to deal with its consequences. Traditional humanitarianism, therefore, does not attempt to stop the killing but rather to limit the suffering and dying. And war being war, violations of these rules could be expected, but the overall aspiration was credible in the environment that gave birth to it—all the important players were playing in the same game. In the century and a half that followed, however, both the nature of wars and the scope of humanitarian action have evolved in ways that belie this fundamental assumption.

References

Ahtisaari, M., et al. (2003). Report of the Independent Panel on the Safety and Security of UN Personnel in Iraq. United Nations.

Barnett, M., & Weiss, T. (2011). *Humanitarianism Contested: Where Angels Fear to Tread*. Oxon: Routledge.

Dunant, H. (1939). *A Memory of Solferino*. Geneva: International Committee of the Red Cross.

Finnemore, M., & Sikkink, K. (1998). International Norm Dynamics and Political Change. *International Organization, 52*(4), 887–917.

Harmer, A., Stoddard, A., & Sarazen, A. (2018, December). *Humanitarian Access in Armed Conflict: A Need for New Principles?* New York: Humanitarian Outcomes.

International Committee of the Red Cross (ICRC). (1977). *Protocol Additional to the Geneva Conventions of 12 August 1949, and Relating to the Protection of Victims of Non-international Armed Conflicts (Protocol II)*, 8 June 1977. Commentary 4872. ICRC.

International Committee of the Red Cross (ICRC). (2015). *Rule 55: Access for Humanitarian Relief to Civilians in Need*. Geneva: ICRC.

Kilcullen, D. (2009). *The Accidental Guerilla: Fighting Small Wars in the Midst of a Big One*. Oxford: Oxford University Press.

Ollivant, D. (2016). *The Rise of the Hybrid Warriors: From Ukraine to the Middle East*. warontherocks.com. Retrieved from https://warontherocks.com/2016/03/the-rise-of-the-hybrid-warriors-from-ukraine-to-the-middle-east/

Pfanner, T. (2005). Asymmetrical Warfare from the Perspective of Humanitarian Law and Humanitarian Action. *International Review of the Red Cross, 87*(857), 149–174.

Power, S. (2008, January 27). The Envoy: The United Nations' Doomed Mission to Iraq. *The New Yorker.*

Slim, H. (2015). *Humanitarian Ethics: A Guide to the Morality of Aid in War and Disaster*. New York: Oxford University Press.

Stoddard, A., & Harmer, A. (2006). Little Room to Maneuver: The Challenges to Humanitarian Action in the New Global Security Environment. *Journal of Human Development, 7*(1), 23–41.

Stoddard, A., Harmer, A., & DiDomenico, V. (2009). *Providing Aid in Insecure Environments: 2009 Update*. London: ODI.

Terry, F. (2002). *Condemned to Repeat? The Paradox of Humanitarian Action.* Ithaca: Cornell University Press.

Traub, J. (2006). *The Best Intentions: Kofi Annan and the UN in the Era of American World Power* (1st ed.). New York: Farrar, Straus and Giroux.

UCDP/PRIO Armed Conflict Dataset Codebook. Version 17.2, Uppsala Conflict Data Program (UCDP). www.ucdp.uu.se, International Peace Research Institute, Oslo (PRIO), www.prio.no

United Nations. (2003). *Report of the Independent Panel on the Safety and Security of UN Personnel in Iraq*. New York: United Nations.

United Nations. (2015). *Meetings Coverage and Press Releases, Human Cost of Illicit Flow of Small Arms, Light Weapons Stressed in Security Council Debate*, 13 May 2015. https://www.un.org/press/en/2015/sc11889.doc.htm

CHAPTER 3

Contending with Non-state Forces

A Kidnapping in Basilan

On 15 September 2008, Merlie B. "Milet" Mendoza[1] woke up early to begin what was supposed to be her last working day in Basilan before returning home to Manila. She had a busy day ahead: the local NGO she was assisting was wrapping up a household survey, and then they were to meet with community leaders to work out the details of a new aid program. Her day, however, would not go as planned. By nightfall, she would be stumbling through a dark, muddy forest at gunpoint.

Basilan is the largest island of the Sulu Archipelago in the southern Philippines, in the heart of the Autonomous Region in Muslim Mindanao. A tropical idyll, with palm-lined, white sand beaches rimming an inland rain forest that stretches across rolling hills and volcanic peaks, the island has been at the center of a bloody civil conflict since 1972. In the early 1990s, the armed insurgent groups that formed the Moro Islamic Liberation Front were joined by a new jihadist organization known as the Abu Sayyaf Group (ASG), an extremely violent movement that would some years later pledge its allegiance to the Islamic State.

Mendoza was in Basilan to help organize assistance for 200 families displaced by the conflict. An energetic woman with full cheeks and a

[1] In addition to my 2012 and 2019 interviews with Milet Mendoza, this case narrative draws from news accounts and her own published writing about the incident. Quotes drawn from those pieces are referenced.

A. Stoddard, *Necessary Risks*,
https://doi.org/10.1007/978-3-030-26411-6_3

habitual smile, Mendoza appeared much younger than her 44 years, though this did not detract from her ability to lead humanitarian teams and work effectively with local government authorities. She knew Basilan and its people well, having spent many years as a program coordinator for the humanitarian organization Tabang Mindanaw, overseeing relief projects throughout the Sulu Archipelago. Despite her status as an outsider—she was Filipina but a Catholic from a middle-class family in the capital—Mendoza felt drawn to the area and the communities she had come to know. As a deeply religious person, she felt a spiritual kinship with the Muslim families she saw living lives of devotion and prayer. At the same time, she was well aware of the security risks involved in her work—risks she had chosen not to communicate fully to her parents and siblings back in Manila. The ASG funded their insurgency through illicit drug sales, extortion, and ransoms, so kidnappings were a regular occurrence. Her own mentor, a peace worker and humanitarian named Father Jesus Reynaldo "Rey" Roda, had been shot and killed earlier that year in an attempted abduction by ASG fighters in a relatively peaceful island further south, in the province of Tawi-Tawi.

At about 1:00 p.m., Mendoza and her colleagues were on the road, having just concluded their meeting with community leaders. Mendoza rode with two co-workers in the back of a Toyota pickup owned by the local NGO, while ahead of them was a rented van with government social workers whom they had been training. The co-worker sitting next to her was a woman named Esperanza Hupida, who had become a friend. Hupida had been born and raised in Basilan, but to a family belonging to the Christian minority, so in her own way Hupida was an "outsider" like Mendoza. They had been driving only a short while when a group of men with machine guns and a grenade launcher suddenly appeared on the road ahead of them. Mendoza was looking down at her phone and didn't see the ambush coming until Hupida screamed. The men were aiming their weapons at the vehicles and shouting for the riders to get out. Feeling panic rising in her chest and tightening her limbs, Mendoza fumbled as she frantically tried to hide her cell phones. She was the last to get off, prompting one of the men to threaten to shoot her if she didn't move faster. Mendoza watched as her colleagues from the first vehicle recited Islamic prayers in front of the men and pleaded with them to be released. They were allowed to go. The armed men then forced the remaining hostages—Mendoza, Hupida, and three others—to start walking.

After a few hours, it began to rain, and their captors allowed the group to stop for a while under some trees. Mendoza and her colleagues were trying to explain that they were humanitarian workers and were pleading to be released. "They took away all our valuables and asked us to write down our names. I was the first to write down my name, and as they read it, I noticed they nodded their heads and pointed to me."[2] They knew the "foreigner" from Manila stood to be the most valuable of their hostages. The men told them they were taking them to the mayor's home in Tipo-Tipo, where they would then be released, and for a while, Mendoza had cause to hope they were telling the truth. She watched as three of her colleagues were ridden off on motorcycles, leaving just her and Hupida alone with the men. The walking continued, deeper and deeper into the forest as night fell. The men had taken Mendoza's glasses, along with her other possessions, and her nearsighted eyes couldn't focus on anything further away than her own feet. So she kept her eyes on her feet, watching each muddy step, as she quietly recited the Hail Mary to herself, over and over. For a time this helped to quiet her mind and ward off the panic. Around midnight, they finally stopped at a hut, where the women—exhausted, hungry, and wet—were given a single small fish to share and a windowless room in which to sleep.

ASG fighters, like those in many other guerrilla insurgencies, operate from small cells in remote rural areas. With their wives and children in tow, they change locations frequently, squatting in or commandeering houses in each new location like a traveling, heavily armed village. It wasn't until the night of the third day of walking that Mendoza arrived amid the group where she would spend the remainder of her captivity—a collection of about 15 families along with other young fighters who were still unmarried. Earlier that day the men had taken Hupida away to be held by another cell, and Mendoza was now alone with her guards. When they were separated, Mendoza hugged her friend goodbye, as they both wept, and said to her, "If you get out of this alive, please tell my parents I am very sorry for what I have done to them." She would learn later that Hupida was released after 45 days.

When they arrived that night, drenched by the rain, the men took Mendoza to the house of the Commander, a stocky, balding man with a

[2] Mendoza, M. (2009). *The agonies of an Abu Sayyaf kidnap victim (1). MindaNews*. Retrieved 11 May 2019 from https://www.mindanews.com/c3-news/2009/04/the-agonies-of-an-abu-sayyaf-kidnap-victim-1/

stern countenance, who, it was immediately apparent, exercised a fierce and unquestioned authority over his men.[3] The first meeting with the Commander had the air of formality; she would sleep at his house that night so he could officially interrogate her in the morning. He allowed the exhausted Mendoza to rest for a while in his hammock. This would be the last time in a long while that she would be able to lie down on anything but the floor. As she lay in the hammock in her wet clothes, she tried again to calm her mind by silently praying the rosary, over and over. After a while, when she needed to pee, she was handed a pot and told to find a far corner in the house, as she was not to go outside. The Commander warned her, "You may see a woman back there. Do not mind her." In the shadows, Mendoza saw the black-draped figure sleeping on the floor and realized with a chill that this must be another captive, perhaps a local woman taken as a slave. She never found out, and would never see the woman again.

When she woke up the next morning, however, Mendoza encountered a different woman in the house. It was the Commander's most recent wife, a warm and lively young woman who smelled of perfume. Mendoza would come to learn that this new wife was not a local rural inhabitant but an educated Muslim woman from the city. Still in her twenties, she seemed savvier than most of the other women and did not enjoy mingling with the other ASG members when they visited the Commander. When there was food and tea to be served, she made a point of serving only her husband. Mendoza mostly never saw her face—all the women, including Mendoza, had to wear the full niqab (head and face veil)—but word had it that she was very beautiful, and the Commander, in his fifties, was deeply smitten with her. That first morning in the Commander's house, Mendoza watched intently how the man treated his wives, and his evident affection for this young woman gave her a small sense of safety.

Kidnappers generally do not want to encourage feelings of safety among their captives, however; it is preferable that they should always remain in some degree of fear for their lives. So it was that in the first week of her captivity Mendoza was subjected to an act of psychological torture. She had been resisting giving up the names of her friends and family for the ASG to send ransom demands, hoping to spare the pain and fear it would cause her parents. One night, on the fourth or fifth day, two men barged

[3] The Commander's name, Mendoza would learn later, was Khair Mundos. Mundos was on the US government's list of most wanted terrorists and was captured by Philippine authorities in 2014.

into the house where she was confined and dragged her outside. They tied her arms behind her back, put a piece of tape over her mouth, and pushed her down on her knees in the mud. One of them stood behind her, pushing the barrel of his rifle against her head, while the other raised his machete high over her head. She remembers him shouting, "Mabuti pa ikaw ang mamatay kaysa kami!" ("Better that you should die than us!")[4] Frantic thoughts raced through her mind: "Tears aren't coming. I wish I could show them tears." "He looks so angry; angry enough to kill me—an aid worker, a woman, someone who could be his sister—what have we done to make him so angry?" And another thought: "Oh God, is it sharp?" She hoped the machete would be able to do the job in one blow; that her head would not need to be sawn off, as in the stories she had heard from people in Sulu who had witnessed beheadings. Words started pouring out of her mouth, muffled by the tape. She begged for forgiveness for the sins of the Christians against the Muslims, she spoke of her gratitude for the Muslims who had cared for her and made her a better Christian through demonstrating their own deep faith, and she spoke of the respect she would always have for Muslim people. She kept talking, even as she accepted that this was the moment of her death.

After a moment, the machete was lowered and the rifle removed from her head. "We will execute you tomorrow," they said.

Every night after the mock execution, Mendoza went to sleep in fear of the men coming to her door. When they did show up, as became a regular occurrence, it was to march her up to a hilltop, where there was a cell phone signal, to make ransom calls. These hikes lasted more than two hours each way, and Mendoza, who was kept in a small, dark space and not allowed out during the day, was weak from lack of exercise as well as fear. "My body would not cooperate. My knees seemed to be like jelly. I would get nauseous easily and would run out of breath quickly." During these trips, always made at night, Mendoza would be covered in her niqab and one of the men would be assigned to stay close to her, presumably so that any local they came across would assume she was his wife. This seemed laughable to Mendoza; she was one woman, accompanied by sometimes dozens of heavily armed men. She was fairly certain that any passerby would assume she was a hostage.

[4] Mendoza, M. (2009). *The agonies of an Abu Sayyaf kidnap victim (1). MindaNews.* Retrieved 11 May 2019 from https://www.mindanews.com/c3-news/2009/04/the-agonies-of-an-abu-sayyaf-kidnap-victim-1/

The calls continued over a long period, but Mendoza still resisted the ASG's demands that she plead to friends and relatives in Manila to pay ransom. She also knew that kidnappings of aid workers are often resolved in unconditional release when local contacts and community leaders intervene on their behalf. "After all, I had worked among Muslims for many years. I was sure many of my friends were exerting their efforts, looking for contacts who could convince our captors to release us." And indeed, many were. There were NGO heads, community elders, even members of the Moro Islamic Liberation Front advocating for her. She had spent four years working in Sulu, and her former organization, Tabang Mindanaw, was prominent and well-liked for its work in the region. Paradoxically, the response by so many might have reinforced Mendoza's economic value in the minds of her captors, who approached their hostage-taking very practically ("It's a business thing," said Mendoza with a wry laugh). Perhaps they believed they would eventually obtain a larger ransom if they held out long enough.

As days became weeks, Mendoza endured most of the intensely hot days and cold nights inside a 16-square-meter hut with a corrugated metal roof and a tarp covering the window. There was no furniture, nothing to read or listen to, and no toilet. "Not being allowed to leave [the hut], everything had to be done there. For a long while, everything had to be done in plastic bags—'cellophane' as they referred to it—which came in short supply."[5] Before malnutrition stopped her cycle, Mendoza made use of recycled baby wipes for sanitation—something Hupida had recommended to her before they were separated. The simplest acts of keeping clean now became a consuming preoccupation as Mendoza tried to cling to a sense of personhood. As she described it in her written account, "Little by little the layers of self-worth that we build onto our self-image are gouged away by the indignities."[6] When meals came, usually rice with some tuyo (salted fish), Mendoza would chew as slowly as she could, taking an hour or more to finish her food. When the eating was over, there would be nothing else to do.

Thoughts of suicide were unavoidable, but Mendoza never made an attempt. Instead, to cope, she sank deeper into faith and spirituality. Vivid

[5] Ibid.

[6] Mendoza, M. (2009). *Post-Lenten reflections of an Abu Sayyaf kidnap victim: Moving forward (1). MindaNews.* Retrieved 13 May 2019 from https://www.mindanews.com/c3-news/2009/04/post-lenten-reflections-of-an-abu-sayyaf-kidnap-victim-moving-forward-1/

thoughts and dreams would take on profound significance, and she would often "see" and talk with loved ones and her late mentor Father Rey. She started to notice coincidences ("little miracles," as she thought of them), piecing them together to construct a narrative of meaning and hope out of her experience.

> One evening I asked Father Rey if I could have an egg with my meal. And, voila! The following morning I was given half a hard-boiled egg to eat with my rice for breakfast, the first and only time I had egg during my captivity. I told myself it was typical of Father Rey to tease. The ASG man who handed me my breakfast plate could probably not figure out why I had a big smile on my face over half an egg.[7]

She was not completely isolated, though. In the ASG community, the men would mostly spend their days reading the Quran and drilling with their weapons, while the women did chores. Although they were not supposed to, sometimes one or two of the women would come to visit Mendoza out of curiosity or boredom, usually when the Commander was not around. Though the women made it clear that they were in no position to help her ("we are only women," as they said), they would often try to raise Mendoza's spirits. "Don't worry," they would say. "This is all just drama. It is being arranged, you will be going home soon."

The Commander's young wife was her most frequent visitor; she seemed to prefer Mendoza's company to that of the other ASG women. She brought Mendoza a change of clothes she had taken from one of the Commander's other wives, and once or twice, she would gift her with an item from the kitchen or the market. In these brief visits, the two women would tell each other about their lives. When she couldn't visit, the Commander's wife would sometimes hang her laundry outside the house where Mendoza was confined, singing popular love songs in English that she knew Mendoza would know. One day, when she was paying a secret visit, the wife embraced Mendoza and confided, "I am not happy here." She was used to urban life, and the marriage had not been of her own accord. Her mother had been a scholar of midwifery, she told Mendoza, who had also been taken by the ASG in a forced marriage. She sometimes

[7] Mendoza, M. (2009). *The agonies of an Abu Sayyaf kidnap victim (2): Coping with Captivity: One victim's story. MindaNews.* Retrieved 11 May 2019 from https://www.mindanews.com/c3-news/2009/04/the-agonies-of-an-abu-sayyaf-kidnap-victim-2-coping-with-captivity-one-victims-story/

spoke fondly of the Commander, however, recounting days early in the marriage when they would go together to bathe in the river. As she spoke, Mendoza pictured the river and thought about how she had not been able to bathe for more than a month.

There were other moments of kindness and connection. One of the other wives was a converted Christian named Mary, who had a baby daughter who was the light of everyone's eyes in the village. She had the hut next to Mendoza's and would sometimes bring her tea when the men were not around. Mary once took Mendoza's hand and asked her, when she was released, to please tell the military not to bomb their encampment. She was afraid for her baby. "Tell them there are women and children here," she entreated. On another day, one of the young ASG fighters, a good-looking youth of about 18, passed Mendoza a couple of pieces of hard candy through a hole in her wall. She gratefully stored them away to help give her energy for the next hike up the hill. That evening, the same youth delivered Mendoza her dinner and sat inside with her as she ate it in the darkness. He was sad and anxious and needed to talk to someone. He had been taken by the ASG when he was in the third grade, he told her, and he missed his mother terribly. He confessed that the noise of gunfire gave him attacks of migraine and made him feel like he was going crazy. He wanted to go back to his town, to go back to school. "You resemble my mother," he said. "I miss home."

During the second month of Mendoza's captivity, the Commander's wife escaped. As Mendoza learned from the gossiping ASG men, the wife had fled from the foot of the hill where she was meant to be awaiting her husband's return from a mission. The Commander was bereft. Mendoza remembers how the Commander's grief over the loss was met with unkind remarks, even laughter, from the other men. They had always thought that he allowed the pretty young woman to have too much sway over him. For Mendoza, it was bittersweet. She too missed the bright presence of the young woman, but at the same time, she was thrilled by the boldness of the escape and happy that her friend was free.

Kidnapping is a relatively easy, low-tech stratagem in asymmetric warfare, and can be a hugely useful source of revenue. When it goes on too long, however, there are diminishing returns. Keeping a hostage alive requires some costs; there is the food, the arrangements for accommodations and constant guarding, and occasionally medicines that need to be purchased. A UN security professional experienced in many lengthy hostage negotiations told me he knew of cases where eventually the captors decide to cut their losses and leave open a door, allowing the hostage to simply "escape." By the third month, Mendoza was getting a strong sense that the ASG men were growing impatient with the process. More than one ASG cell was involved in her case, and they were to split the proceeds, but her cell's commander was always in charge of the negotiations. He was one of the most mature and sophisticated of the ASG leaders; he spoke multiple languages and had a background in finance. The hilltop cell phone conversations always took place on speaker, so that everyone could hear both sides, and Mendoza's only role was to plead for help and not let slip any information regarding where she was and who was holding her. (Once, making the mistake of mentioning they were in Basilan earned her a painful blow on the back.) Mendoza's friend and NGO colleague was one of the primary contacts negotiating in her behalf. This colleague was a calm and measured presence on the phone. He was unemotional and business-like when speaking to her captors, reasoning with them pragmatically, trying to work things out. His approach went over well with the Commander. Mendoza remembers one time, after finishing a call with him, the Commander remarked: "This guy is very good. He respects the trade."

What finally clinched the agreement for Mendoza's release is unclear, but the ASG never did get the huge ransom they were hoping she would fetch. One night, on the 61st day of her captivity, Mendoza woke up to the Commander himself entering her hut. Her limbs numb from lying on the floor, Mendoza pretended to still be asleep. "How are you?!" he boomed. She answered that she didn't feel well. She had stopped eating some days earlier, and on top of that, her stomach was beginning to churn with the familiar pain and nausea that greeted every late-night hike. The Commander kicked her feet and said, "Well, if you don't get up and get well, then you cannot be released."

This last encounter with the Commander fit a pattern. Since the first day, his behavior toward Mendoza had alternated between anger and something almost like caring; sometimes casting himself as her biggest threat and other times as her only hope for protection. This was surely intentional, designed to keep her off balance. For her part, over the course of their relationship, Mendoza had some small moments of defiance; one time she had screamed at him that if he was going to kill her, he should do it now, and quickly. Another time her anger emboldened her to report to him that his right-hand man—a coarse and loutish soldier that none of the ASG women liked—had attempted to molest her. How could he answer for such behavior by his men, she asked the Commander severely, under the values of Islam? But mostly, of course, she was powerless, and that powerlessness defined the external experience of her captivity; it was a feeling of being less than human. As she was being walked away from her hut, and the Commander, for the last time, Mendoza looked back and saw the candlelit silhouette of Mary, holding her daughter, watching her go.

Later that night on a dark road, she was handed over to the vice-governor of Basilan and his brother, who had helped to negotiate the release. The politician insisted on taking photos. In one grainy image, a man with a machine gun is seen holding the arm of a woman draped in black. The next photo shows a gaunt and stunned-looking Mendoza, her niqab removed, being helped on with a bright yellow sweatshirt. Her friend who had led the negotiations was there to welcome her back, along with many other friends and NGO colleagues from Sulu, all waiting to take her inside the vice-governor's house, where she would wash her feet and call her parents.

Milet Mendoza continues to work with the communities of Mindanao and has returned to Sulu many times, though not yet to Basilan. Like many national aid workers who have survived kidnappings, she received little in the way of after-care and psychological trauma support, but she credits her friends, family, and faith for her recovery, and currently advocates for other survivors. And like some other people who have experienced severe traumatic events, she believes it has led to personal growth. A decade later, she still finds meaning and connection in little details, and gratitude for things as simple as a cup of water. As she said in our most recent conversation, "Everything about freedom is so *sweet*." She also has no regrets over her choice of profession.

> The best part of my career in peace-building and humanitarianism was the moment when I went to the grassroots because I had to unlearn all my bias. The best part of my life is immersing myself in these communities. The face to face encounter allowed me to see the best in the Islamic faith. There is always hope in organizing these marginalized communities.

Proximity, Opportunity, and Vulnerability: The Practical Logic of Targeting Aid Providers

Non-state armed groups engaged in asymmetric conflicts will have a variety of political and strategic incentives for striking at humanitarian organizations working in their sphere of operation. But before we delve into the complex motivations of different insurgent groups, we must acknowledge certain practical realities of aid operations and environmental factors that conspire to make humanitarians such easy and appealing targets.

When deciding what and whom to attack, an insurgent force's decision-making differs in important ways from that of national militaries. The US Army's Special Operations Forces, for example, have codified the criteria for target selection, using the acronym CARVER: Criticality, Accessibility, Recuperability, Vulnerability, Effect, and Recognizability.[8] By this rubric, a good target would be an asset that is of major importance to the enemy ("criticality"), one that will take a long time to replace or recover from once hit ("recuperability"), and that, by striking it, you will have made a meaningful impact ("effect") toward your strategic objectives. At the same time, for the strike to be successful, the target must be readily identifiable ("recognizability"), open to attack ("vulnerability"), and reachable by your striking force ("accessibility"). In selecting their targets, Special Operations Forces planners assign numerical values to each of the CARVER criteria in order to prioritize the most efficacious targets among multiple possibilities.

Much smaller and weaker fighting groups, of course, face a much more limited set of options, and their targeting criteria reflect this. Target selection from this "point of view" may be better represented through a different acronym—POV: Proximity, Opportunity, Vulnerability. Because most insurgent groups possess far less geographical reach and capacity than their state counterparts, their target selections are mainly determined by (1) the proximity of the target to their bases, (2) the opportunity afforded to them by striking it (which often comes in the form of terrorist-style visibility and/or economic benefit as opposed to a traditional military strategic advantage), and (3) the vulnerability of the target to their limited means of attack. In many conflict areas, unfortunately, humanitarian organizations check all of these boxes.

Proximity

Geographical proximity might seem at first to be such an obvious component of targeting as to omit mention, which may be why it has not been extensively studied in the literature on insurgent fighting behavior. Instead, most analysts who write about target selection by non-state forces focus

[8] U.S. Army Special Operations Forces Field Manual (FM 34–36 Appendix D).

on the symbolic value of their targets in terms of their usefulness for political messaging, in the standard "terrorist" frame. This approach unhelpfully conflates all asymmetric fighters with terrorists, whereas the symbolic criterion is primary really only for a narrow slice of non-state actors, such as Al Qaeda and the Islamic State of Iraq and Syria (ISIS), employing spectacular attacks to advance a global ideological agenda. It is of secondary importance to insurgent fighters on the ground whose main objectives are gaining local control while keeping government or occupying forces on the back foot. For them, political symbolism takes a back seat to the more practical concerns of guerilla warfare.

Unless they control significant swathes of territory, as the Islamic State did for a time in Syria and Iraq, insurgent forces typically cannot defend, and so do not attempt to establish, large military bases, relying instead on "security by obscurity" in small and hidden bases in non-contiguous locations. This has direct implications for what they choose to target for attack. For field-level commanders in the Taliban, Al Shabab (AS), or Boko Haram, the "access" criterion is much more circumscribed, and is essentially dictated by the distance of the target from the group's nearest base of operations. Tamar Mitts, a political scientist at Columbia University, demonstrated the critical importance of proximity in her 2012 analysis of insurgent group targeting.[9] Using detailed geographical data and comparative utility analysis, she demonstrated that the location of insurgent bases played a key role in determining where they chose to strike. In part, Mitts' analysis was a response to the newly popular "contagion" theories on violence, which used location data to show that violence spreads in patterns similar to contagious disease. While an intriguing idea, the contagion theories fell short of providing a credible explanatory mechanism, treating violence as if it were truly a biological organism perpetuating itself, delinked from human agency and strategic considerations.[10] Mitt's mapping showed that, on the contrary, insurgents had very practical interests served by striking in the patterns that they did. Specifically, they needed the target to be close enough to be accessible from their base and

[9] Mitts, T. (2012). *Targeting and the Spatial Spread of Insurgent Violence A Study on Jammu and Kashmir, India*. (Unpublished thesis).

[10] For example, contagious patterns of diffusion were found in Bosnia, Kosovo, Burundi, and Rwanda (Schutte and Weidmann 2011; Weidmann and Ward 2010), as well as Chechnya, the North Caucasus (O'Loughlin and Witmer 2011; Zhukov 2012), and Iraq (Townsley et al. 2008).

not too costly to carry out, but still far enough away to protect that base from exposure to retaliatory attacks.

Mitts showed further that in complex attacks the likelihood of retaliatory action figures more prominently into the calculus. Recall that complex attacks are the larger, more sophisticated strikes that require more manpower, matériel, training, and coordination, as opposed to simple acts of violence that could be carried out by a single individual, such as a shooting or suicide bombing. With simple attacks, according to Mitts, there is far less risk of serious retaliation by the larger force, and therefore they entail a simple, straight linear function between distance and cost; the further away the target, the more costly it will be to attack it. "The implication of the strategy…is that insurgents will choose to carry out simple attacks in locations that are close to their base and complex attacks in locations that are not too far and not too close to their base."[11]

The humanitarian sector has suffered its share of complex attacks in recent decades. The Aid Worker Security Database records at least 20 cases where aid agency compounds were raided by assailants using a sophisticated and carefully planned combination of explosives (sometimes vehicle-borne and sometimes body-borne suicide bombs) and teams of gunmen, always resulting in aid worker fatalities. However, when looking at the totality of attacks we have recorded, we see far more attacks of the simple variety, including ambushes, drive-by (or walk-up) shootings, kidnappings, IED detonations, and violent robberies. The data suggest that insurgent groups will normally reserve their manpower and heavy weaponry for higher value and harder targets, such as police stations, military bases, government buildings, and airports, while launching simple attacks as the opportunities arise within their local scope of operations. This helps explain why humanitarian actors often end up in the crosshairs: they are frequently the only game in town. In many far-flung rural places where the attackers are based, humanitarians are the best or only option to use as a proxy for the enemy forces.

Opportunity

In addition to being proximate, humanitarian organizations and their projects in the field offer multiple opportunities for furthering the agendas

[11] Mitts, T. (2012). *Targeting and the Spatial Spread of Insurgent Violence A Study on Jammu and Kashmir, India.* (Unpublished thesis), p. 13.

of non-state actors. Unlike their state counterparts, insurgent forces do not have large tax bases and military budgets to fund their military campaigns, and so it behooves them to dual-purpose their operations. In coding the attacks recorded in the Aid Worker Security Database for motives (whenever it was possible to reasonably determine this from the available evidence), we found that a great many of the attacks had political or military motivations while at the same time serving the attackers' economic purposes, and vice versa. For instance, an attack on a compound to punish the delivery of aid in a certain area and to drive out other humanitarian actors also has the benefit of looting supplies, vehicles, laptops, and cash.

Kidnappings excel as a multi-opportunity tactic for insurgents. Not only do they bring revenue in the form of ransoms (particularly when the victim is an international) but they also can be used as leverage for prisoner exchange or other government concessions while at the same time sending a powerful message to local inhabitants and other humanitarian organizations about who is in charge. They are also a fairly cheap and uncomplicated attack to pull off, and only become onerous and potentially costly if they are prolonged, requiring months of guard payments and hidden locations. In its kidnappings of Western humanitarians and journalists, ISIS collected ransom from those it could and executed the hostages whose governments refused payment, recording their murders to use in their propaganda materials and social media recruitment campaigns. For obvious reasons, no government or organization would admit publicly that they pay ransoms to secure the release of its nationals or staff. However, the armed groups know well that a great many do, if not directly then through intermediaries arranged through local contacts or by private companies and crisis teams funded by insurance policies. KRE (kidnap, ransom, and extortion) insurance coverage is now quietly standard across the sector.[12]

[12] The US government, which takes a tougher line than many other nations on its refusal to pay ransom or grant concessions to hostage takers, has recently softened its stance. While it maintains a strict no-ransom policy, it will no longer threaten to prosecute family members of kidnap victims for doing so, and has established a government "fusion cell" to "communicate and negotiate with militants holding American hostages and help family members to secure the safe return of hostages." See Dunham, W. & Rampton, R. "U.S. will not prosecute families for paying hostage ransom." (2019). *U.S.* Retrieved 20 March 2019 from https://www.reuters.com/article/us-usa-security-hostages/u-s-will-not-prosecute-families-for-paying-hostage-ransom-idUSKBN0P31Q720150623

National-level insurgent groups like the Taliban will often use kidnappings for local control and information gathering. In Afghanistan, the data show patterns of multiple kidnappings of NGO staff members, who are typically held for a few days and released upon the intervention by community elders who negotiate on behalf of the organization affected. During the detention period, hostages are questioned at length about their organization and its activities in the area. These kidnappings became so commonplace in Afghanistan that security professionals have referred to them as the Taliban's means of "informal registration"[13] (an object lesson, it would seem, on the need to reach out to and negotiate with the relevant armed groups in an area before starting aid programs).

Vulnerability

The perpetrators of the Canal Hotel bombing no doubt recognized the opportunity that such a spectacular strike would afford to deliver a reverberating blow to the international community. The site also had the distinction of being much easier to hit than the occupying forces' assets in Baghdad. The relative vulnerability of aid organizations among other potential targets in conflict zones is hard to overstate. If there is more than one target in a location, say a government office or an aid agency compound, the one that is softer by comparison will automatically be more attractive. If your house is the only one on the block without outdoor lights, it will be the one the burglars choose to break into. If you add lights, but all your neighbors simultaneously install bars on their windows, yours is still the house most likely to be hit because it remains the softer target.

In many developing countries, a typical aid organization compound will have high walls, often topped with barbed wire, an unarmed security guard or two, and various physical security implements designed to harden the target. This level of protective security is often in keeping with the surrounding residences. Yet when compared to government buildings, military bases, or a private contractor's facilities, aid organization compounds always remain the comparatively softer target because, as a rule and a matter of principle, they are the only ones without guns. Later we will discuss the basic concepts of the "acceptance" security approach favored by

[13] Stoddard, A., Harmer., A., & Toth, K. (2013). *The new normal: Coping with the kidnapping threat.* Humanitarian Outcomes, October, p. 7.

humanitarian groups, and how it is seen as preferable to whatever short-term security gains may be gotten through the deterrence factor of employing armed protection. For now, suffice it to say that the inherent softness of humanitarian organizations is a feature, not a bug.

Regardless of how well or weakly protected their compounds, humanitarians are made vulnerable by the extent to which their work involves their being out on the road. Aid work typically involves extensive road travel, as staff must travel between their various office locations and far-flung project sites, as well as to assess humanitarian needs and scope out new areas for work. Roads are also critical for insurgent forces, and as Mitts's geographical analysis of their targeting preferences demonstrated, utterly central to their strategy of fighting a state power from their non-contiguous bases and cells. "[I]nsurgent cells are distributed across the conflicted region in different bases and carry out attacks in locations that are accessible by roads." Oftentimes the location of attack is the road itself, since it can provide the ideal conditions for hitting vulnerable targets outside the reach of law enforcement or security forces. As the data on aid worker attacks consistently show, humanitarian personnel are at their most vulnerable when they are traveling by road. Often they are ferrying goods, cash, or equipment in vehicles (such as the stereotypical white Toyota Land Cruisers) that readily identify them as aid organizations. Since 1997, close to 50 percent of all attacks where the location was known have been on the road, in the context of an ambush or other type of road attacks, such as IED detonations and shootings from other moving vehicles. Roads as the context for aid worker attacks have been so frequent and new thinking on how to secure humanitarians in transit so lacking in the sector, that we made this topic the thematic focus of one of our annual reports on aid worker violence.[14] As we noted in that report:

> The exposure this creates is obvious—personnel are outside the protection of gates and walls; they are visible, observable, and hence vulnerable to opportunistic and premeditated attacks as well as incidental violence. … As one aid worker put it, roads represent 'massive real estate,' and it is impossible for most governments, much less one that is undergoing crisis and lacks basic security sector capacity, to effectively police or survey entire stretches of road.

[14] Stoddard, A., Harmer, A., Ryou, K (2014). *Unsafe Passage: Road attacks and their impact on humanitarian operations.* Humanitarian Outcomes.

Today's non-international conflicts can persist for years or decades with low-level or periodic fighting in remote areas, as seen with the numerous militias scattered throughout the eastern forests of the Democratic Republic of the Congo. Or, insurgent forces may augment a campaign of rural fighting with occasional spectacular strikes in urban centers or against high-profile targets; Boko Haram in northeast Nigeria and the Taliban, and more recently ISIS, in Afghanistan have all displayed this pattern. Some armed insurgencies proceed in a systematic campaign of territorial acquisition progressing from remote villages to provincial capitals, such as ISIS in Syria and the Taliban in Afghanistan who have demonstrated the ability to gain and hold significant geographic areas. This type of warfare naturally lends itself to finding and exploiting the nearby and vulnerable targets that humanitarians represent. When we asked the insurgents themselves, however, we learned they could point to additional reasons to attack aid workers and their programs—as well as reasons to let them be.

"A Kind of Payment": Navigating the Motives and Motivation of Insurgent Forces

In 2017, a low-ranking Taliban soldier in the Helmand province of Afghanistan spoke to our research team about the humanitarian organizations that were working in his country and the most appropriate way to deal with them. This mujahid (as was the only identification he gave to his interviewer) had a sixth-grade education and had lived in a war zone for nearly all of his life. At just 19, he had already been fighting with the Taliban for 3 years and had recently volunteered for training as a suicide bomber. Whenever his commanders should give the word, he said, he was ready to sacrifice himself "without hesitation." His older brother, also a member of the Taliban, had already been martyred to the cause, killed by a drone strike in Uruzgan.

In the interview, this young soldier named a few humanitarian aid agencies that he believed were "truly neutral" and doing good work. The rest of them—some of whose names he knew and some he didn't—were mostly spies, he said, and enemies of Islam. Like most of his comrades, he particularly objected to their practice of hiring female employees. When asked if the aid workers were ever appropriate targets of violence, he stated firmly: "Yes, it is always legitimate to use force against these groups, if they are non-Muslims and doing things against Islam, against our culture, against our people, against our religion, against our norms and standard of life… In fact, this is our duty to use it."

When one considers the structural incentives for insurgents to attack humanitarians, discussed in Chap. 2, as well as the more immediate reasons related to proximity, opportunity, and vulnerability, it may seem incredible that aid organizations are able to operate in war-torn nations at all. Yet in a two-year study on humanitarian access in civil conflicts, which my colleagues and I conducted for the UK government,[15] we found that even in some of the most violent places, a small number of local and international humanitarian organizations were able to keep relief programs running.[16] In our research, we measured the operational footprint of the humanitarian response in the worst conflicts at the time: Afghanistan, south-central Somalia, South Sudan, and Syria. Although we found that the operational presence of aid organizations was undeniably sparse in the more dangerous areas, leaving many critical gaps in the coverage of people's needs,[17] it nonetheless affirmed that some relief activities can take place even under extremely hostile conditions.

Part of the answer as to how this is possible lies in understanding the nuances of the warring parties' political and strategic motivations. As security professionals know, before you can weigh the likelihood and impact of the various dangers that may befall your personnel in the field, you must develop a good grasp of the "human terrain" in an area. Actor-mapping is a systematic way to go about this research, and thus a crucial first step in any risk assessment. The purpose is to glean, as far as possible, the interests, incentives, and ambitions of all those who may pose a threat to you, and if and how they interconnect.[18] In 2017, we took the behaviors and motivations of perpetrators as the topic of our annual *Aid Worker Security Report*.[19] In an attempt to achieve something like actor-mapping on a

[15] The research products from Humanitarian Outcomes' Secure Access in Volatile Environments (SAVE) project can be found at saveresearch.net

[16] Stoddard, A., Jillani, S., Caccavale, J., Cooke, P., Guillemois, D., & Klimentov, V. (2017). Out of Reach: How Insecurity Prevents Humanitarian Aid from Accessing the Neediest. *Stability: International Journal of Security and Development*, *6*(1). doi:https://doi.org/10.5334/sta.506

[17] See Stoddard et al. (2017a, b) and Jackson, A., & Zyck, S.A. (2017). *Presence & Proximity: To Stay and Deliver, Five Years On*. UN OCHA, June 22.

[18] Various Authors (2010). *Operational Security Management in Violent Environments (Revised Edition)*. Humanitarian Practice Network, Overseas Development Institute.

[19] Stoddard, A., Harmer, A., & Czwarno, M. (2017). *Aid Worker Security Report 2017: Behind the Attacks: A look at the perpetrators of violence against aid workers*. Humanitarian Outcomes.

wide scale, we used the data that we had on perpetrators to examine the different types of threats posed by different groups, and how humanitarians might best respond.

The perpetrators of attacks against aid workers come in many forms. Some are simply common criminals (such as armed robbers or bandits) or members of more sophisticated criminal gangs (including, occasionally, pirates). Others are disgruntled ex-employees of the aid agency or individuals with personal vendettas against specific aid workers. Even aid recipients can sometimes be perpetrators, as in a small number of cases where riots and mob violence have occurred in displacement camps and project sites. However, most of the major attacks against humanitarian staff and operations, where the perpetrators are known, are committed by organized non-state groups that are parties to an ongoing armed conflict.

"Between 2011 and 2016," our report found, "the non-state entities responsible for most major attacks on aid workers were the Taliban (51 attacks), Al Shabab (21), Islamic State (IS) (12), and Al Qaeda in the Islamic Maghreb (AQIM) (5). Other significant perpetrator groups included the Anti-Balaka groups in the Central African Republic (four incidents) and Syria's Jabhat Al Nusra, the Democratic Front for the Liberation of Rwanda and Mouvement pour l'unicité et le jihad en Afrique de l'Ouest (Movement for Oneness and Jihad in West Africa) (three incidents each)."[20] Our report included a table (slightly modified below) listing different types of organized groups along with the number of major attacks against aid workers they committed during the period. It also classifies them according to their scope of operations and level of ambition: global insurgency, national insurgency, subnational or local insurgency, and organized criminal groups (Fig. 3.1).

Why is it important to have information on the would-be attackers' motivations and scope of ambition? In the case of "common criminal" incidents, while they can sometimes entail brutal violence, the motive is self-evident: economic gain. To reduce vulnerability to this sort of attack, therefore, aid organizations need only to identify and curtail the criminals' potential opportunities to strike—for instance, weakly guarded facilities, isolated roads with geographic features amenable to ambush, or staff members traveling alone or out late at night. By implementing stricter security protocols and beefing up protective measures on their physical

[20] Stoddard, A., Harmer, A., & Czwarno, M. (2017). *Aid Worker Security Report 2017: Behind the attacks: A look at the perpetrators of violence against aid workers.* Humanitarian Outcomes, p. 7.

Type/Level of NSAG*	Motivations/power-ambition	Examples**	Areas of operation
Global	Overthrow of current world order on behalf of a universal absolutist ideology	Islamic State	Afghanistan, Iraq, Syria
		Al Qaeda (core)	Afghanistan, Pakistan
		Al Qaeda in the Arabian Peninsula	Saudi Arabia, Yemen
Regional/ transnational	Control or influence over a territory overlapping current national boundaries on ethnic or ideological grounds	Al Qaeda in the Islamic Maghreb	Northwest Africa
		Boko Haram	Northern Nigeria, Cameroon, Chad, Niger
National	Overthrow and replacement of current government within the existing state	Al Shabab	Somalia, Kenya
		Taliban	Afghanistan
		Tehrik-i-Taliban	Pakistan
Sub-national (local)	Autonomy or control over areas within the existing state	Mai Mai Militias	DRC
		Haqqani Network	Northeast Afghanistan
Criminal enterprise	Economic gain	"Pirates"	Somalia

* *Some NSAGs do not fit neatly into one category, but contain features of two. As depicted above, Al Shabab is primarily a nationalist movement but has some global jihadist links, and the Haqqani network has criminal elements.*

** *Not an exhaustive list*

Fig. 3.1 Non-state armed groups. (From Humanitarian Outcomes' *Aid Worker Security Report 2017*: *Behind the Attacks: A look at the perpetrators of violence against aid workers*)

facilities and vehicles, aid organizations can dramatically reduce their risk of economically motivated attacks.

Political perpetrators, on the other hand, have a different and more extensive set of motives. To contend with the threat they may pose, aid workers need to forge a more detailed understanding of who the potential attackers are and what they want. For example, what are the group's military and strategic objectives, as stated or as demonstrated by their past actions? What level of power and control are they seeking—local, provincial, national, or even global? To what degree does the group demonstrate internal cohesion—or, in other words, does it exhibit sufficient command and control that an agreement with a commander will be transmitted down to and respected by local foot soldiers? These group features are necessary to understand because they offer clues to their scope of potential targets, the means and tactics they may use to strike, and how positively or negatively they perceive various humanitarian actors.

Understanding group motivations can lead to surprising conclusions about the proper tactical response. Consider two national-level insurgent groups, the Taliban in Afghanistan and Al Shabab in Somalia, who between them are responsible for the largest number of recorded attacks in which the perpetrators are known. Both of these groups are fighting in "internationalized conflicts," both have been aligned with and received support from global jihadist movements, and Al Shabab has conducted significant terrorist strikes outside its borders (in neighboring Kenya). However, both groups are fundamentally national insurgencies, engaged in campaigns of concrete strategic measures aimed at seizing control of their country's government in the foreseeable future. For this reason, even though they have the highest number of aid worker casualties to their names, they are also the most likely of the non-state armed groups to forge agreements for the secure access of humanitarian operations.

International jihadist movements such as Al Qaeda and IS, on the other hand, require a different approach, given their distinct methods and objectives. Although these extremist groups are responsible for smaller absolute numbers of aid worker casualties, their attacks can be more sophisticated and, when executed successfully, cause higher numbers of fatalities. In addition to being more lethal in their tactics (often employing explosives and suicide elements), such groups have also been known to specifically target foreign aid workers and organizations in order to gain international media visibility and promote their propaganda objectives. Global insurgent groups are also, by definition, more sweeping in their ambition and thus naturally have fewer incentives to engage in negotiations with aid organizations on the ground. To the contrary, in many cases they will exploit the visibility of high-profile attacks on aid workers to advance their agenda of terrorizing local populations, broadcasting ideological messages throughout the world and, in the case of hostages, often generating income from ransom. The data reflect the balance of these incentives, showing that these groups are responsible for more deaths per incident and a higher proportion of international victims than other perpetrator groups.

To make matters worse, many of today's global insurgent movements lack a true top-down leadership hierarchy that could serve as a reliable negotiating partner even if they wanted to. Since the US routed its bases in Afghanistan in the post-September 11 military campaign, Al Qaeda has relied on a network of underground cells and "lone-wolf" operators to plan and implement terrorist strikes against the West, while also providing support to help foment fundamentalist Sunni uprisings around the world. It does not attempt to capture territory and build a state apparatus from which to confront its enemies. This strategic orientation, which Al Qaeda members note has a long historical precedent in the Muslim world,[21] stands in contrast to the "open fronts"[22] jihadist warfare it engaged in prior to 2001, which included Bosnia, Chechnya, and Afghanistan during the control of the Taliban. From its current decentralized global perch, Al Qaeda takes a sweeping, ideological view of the international humanitarian sector, conflating all aid entities as mere tools for extending US hegemonic power. In a typical expression of this view, a 2010 article in Al Qaeda's magazine *Inspire*, written in the form of a letter to President Barack Obama, includes among its demands that "you must seize [*sic*] all interference in the religion, society, politics, economy, and government of the Islamic world. This means putting an immediate stop to the deployment of your Economic Hit men, CIA jackals, Peace Corp volunteers, US Aid Employees, and UN and US sponsored nongovernmental organizations. All of which put together represent the vanguard of American interference in our region and the world."[23]

The other major global insurgent group, the Islamic State (IS)—also known as the Islamic State of Iraq and Syria (ISIS), the Islamic State of Iraq and the Levant (ISIL), or by the pejorative moniker Daesh—in some ways resembles a more traditional national front but has proven over its history to be as unpredictable as Al Qaeda. The Islamic State evolved from a smaller Jordanian jihadist group called Jamā'at al-Tawḥīd wa-al-Jihād in response to the American-led invasion of Iraq in 2003. For a time, the group acted as an official Al Qaeda satellite, coordinating attacks against occupation military and civilian outposts in Iraq. While retaining an internationalist campaign with a sophisticated social media strategy to reach out to and groom receptive individuals in the West, on the ground the group's forces were conquering and governing, and they eventually distanced themselves from the larger Al Qaeda network. For them, the global caliphate became a concrete plan of action, as opposed to Al Qaeda's more abstract idea of an eventual prophesied historical outcome, and for a few years, the former satellite group seemed to be making serious strides

[21] "This jihadi school is very old… maybe its first experience was the unit of the Prophet's great companion Abu Basir." From Al-Suri, A. (2010). "The Jihadi Experience." *Inspire*, Issue 2, Fall 2010, p. 14.

[22] "The meaning of Open Fronts is that there are mujahidin forces whose presence is overt and linked to permanent bases. They fight the enemy forces on open battle lines, or they fight a guerilla war from those fixed positions." From Al-Suri, A. (2010). "The Jihadi Experience." *Inspire*, Issue 2, Fall 2010, p. 14.

[23] Gadahn, A. (2010). *Inspire*, Issue 2, Fall 2010, p. 70.

toward its goal of constructing a new state through conquest. At its height, the rebranded "Islamic State" encompassed roughly a third each of the landmasses of Iraq and Syria, in a narrow and meandering but mostly contiguous sweep of territory roughly the area of Great Britain.[24] By 2014, it had approximately 900 million people under its control.

The new state required systems of government, social services, utilities, and so on, and IS was surprisingly successful in filling a significant portion of these roles through coercion, economic incentives, and foreign recruitment. Humanitarian needs in the conquered areas, however, were too extensive for the group to manage completely on its own. Humanitarian organizations working in Syria and across borders reported that, in the beginning, IS members had shown some willingness to negotiate with them and arrange for humanitarian operations to take place in the areas under their control. Our researchers found an example where, after expelling a Western NGO, IS had trouble meeting the costs for the medical supplies and health workers' salaries that the NGO was providing, so they invited the organization back. However, the humanitarians soon discovered that IS was a highly unreliable negotiating counterpart and would frequently violate the terms of the agreement without warning. Ideology trumped the group's nationalist ambitions, and after several high-profile kidnappings and killings, international organizations ceased attempting to work with IS altogether.

The organization Geneva Call, which has done extensive research into negotiations between non-state forces and humanitarian actors,[25] does not include either Al Qaeda or IS in its database of nearly 250 non-state armed groups, perhaps indicating the futility of the prospect of successful negotiations with either group. Our own researchers were not able to arrange interviews with members of the Islamic State or Al Qaeda, and instead scoured their public statements and written materials, including their magazines *Dabiq*, *Rumiyah*, and *Inspire*. In them, we found little to suggest anything approaching a nuanced view of, or much interest in, the international aid sector. Instead, these groups are more inclined to tar humanitarians with a broad brush. One of the few references to humani-

[24] Johnson, H. (2016). *Mapped: The Islamic State Is Losing Its Territory – and Fast. Foreign Policy*. Retrieved 24 February 2019 from https://foreignpolicy.com/2016/03/16/mapped-the-islamic-state-is-losing-its-territory-and-fast/

[25] Geneva Call, "Their Words: Directory of Armed Non-State Actor Humanitarian Commitments." Available at http://theirwords.org/

tarians in *Dabiq* came in a story about the American-Israeli journalist Steven Sotloff, whom IS held hostage and ultimately executed. "The case of Steven Sotloff contains a direct refutation against those who portray western journalism and humanitarian aid as purely innocent, for this man was a Jew and citizen of the Jewish state."[26] Even erstwhile local allies have criticized their extreme measures and gratuitous cruelty. Said one Taliban soldier in Helmand, Afghanistan, "IS kills anyone that they think is not supporting them, without having any evidence. They even kill children and elders, whom we respect and protect."

It is a different story with local- and national-level insurgencies. Some of them may share the political ideology and extremist religious values of the globalist groups and frequently work in cooperation with them toward specific objectives, but national-level insurgent groups are more immediately concerned with fighting against their own government and occupying forces than a global Western hegemony. These groups, which are bent ultimately on seizing control of the state, will have more scope to negotiate and, in some circumstances, compelling reasons to cooperate with aid organizations. Once territory is secured, it is in the insurgents' interest to bring in humanitarian aid groups to help meet the needs of the population, as long as the humanitarians toe the line. Stathis Kalyvas, an expert in civil conflict, has published research showing that insurgent groups use violence more indiscriminately in areas they do not control, whereas in areas under their control the violence is less necessary and used only selectively, to maintain pressure for local populations to cooperate and to gain information on potential defectors.[27] Humanitarians can thus expect more cooperation and fewer attempted attacks from a "governing" insurgent group, and, conversely, will see instability and violence ramping up again when the government side of the conflict attempts to regain control.

The distinction between global and national insurgent groups, however, is often not so clear. Al Shabab (AS) is primarily a Somali nationalist movement, but it also possesses some internationalist elements similar to the global jihadist groups. The name Al Shabab means "the youth," and Islamist values allowed the organization to form by transcending clan affiliations, in a rebuff to the various clan elders who had shut young Somalis out of power and opportunity. Today, AS leadership exhibits its own gen-

[26] "A Message from Sotloff." *Dabiq*, Issue 4, 2013.

[27] Kalyvas, S. N. (2006). *The Logic of Violence in Civil War*. Cambridge; New York: Cambridge University Press.

erational split, between the younger elements, which tend to be more extremist in ideology and more interested in global jihad, and their elder counterparts, who have spent decades devoted to seizing control of the Somali government and remain principally nationalist in their aims. Not unlike the clans who still exercise control in the non-AS-held parts of Somalia, AS leaders often approach negotiations with humanitarian organizations as an economic transaction, requiring payments for access for humanitarians to work, essentially "demanding their cut of the aid work business taking place in their territory."[28] AS has also used humanitarian agencies to demonstrate their power and control over their territories, through harassment and periodically expelling entire organizations from working in their regions.

The Afghanistan Taliban is another national-level insurgency that has been fighting a civil war for decades but also has ties to global jihadist movements. Since being ousted from its short reign of control (1996–2001) by the US-led invasion after 9/11, the Taliban has waged a campaign of guerrilla warfare to claw back districts and provinces across the country, creating shadow government structures and using terrorist modalities to strike at government-allied international targets. Since Afghanistan remains one of the most underdeveloped nations in the world, the Taliban has a long history with humanitarian organizations. Historically, they have allowed and encouraged aid projects they deemed necessary and worthy, such as medical facilities and health care, while rejecting others, especially girls' education. Like Al Shabab, however, the Afghan armed opposition is not a monolithic organization. The Haqqani network joined forces with the Taliban in the 1990s under the Islamic Emirate of Afghanistan (IEA) but retains its unique characteristics that make it somewhat of a hybrid between an armed militia and a criminal gang. It is responsible for numerous kidnappings, targeting nationals of countries whose governments are known to pay (or facilitate payments of) ransoms. Humanitarian security professionals have found Haqqani network members, historically less concerned with seizing and governing territory, to be more unpredictable and generally less willing to negotiate than their Taliban counterparts.

In 2017, my colleagues and I arranged interviews with members of three of the armed groups described above: Al Shabab in Somalia and the Taliban and Haqqani Network in Afghanistan. Our research partner orga-

[28] Ibid, p. 11.

nizations[29] in the two countries reached out to these groups, using their local networks of contacts to identify people who were willing to speak on the topic, and conducted the interviews using our questionnaire. We sought these first-person perspectives in order to contextualize the data we were seeing; so we asked these individuals why their forces had used violence against humanitarians, under what circumstances did they see this violence as justified, and what would be required for them to allow aid groups to operate safely. In doing so, we built upon and benefited from the pioneering research of Ashley Jackson, in a series of reports she wrote for the Overseas Development Institute and Geneva Call,[30] *Talking to the Enemy* and *In Their Words: Perceptions of Armed Non-State Actors on Humanitarian Action.*

The interviews offered new insight on how these groups perceive humanitarian aid workers, who can alternately represent obstacles, threats, and potential benefits to the insurgents' agenda. While we cannot claim that our sample is representative, the interviewees of the different groups expressed sentiments about aid organizations that were remarkably consistent. The most significant discrepancy among them seemed to be the extent to which they differentiated among aid organizations, with some interviewees lumping all organizations together as bad actors and others drawing careful distinctions around what they saw were the one or two groups worthy of respect and protection. One Taliban soldier told us that the aid groups were "different from each other in terms of services, intention, and purpose." He cited the Afghan Red Crescent specifically as "one of the organizations which provide exceptional humanitarian services in any kind of situation. It provides healthcare services for the victims of war." The Afghan insurgents were more likely to take this somewhat more nuanced view of aid organizations than were Al Shabab members, likely because of the Taliban's history of being in control of the government at one time, when they cooperated more extensively with the international humanitarian sector. Even so, the positive attitudes were reserved more

[29] In Afghanistan, we partnered with The Liaison Office (TLO) and in Somalia with Hikmah Consulting.

[30] Jackson, A., & Giustozzi, A. (2012). Talking to the other side: Humanitarian engagement with the Taliban in Afghanistan. London: Humanitarian Policy Group, ODI.

Jackson, A., & Aynte, A. J. L. (2013). Talking to the other side: Humanitarian negotiations with Al-Shabaab in Somalia. Humanitarian Policy Group, ODI.

Heritage Institute for Policy Studies; Jackson, A. (2016). In their words: Perceptions of armed non-state actors on humanitarian action. Geneva: Geneva Call.

for national NGOs and the Afghan Red Crescent than for international ones.[31] We also noticed that high-ranking interviewees had a fairly detailed understanding of the architecture and funding mechanisms of the humanitarian sector and shaped their opinions of its constituents accordingly. For example, a senior Al Shabab member had this to say:

> All UN agencies are banned. Almost ninety percent of INGOs and about fifty percent of Muslim and national NGOs are also banned. If a national NGO approaches us with projects to implement, we look at the source of the funding. If it is a UN agency or other NGO that is banned, then we reject their application. Because the source is the same and this NGO is acting on behalf of a banned organization. It is just the banned organization with another face.

The interviewees expressed little disagreement in terms of the negative perceptions they held of humanitarian actors, though, which we grouped into the following three categories: "agents of the enemy," "rivals for authority/creators of dependency," and "violators of religious and cultural norms." Regarding the enemy agent perception, it became clear in interview after interview that this was the most commonly held suspicion of humanitarian organizations. An Al Shabab interviewee who had previously held the position of Social Affairs Officer for the organization explained: "Principally, AS believes that all NGOs work for spying agencies and it is AS policy to make it difficult for NGOs to work in AS-controlled area. They say they are here for humanitarian purpose but what they are actually doing is spying, measuring the land, and reconnaissance." Striking a similar note, an Afghan Taliban member said, "We also know … some organizations who were intending to work here for spying over us. As soon as we identify those entities, we arrest their employees, and based on sayings of our Ameer, Mullah Muhammad Omar, we then would be allowed to give them any punishment, including the death penalty and that organization will never be allowed to come and work in the areas under our control." Another, from Khost Province, echoed these sentiments: "They say that they are working for promoting people's rights, but in reality they are spying for foreigners or government. It means many

[31] However, a few international organizations made the worthy list as well: CARE, the Danish Committee for Aid to Afghan Refugees (DACAAR), MSF, and UNHCR are examples of organizations cited by interviewees.

organizations working here are spying for the puppet government, but a small number are serving people."

Viewing the humanitarians as in league with their enemies provides the necessary justification for attacking them. Even for the most extremist of the insurgent groups, having justification for violence is important for public relations reasons as well as for the mental condition of the fighters committing it. In war, of course, violence against one's enemy is inherently justified, and our interviewees made clear they had no compunction against using force against aid workers if they fit this role. Suspicion of spying (a hostile military act) is one such rationale, as is defaming or proselytizing against Islam if the insurgent group also embraces a concept of holy war in their mission. In his audio statement claiming responsibility for the Canal Hotel bombing, Al Qaeda leader Abu Musab al-Zarqawi took pains to provide an additional political-religious justification for the killing of Sergio Viera de Mello, saying the diplomat had been specifically targeted in part for his role in negotiating independence for East Timor, the heavily Catholic territory formerly under the control of Muslim-majority Indonesia.[32] Al Shabab stretched the holy war logic further to raise the stakes for humanitarians working in their territories, declaring that refusal to pay bribes would mark the aid organization as an enemy of Islam. A former commander in Kismayo explained, "Because they see aid agencies as businesses, they also ask them to contribute to the jihad effort periodically as they do with all businesses in their area of control. If you don't pay, you are against them and that makes you a legitimate target."

In addition to using humanitarians as direct and proxy targets, the insurgents have also found use for them as pawns in prisoner exchange negotiations with the other side. Al Qaeda leaders have explicitly called for the kidnappings of Westerners for this purpose,[33] but national-level insurgent groups use this strategy as well. The director of an Afghan NGO I spoke to, who requested anonymity for himself and his organization,

[32] The statement came after the attack, and this particular rationale was most likely post hoc. It is not even clear whether Al Qaeda in Iraq (AQI) knew that they were parking the truck bomb directly under Viera de Mello's office or if it was merely a matter of that left-side access road being the best or only assault position.

[33] An article on Al Jazeera's website "New al-Qaeda tape urges kidnappings," quoted Zarqawi's (short-lived) successor Abu Hamza al-Muhajir from an audio recording: "I call on every holy fighter in Iraq to strive during this holy month [Ramadan]… to capture some dogs of the Christians so that we can liberate our imprisoned sheikh," Retrieved from https://www.aljazeera.com/archive/2006/09/2008410927465173 83.html

told me that in 2007 a team of local aid workers in his district was kidnapped by the insurgent forces specifically to pressure the government to release the body of one of their fighters. The government acceded to the demand, he said, after one of the hostages was beheaded.

The idea that the humanitarian organizations were using their assistance to create dependency and exercise control over local populations was particularly salient among the Somali insurgents interviewed, who have all lived through decades of food insecurity and periods of full-blown famine. This belief feeds a larger narrative of Western powers seeking to dominate Somalia and other countries through soft power modalities. Adding insult to injury, they believe the aid provided is not even of decent quality. As a senior Al Shabab commander said, "The food they bring is expired food and they bring sacks of maize from America to undercut the Somali production, to cheat and humiliate our people. The purpose is to make the Somalis people who can do nothing for themselves."[34]

The third negative perception held by some insurgent groups—that aid workers in their countries trample on their socio-religious norms—sits especially uneasily with the international humanitarian sector, whose members like to believe that their work is in service to a universal set of altruistic values. But humanitarian organizations that overlook or underplay the normative and cultural motivations of the insurgent groups do so at their peril. Aid workers attached to Western organizations, whether secular or faith-based, often live and work in ways that are antithetical to local values or the religious beliefs of the would-be attackers. Depending on the location, this could include consumption of alcohol, inappropriate dress, social mixing of male and female staff, or the hiring of female staff members at all. One international NGO in Afghanistan had a grenade lobbed over their compound wall in response—they later learned—to a staff party where males and females socialized together and played music. Another NGO in Pakistan built a new wall in their compound to separate their male and female staff after receiving a threatening letter. There have also been cases where religious NGOs have been threatened and attacked for allegedly proselytizing and seeking converts to Christianity. Attacks designed to punish these behaviors are opportunities for the insurgent group to signal their moral values and to warn local inhabitants not to

[34] Interview conducted for Stoddard, A., Harmer, A., & Czwarno, M. (2017). Aid Worker Security Report 2017: Behind the attacks: a look at the perpetrators of violence against aid workers. Humanitarian Outcomes.

similarly transgress. Such attacks may even gain some sympathy among the local population if the behavior of the aid group ran strongly afoul of local mores.[35]

Among the various reasons the insurgents cited to explain the use of violence against humanitarian operations, one stood out as especially chilling. An Al Shabab member admitted that attacking aid workers was offered as a kind of perk to their zealous young soldiers—a chance for them to see some action and let off steam. "Most of the members are youngsters who are not paid regularly and are highly charged and emotional as a result of the constant indoctrinations to keep them going," he explained. "The older members can distinguish and know the differences and exceptions [among aid agencies] but the youngsters don't, and actually don't care. They are looking for an infidel to kill and when they can't find them, Muslims are tagged as infidels. This freedom they have, to do what suits them with impunity, is also [a way to keep them] highly motivated. They are not paid, hence are left to follow their instincts to destroy and feel high. This is a kind of payment."

Al Shabab's ability to use violence against "infidels" as a motivator and a unifying force for its young soldiers shows the particular potency of religious fervor to fuel and sustain insurgent warfare. The Taliban interviewees placed more emphasis on due process and having evidence of transgressions before committing violence against the humanitarian staff, but they too stressed religious justifications. In a typical answer to our question of "When is it permissible to use force against aid workers?" a 33-year old soldier in Khost answered, "Those organizations who are working against our religion and want to spread the democracy, if we would find any of their workers with proof, we can give them any kind of punishment."

Jihadists have also relied on religious justifications to break in new recruits and get them past their initial revulsion to physical violence. A young Canadian recruit to IS called Abu Huzayfah, who was profiled in the *New York Times* podcast "Caliphate," described a systematic process of desensitization, where he and his fellow recruits were progressively exposed to violence, while being reassured by their commanders that this was part of their sacred duty. "They would say to us, 'It's going to be hard

[35] Stoddard, A., Harmer, A., & Czwarno, M. (2017). Aid Worker Security Report 2017: Behind the attacks: a look at the perpetrators of violence against aid workers. Humanitarian Outcomes, p. 7.

for you guys. The first time, it's going to affect you a lot. You're going to be sad, you're going to be sick, and you might even faint from the blood. But what you have to do is you just have to drink down those emotions. Remember you are doing this for God.'"[36]

For humanitarians to negotiate successfully—or to recognize the times when negotiation is impossible—they must understand both the overriding motivations and the immediate, practical interests of the armed groups. And further, they must assess which of these holds more sway over the group's behavior at the current time.

Getting (Close Enough) to Yes: Developing the Art of Humanitarian Negotiation

When humanitarians are able to establish secure and successful operations in civil conflicts, we can generally assume it is not because the fighting forces have decided to honor the spirit of the Geneva Conventions. Rather, it is because they have concluded that allowing the humanitarians to operate is in their interest. A small but growing number of aid agencies have come to understand that if they seek to work where ongoing conflicts are creating the worst humanitarian needs, it is not enough to "advocate" for access based on abstract humanitarian principles; they must forge agreements in which both sides get something they want. The successful outcome of a negotiation is a mutually beneficial agreement that you can be reasonably confident that the other side will not violate without causing themselves some harm.

In the past, most of the work on humanitarian advocacy and civil-military engagement has focused on formal state militaries and governments, simply because it is much easier than dealing with non-state armed groups. With state entities, there are clear points of engagement and leadership structures wherein programs of education and indoctrination can have a measurable impact on the battlefield conduct of soldiers. Unfortunately, these national militaries are only one part of the problem, and the smaller part, given the majority of warring parties in today's armed conflicts, are non-state groups. It is immensely more challenging to work with armed forces that are loosely organized or decentralized, poorly paid, and far less disciplined. In some recently published research, the

[36] *New York Times* podcasts, *Caliphate*, Chapter 4: "Us vs. Them." https://www.nytimes.com/2018/09/20/podcasts/caliphate-transcript-chapter-four-us-versus-them.html

International Committee of the Red Cross (ICRC) has acknowledged that its work to promote understanding and respect for international humanitarian law has been overly focused on national militaries.[37] In their 2018 report for the ICRC called "The Roots of Restraint in War," Fiona Terry and Brian McQuinn laid out the challenge of the different constellation of warfighters in the current age: "ICRC data show that only one-third of conflicts today are between two belligerent parties: 44 percent have between three and nine opposing forces, and 22 percent have more than ten. Some conflicts have hundreds."[38] Further, they write, "In 2017, some 40 percent of states experiencing armed conflict were confronting jihadi groups, and the vast majority of all foreign interventions are currently against armed groups with a jihadist agenda."[39]

Coming to grips with the reality of these conflicts, the conflict actors, and their own roles is essential for humanitarians if they are to successfully negotiate secure access for their operations. Larissa Fast, in her book *Aid in Danger: The Perils and Promise of Humanitarianism*, writes that humanitarians see themselves and their project as external to the conflict and political dynamics swirling around them, rather than as players within it. This "humanitarian exceptionalism," as she calls it, leads humanitarians to overlook relationships between themselves and the actors around them, and to pay insufficient attention to their own behavior, all of which directly affect their security.

In March 2019, Clémence Boutant-Willm, an expert on humanitarian access negotiations at the Norwegian Refugee Council, died tragically along with dozens of other aid workers in the crash of an Ethiopian Airlines 737 MAX 8 plane. She and a colleague, Sam Pegram, were en route to Nairobi to run trainings for humanitarians on how to negotiate with armed groups. A few months before the crash, Boutant-Willm spoke to us about what it takes for aid workers to negotiate secure access successfully. Commitment to principles, altruism, and good faith by humanitarians are not enough, she explained—there are practical skills they must learn. "Principles are for us, but when we explain them to interlocutors, they have to be adapted," she said. "Where we see gaps [in the humanitarian sector], it isn't in the area of principles, but capacities." Sean Healy, a humanitarian adviser at Médecins Sans Frontières (MSF)-Holland, agrees.

[37] Terry, F., & McQuinn, B. (2018). *The Roots of Restraint in War*. Geneva: ICRC.
[38] Ibid., p. 13.
[39] Ibid., p. 14.

"I can't think of one situation where [international humanitarian law] was used for a negotiation tactic or strategic framework for dealing with access," he said in an interview with me. "MSF has moved to a transactional framework on how, why and on what parties will agree."

To this end, a few organizations are adapting the principles of negotiation theory popularized in books like Fisher and Ury's *Getting to Yes* for use by their field teams in communicating with armed groups. Respect for law and core humanitarian principles are not abandoned in these efforts, but neither are they the meat of the talks. Instead, they constitute the identity position of the humanitarians at the outset of the negotiation; they are "the way we [humanitarians] promote ourselves and how we seek to engage with the parties we are negotiating with," says the Danish Refugee Council's Access Adviser, Ross Allen. "Once the engagement is made, then we start talking about compromises."

Compromise is central to negotiation, of course, and represents a key point of departure from advocacy. Negotiation entails that for both sides to get something, they must also both sacrifice something. For the armed group, it may be a question of tolerating the presence of international entities they don't entirely trust to mix with their population in exchange for needed services. As we have seen, local- or national-level insurgent groups that have decisively seized control of an area may have a keen interest in providing services to the population they now control. The armed group's new incentive to provide governance functions makes humanitarian organizations useful to them and provides humanitarians with an entry point.

In actively contested areas, by contrast, the incentives of the insurgent forces may lean more toward attacking humanitarians than cooperating with them. Even in these phases of conflict, however, it can be possible to gain the tolerance, if not the welcome, of the armed groups. The International Committee of the Red Cross (ICRC) and Médecins Sans Frontières (MSF) are examples of humanitarian organizations that have managed to work in some of the most extreme conflict environments by continually and assiduously negotiating with belligerents. This requires employing dedicated negotiators with the appropriate expertise and skills, an investment both organizations have made. At the same time, it should not be forgotten that the types of services these organizations provide give them a leg up in most negotiations. Both organizations adhere strongly to the Dunantist humanitarian principles, and also provide direct, tangible value to insurgent groups that most other aid organizations do not. MSF field hospitals treat wounded fighters, from all sides, as well as civilians. It is not hard to see why an insurgent force would allow this to continue. As an Al Shabab district commander told our interviewers, "When MSF was here, they were useful to us. They were helping our injured soldiers as well as the general public." ICRC provides similar medical services and also arranges care for prisoners of war, exchange of hostages, and the return of bodily remains of soldiers—again, services of direct value to all sides of a conflict. The investments and inherent advantages of ICRC and MSF have not, unfortunately, averted all attacks against them, and both organizations have decided to pull out of areas in response to violence. Overall, however, the two organizations have demonstrated their ability to work in more hostile conditions than a great many of their counterparts.[40]

When speaking with members of Al Shabab, the Taliban, and the Haqqani network, our interviewers asked them to define the conditions under which they would tolerate humanitarian organizations working in their areas. As we wrote in our report, "Their answers ranged from the broad ('They should never do any activity that is against Islam') to the specific ('They should submit their beneficiary list to us before they give anything'). On balance, the respondents were broadly consistent that agencies should defer to their authority and their interpretation of Islamic law, should explain clearly what they intend to do, should perform up to a certain standard, and should make some level of concession or payment."[41] In addition, they expressed genuine concern that the aid delivered should be of high quality and relevant to what the local population wants and needs. In short, their conditions for acceptance of humanitarian operations were: "Obey the rules, address the priority humanitarian needs (as we define them), and pay up."[42]

While they did not always mention requiring payments, the members of the armed groups made it very clear that permission for the humanitarian organizations to work safely was entirely at their discretion. As one Taliban member said, "If an NGO wants to work here, first it should contact us to

[40] Stoddard, A., Jillani, S., Caccavale, J., Cooke, P., Guillemois, D., & Klimentov, V. (2017). Out of Reach: How Insecurity Prevents Humanitarian Aid from Accessing the Neediest. *Stability: International Journal of Security and Development, 6*(1). doi:https://doi.org/10.5334/sta.506

[41] Stoddard, A., Harmer, A., & Czwarno, M. (2017). *Aid Worker Security Report 2017: Behind the attacks: a look at the perpetrators of violence against aid workers.* Humanitarian Outcomes, p. 15.

[42] Ibid.

understand their plan and activities. After that, we will find information about their background and understand their main intention about their plan. Finally, we will let them proceed if their activities are not against Islam and for the benefit of our people." Some of them rattled off a clear list of their expectations, like this Haqqani network member: "The first condition is that they should never do any activity that is against Islam or for the defaming of Islam. Secondly, they should not have any female employee and they should come to our area with Islamic clothes on. Thirdly, they should contact the tribal elders of the area and then they will contact us, and we will give them permission through the local elders of the area. Fourthly, they should work purely to help the local people."

This brings us to the compromises that humanitarians are forced to make when negotiating access, which often take the form of uncomfortable infringements to the humanitarian principles.[43] They may find themselves having to decide, for instance, if they are willing to provide payments or other concessions to armed forces (or other powerful actors and gatekeepers) in exchange for being allowed to reach a needy population with relief aid. My colleagues Katherine Haver and Will Carter found evidence that the types of compromises commonly facing humanitarian organizations include paying "tolls" or "customs" fees to armed groups at checkpoints; paying "taxes" for the privilege of working in certain areas; adding to or otherwise altering their targeted lists of aid recipients to favor specific populations or individuals, putting local militia members on their payroll; and avoiding certain areas or types of programming "so as not to antagonise a local authority, armed actor or dominant community."[44]

These are not easy decisions, and different organizations might well make different choices. What Haver and Carter's research makes clear, however, is that humanitarians cannot realistically avoid such decisions in contested environments. The organizations that make them consciously and deliberately, weighing the costs against the opportunity to provide aid, tend to be more successful in maintaining their access.[45] Unfortunately, most humanitarian organizations do not formally engage in negotiations with armed groups, due to lack of skills, resources, or will, which goes a long way to explaining why so few organizations are operational in conflict

[43] Haver, K., & Carter, W. (2016). *What it Takes: Principled pragmatism to enable access and quality humanitarian aid in insecure environments*. Humanitarian Outcomes.

[44] Ibid., p. 11.

[45] Ibid., p. 61.

zones. An NGO staff member working in the Democratic Republic of Congo told our research team that more than half of the NGOs working there had not made any contact with any of the multiple armed groups that could potentially pose a threat to them. Attacks and kidnappings of aid workers were now on the rise there, he said, as the predictable result. When organizations are unwilling to make explicit decisions of what they will and will not accept, they tend instead to adopt an attitude of willful blindness. They allow for low-level arrangements to be made, often by their local staff or partner organizations, and choose not to ask questions. This is an inadvisable way to conduct bilateral negotiations, and moreover makes multilateral negotiations impossible, since if humanitarian organizations are not sharing information with each other, they cannot coordinate to form common negotiation positions and red lines (non-negotiable points).

To many, the idea of applying any conditions on the provision of aid to needy people is anathema to humanitarian principles and could justifiably be considered a non-starter for an aid organization. For agencies of a more pragmatic bent, the takeaway from this small sample of armed group members may be more positive. The fact that the insurgents could readily list a series of conditions that in their view would make the humanitarian programming acceptable, and that none of them responded that humanitarians would never be tolerated under any circumstance, shows that negotiated access is at least theoretically possible. The small number of agencies that persist in attempting to access hard-to-reach populations rarely think in terms of stark choices, but rather questions of degree. For example, to what degree will they compromise on the principle of impartiality and include additional names on recipient lists dictated by armed group favoritism? To what degree will they go against their egalitarian values to accede to fundamentalist religious dictates about women?

The issue of employing female staff is especially fraught. It is not merely a question of the aid organizations wanting to support equal rights for women; without female staff, it becomes impossible to do the kind of programming that targets women and girls as a particularly vulnerable group. One international humanitarian NGO, which aspires to gender balance in its staff for reasons of both fairness and better programming, says it must regularly compromise such principles in order to make its work possible. In Kandahar, it allows fathers and village elders to inspect its facilities to ensure there is sufficient separation of the sexes. In Al Nusra-controlled territory in Syria, it set a policy of not allowing women in vehicles that had to cross checkpoints. In Iraq, shortly after Mosul was retaken from IS by Iraqi and international forces, the organization lobbied hard with the families of local female staff to let them travel into the city with relief convoys, promising separate accommodations and even allowing male relatives to accompany the female employees on the journey, at significant extra cost.

Sometimes humanitarians will comply with the demands or interference of armed groups on the justification that it is to the benefit of the local population. In Somalia, our colleagues learned, Al Shabab approached a humanitarian organization with a request to de-silt some aging water reservoirs, and the organization, having "determined that the benefits of this work would be community-wide, …was happy to comply."[46] It is also possible for humanitarians to effectively push back on the armed group when it goes too far in capitalizing on the aid projects. In the early days of IS control over parts of Syria, IS members made an appearance at an NGO's health care facility to film propaganda videos. In response, the NGO closed the facility in protest of IS violating the terms of their understanding. "IS reportedly saw this as a fair response, and the situation was resolved over a period of four months."[47]

In summary, before setting to work amid active conflict, humanitarians need a clear-eyed understanding of the hurdles they face and then must work diligently to overcome them in their communications and actions. Once aid agencies are operating in an area, communication and negotiations with the armed groups must continue, lest the agreements for secure access erode with the turnover of personnel or changing conflict conditions. Understand that throughout nearly every interaction, the automatic assumption is you are a spy for, and/or an arm of, their enemy in the current conflict. The onus is on your organization to persuade them otherwise and to continue to cultivate trust. Know their red lines. Take them at their word that the most egregious transgression, in their view, is "disrespect" of Islam. Know that you will not achieve "acceptance" so much as tolerance, and only if you are seen to provide the services they want, pay for the privilege, and obey the rules they lay down.

At times, it can be simpler to call for the specific desired behavior without going into the principles that underpin it. An example is MSF's very clear "no guns" policy for their facilities and vehicles, communicated with

[46] Ibid., p. 38.
[47] Ibid.

an unmistakable emblem (a gun with a red line through it). Armed actors in many different countries, while they may not always respect it, understand this clearly as MSF's bottom line, and that violating it will have consequences. Similarly, the free treatment provided to any and all patients in MSF hospitals can be understood and respected without elucidation on the impartiality principle. MSF field workers point to such things as concrete, understandable elements that can anchor negotiations and clear a path for other points of agreement. Long before Robert Painter got to Baghdad, he experienced a similar phenomenon amid the chaos and violence of the civil war in Sierra Leone in the early 1990s. He helped develop a "code of conduct" for humanitarian agencies operating there, which took the form of a yellow laminated card that the aid organizations would put on the dashboard of their vehicles. It was rather audacious—its first point was that aid workers were prohibited from ever handing over goods or cash at checkpoints—but surprisingly successful at deflecting hostility. Aid workers stopped at a checkpoint could point to the card and shrug sympathetically, as if they would like to comply, but their hands were tied. Painter described an almost comical routine, where the checkpoint guards would see the card and throw their hands up in an expression of exasperation to the effect of "oh, damn, it's that yellow card again," and wave the aid workers on.

A pragmatic, transactional approach to humanitarian action need not be seen as the antithesis of international humanitarian law and the core humanitarian principles; on the contrary, it coheres more closely to the original Dunantist pragmatism that led to the founding of the modern humanitarian movement. The spirit of the original international conference in Geneva acknowledged the inevitability of war between nations and counted on all sides knowing it was in their interests to allow relief and protection for civilians, wounded soldiers, and prisoners of war. In this era, less affected by interstate wars than by civil conflicts and global insurgency, humanitarian objectives are not served by reifying and fetishizing the past-era principles as if they were ends in themselves. Fiona Terry, who spent years in the field with MSF and later worked with ICRC, has written at length about the contradictions and compromises that are unavoidable when humanitarian principles meet the realities of aid work. When it comes to the principles, she wrote back in 2002, it is of no use for humanitarians to "recite them as a mantra and treat them as moral absolutes."[48] Better, they should be adapted to better suit the reality of

[48] Terry, F. (2002). *Condemned to Repeat? The paradox of humanitarian action*. Cornell University Press.

non-international, asymmetric conflict. This is not to say that humanitarians have dispensed with making moral arguments, but when they do, they find they are more successful when they frame them within the relevant cultural or religious values. These are just naturally more compelling to the armed groups than appeals to nineteenth-century European battlefield etiquette. Norms of humanity, altruism, and protection of the vulnerable are universal, of course, but there are local routes to this same destination that can be more expeditious.

The challenge for promoting respect to humanitarian law among those who are likely to violate it, as Terry and McQuinn write in *The Roots of Restraint in War* report, is to connect it to ideas that have greater emotional resonance and relevance to the fighters' daily lives. Appealing to more proximate, familiar norms to influence the behavior of fighters, ICRC attempts to encourage them to refrain from committing the most extreme acts of violence, and from targeting the civilians, health care providers, and other aid workers who should be off-limits. In formal militaries with coherent command structures, the adherence to norms requires only the discipline of following orders. When it comes to informal and decentralized armed groups, however, the norms of restraint need to be socialized and internalized to the individual soldiers' sense of morality and the values they grew up with. For example, with fighters for whom Islamic law is paramount, ICRC's trainers and negotiators will "emphasize the correlation between IHL and Islamic principles regarding restraint towards civilians and the prohibition of the use of certain means and methods of warfare."[49] They will point out moreover, that Islamic law predates international humanitarian law (IHL) by more than a thousand years.

It is not clear how successful such a strategy can be, however, when the fighters' comrades and commanders are also using religion to motivate them, citing different parts of the Quran and Hadith to justify violence even against their co-religionists, as IS does. Aversion to violence is something that militaries have meticulously trained out of their fighters for as long as there have been wars to fight. As the young IS recruit recounted in *Caliphate*, he and his fellow soldiers were desensitized through social pressure and incremental exposure to and participation in violence, starting with practicing stabbing and beheading dolls and mannequins, then being tasked with slaughtering the chickens for dinner, eventually building up to a group firing squad-style execution of real people (leaders of a

[49] Terry, F., & McQuinn, B. (2018). *The Roots of Restraint in War*. Geneva: ICRC, p. 34.

Sunni tribe in Iraq) who, the fighters were told, were apostates, and so deserving of death. Once inured to violence and bonded with comrades in the bloody acts, countering these practices with norms of restraint seems challenging to say the least. It is hard to argue with the analysts and negotiation experts who have placed the global-level insurgents like IS aside, as a nut too tough to crack with the tools at humanitarians' disposal.

All our evidence[50] suggests that aid workers believe that the humanitarian principles remain relevant to their day-to-day work, as long as they are not treated as high ideals but rather as valuable but imperfect tools; tools that circumstances cause regularly to conflict with each other, and that often require compromise and judgment calls in their application. As Haver and Carter write, a "principled pragmatism"[51] is what allows humanitarian organizations to navigate the ethical dilemmas and take a realistic, context-specific approach to operationalizing the humanitarian principles in field settings. In some places and circumstances, Islamic law may be the best framing for sought after behavior; in others, it may be medical ethics that is most compelling. Humanitarian actors in Syria, for instance, note the salience of the Hippocratic Oath when justifying medical relief aid to any and all sides in the conflict. The Islamic principles of charity and hospitality are highly resonant in Afghanistan as are the principles of integrity and ethics in Somalia. Like the humanitarian principles forged in Geneva in the nineteenth century, all strive to separate and safeguard the moral duty to help people in need from the political or military duties and allegiances.

References

A Message from Sotloff to his Mother Days Before his Execution. *Dabiq*, Issue 4, 2013.

Al-Suri, A. (2010). The Jihadi Experience. *Inspire*, Issue 2, Fall 2010, p. 14.

Gadahn, A. (2010). *Inspire*, Issue 2, Fall 2010, p. 70.

Geneva Call. *Their Words: Directory of Armed Non-State Actor Humanitarian Commitments*. Available at http://theirwords.org/

[50] Evidence of the perceived relevance of principles to humanitarian work was seen in among scores of interviews of aid workers, and in survey results cited in Stoddard, A., Harmer, A., & Haver, K. (2011). *Aid Worker Security Report 2011. Spotlight on security for national aid workers: Issues and Perspectives.* Humanitarian Outcomes.

[51] Haver, K., & Carter, W. (2016). *What it Takes: Principled pragmatism to enable access and quality humanitarian aid in insecure environments.* Humanitarian Outcomes, p. 68.

Haver, K., & Carter, W. (2016). *What it Takes: Principled Pragmatism to Enable Access and Quality Humanitarian Aid in Insecure Environments*. New York: Humanitarian Outcomes.

Jackson, A. (2016). *In their Words: Perceptions of Armed Non-state Actors on Humanitarian Action*. Geneva: Geneva Call.

Jackson, A., & Aynte, A. J. L. (2013). *Talking to the Other Side: Humanitarian Negotiations with Al-Shabaab in Somalia*. Humanitarian Policy Group, ODI. London: Overseas Development Institute.

Jackson, A., & Giustozzi, A. (2012). *Talking to the Other Side: Humanitarian Engagement with the Taliban in Afghanistan*. London: Humanitarian Policy Group, ODI.

Jackson, A., & Zyck, S. A. (2017, June 22). Presence & Proximity: To Stay and Deliver, *Five Years On*. UN OCHA.

Johnson, H. (2016). Mapped: The Islamic State Is Losing Its Territory – and Fast. *Foreign Policy*. Retrieved February 24, 2019, from https://foreignpolicy.com/2016/03/16/mapped-the-islamic-state-is-losing-its-territory-and-fast/

Kalyvas, S. N. (2006). *The Logic of Violence in Civil War*. Cambridge/New York: Cambridge University Press.

Mendoza, M. (2009a). The Agonies of an Abu Sayyaf Kidnap Victim (1). *MindaNews*. Retrieved May 11, 2019, from https://www.mindanews.com/c3-news/2009/04/the-agonies-of-an-abu-sayyaf-kidnap-victim-1/

Mendoza, M. (2009b). The Agonies of an Abu Sayyaf Kidnap Victim (2): Coping with Captivity: One victim's Story. *MindaNews*. Retrieved May 11, 2019, from https://www.mindanews.com/c3-news/2009/04/the-agonies-of-an-abu-sayyaf-kidnap-victim-2-coping-with-captivity-one-victims-story/

Mendoza, M. (2009c). Post-Lenten Reflections of an Abu Sayyaf Kidnap Victim: Moving Forward (1). *MindaNews*. Retrieved May 13, 2019, from https://www.mindanews.com/c3-news/2009/04/post-lenten-reflections-of-an-abu-sayyaf-kidnap-victim-moving-forward-1/

Mitts, T. (2012). *Targeting and the Spatial Spread of Insurgent Violence A Study on Jammu and Kashmir*, India (Unpublished thesis). New York University, New York.

New York Times Podcasts. *Caliphate*, Chapter 4: "Us vs. Them" https://www.nytimes.com/2018/09/20/podcasts/caliphate-transcript-chapter-four-us-versus-them.html

O'Loughlin, J., & Witmer, F. (2011). The Localized Geographies of Violence in the North Caucasus of Russia, 1999–2007. *Annals, Association of American Geographers, 101*(1), 178–201.

Schutte, S., & Weidmann, N. B. (2011). Diffusion Patterns of Violence in Civil Wars. *Political Geography, 30*(3), 143–152.

Stoddard, A., Harmer, A., & Haver, K. (2011). *Aid Worker Security Report 2011. Spotlight on Security for National Aid Workers: Issues and Perspectives*. New York: Humanitarian Outcomes.

Stoddard, A., Harmer, A., & Toth, K. (2013, October). *The New Normal: Coping with the Kidnapping Threat.* New York: Humanitarian Outcomes.

Stoddard, A., Harmer, A., & Ryou, K. (2014). *Unsafe Passage: Road Attacks and their Impact on Humanitarian Operations.* New York: Humanitarian Outcomes.

Stoddard, A., Harmer, A., & Czwarno, M. (2017a). *Aid Worker Security Report 2017: Behind the Attacks: A Look at the Perpetrators of Violence against Aid Workers.* New York: Humanitarian Outcomes.

Stoddard, A., Jillani, S., Caccavale, J., Cooke, P., Guillemois, D., & Klimentov, V. (2017b). Out of Reach: How Insecurity Prevents Humanitarian Aid from Accessing the Neediest. *Stability: International Journal of Security and Development, 6*(1). New York: Humanitarian Outcomes. https://doi.org/10.5334/sta.506.

Terry, F. (2002). *Condemned to Repeat? The Paradox of Humanitarian Action.* Ithaca: Cornell University Press.

Terry, F., & McQuinn, B. (2018). *The Roots of Restraint in War.* Geneva: ICRC.

Townsley, M., Johnson, S., & Ratcliffe, J. (2008). Space Time Dynamics of Insurgent Activity in Iraq. *Security Journal, 21*, 139–146.

U.S. Army Special Operations Forces Field Manual (FM 34–36 Appendix D). https://fas.org/irp/doddir/army/fm34-36/appd.htm

Weidmann, N., & Ward, M. (2010). Predicting Conflict in Space and Time. *Journal of Conflict Resolution, 54*(6), 883–901.

Zhukov, Y. M. (2012). Roads and the Diffusion of Insurgent Violence: The Logistics of Conflict in Russia's North Caucasus, *Political Geography.* Copy at http://j.mp/sJDRBO

CHAPTER 4

When States Fail

A Raid in Juba

In July 2016, after beating back opposition forces in Juba, South Sudanese government soldiers stormed a residential area of the Terrain Hotel compound, which had been sheltering international humanitarian NGO workers amid the battle. What followed stands out among aid worker attacks both for the large number of personnel affected and for how it mirrored the chaotic and ruthless nature of the South Sudanese conflict in microcosm. As a UN report summarized it, "During the attack, civilians were subjected to and witnessed gross human rights violations, including murder, intimidation, sexual violence and acts amounting to torture perpetrated by armed Government soldiers." An Associated Press article conveyed the brutality even more directly with its lede: "The soldier pointed his AK-47 at the female aid worker and gave her a choice. 'Either you have sex with me, or we make every man here rape you and then we shoot you in the head,' she remembers him saying. She didn't really have a choice. By the end of the evening, she had been raped by 15 South Sudanese soldiers."[1]

In contrast to the orchestrated, complex attack-style raids on international aid compounds in Afghanistan and Pakistan, the Terrain attack left

[1] Patinkin, J. (2016). *Rampaging South Sudan troops raped foreigners, killed local* (August 15, 2016). *AP NEWS*. Retrieved 2 February 2019, from https://apnews.com/52f948f476874cbda6277492a4f8468e

A. Stoddard, *Necessary Risks*,
https://doi.org/10.1007/978-3-030-26411-6_4

only one person dead, and the violence appeared more random and haphazard—the unorganized behavior of rioting soldiers. The most notable thing about the attack, however, was that that the forces committing these crimes belonged not to an armed insurgency but to the government in power, the recipient, and host of the international humanitarian response. In addition, the United Nations peacekeeping forces, informed in real time about what was happening and located very nearby, took no action to stop the violence. The narrative below was pieced together from the accounts of survivors who agreed to be interviewed, supplemented by public reports and press articles. Some names were changed and certain other details omitted in consideration of those who did not wish to be identified.

At age 29, Elizabeth Jones left Washington, DC for South Sudan to take up her first professional humanitarian field position, something she had been keen to do since getting her master's degree in international affairs. The organization she worked for, Internews has an unusual remit for an NGO; rather than food or medicine or material assistance, it provides access to information for people in crisis and supports the development of free and open communications and independent journalism. For Jones, the idea of the free flow of information as both the facilitator and an objective of aid was a fascinating space to work in the humanitarian sector. She admired how the organization staffed the bulk of its emergency information program entirely with members of the community being served—South Sudanese who had fled the violence and who were living in the displaced persons camps. "I found it compelling to give these people a voice," she said. "The media and information landscape was still very underdeveloped in the country, so we were really starting with the basics there." After months of lobbying her bosses in the DC headquarters for a chance to get more field experience, Jones landed a field posting in South Sudan and flew to Juba in March 2016. Just four months later, she would find herself trapped there when an intense battle broke between government and opposition forces.

It was not the first time fighting had come to the capital; South Sudan, the youngest of the world's nation-states, achieved a negotiated independence from Sudan in 2011 after decades of civil war. The initial joy surrounding independence, and the hopes for peace and economic development to follow, had disintegrated within just two years as the new government fractured along ethno-political lines. The conflict drove roughly two million people from their homes, seeking protection from atrocities that followed each skirmish. Civilians who were not able to flee were subject to wholesale massacres. Women and girls were systematically raped by soldiers as a battle tactic; a type of war crime commonly associated with ethnic cleansing or genocide.

Armed conflict occurring in one of the world's poorest countries meant that, for international aid organizations, jobs in South Sudan were considered "hardship posts" and high risk. The expatriate humanitarian community in Juba had its share of seasoned veterans as well as 20-somethings, as yet unencumbered by families, looking to begin their careers and pay their dues in tough assignments. Few stayed very long. The staff of Internews skewed toward more experienced personnel, some of whom had done time in war zones. Jen Taylor was an Australian radio journalist who had joined the organization after several years of field work as a reporter for the Australian Broadcasting Corporation and additional experience in emergency broadcasting for disaster response. She had first come to Juba in 2013, to work with the UN and was there to experience the last time major fighting had erupted within the city limits, which prompted a temporary mass evacuation of international personnel that same year.

In early 2016, the security situation in Juba, and for aid workers throughout the country in general, was hard to predict. Sporadic combat and ensuing atrocities against civilians continued in other regions of the country, but unlike in other of the world's conflict hotspots, South Sudan was unique in that the internationals seemed far less likely to be targeted than their national colleagues, who faced the threat of ethnically based violence in the parts of the country where there was active fighting. Prior attacks on food distributions, while sometimes violent, seemed to be more about accessing the goods than punishing the deliverers. The aid organizations based in Juba had to contend mostly with economic crimes, such as burglaries and muggings, and the security incidents affecting international staff tended to involve people who had stayed out past curfew or were drinking in a prohibited bar. Taylor recalled that these incidents were viewed as isolated events of the "wrong place, wrong time" variety, and the sense among her colleagues in the international aid community was that, "if people had complied with security protocols this wouldn't have happened."

The Terrain Hotel was a gated compound containing several low buildings that served as residences for the international staff of Internews and a few other international NGOs. From a security standpoint, the site had initially been highly attractive. It was on the northern end of the city, away from the denser downtown area that had seen the worst of the fighting in 2013. It was located along a main road, nearby to one of the UN peace-keeping mission (UNMISS) bases, which presumably would provide an extra layer of protection and deterrence. As it turned out, when the fighting started, the opposition forces set up their cantonments on that same stretch of road, and the Terrain's residents found themselves right between the opposing forces, in the most dangerous possible place.

In addition to the international NGO staff living there, the Terrain compound was populated during the day by local workers who maintained the facilities and worked in the compound's restaurant. On Fridays, after work the residents would gather at the restaurant for drinks, joined by friends from other international organizations from around the city looking to socialize and unwind at the end of the week. On Friday, July 8, just as they arrived back from work and were getting ready to head over to the restaurant, Taylor and her colleagues heard the first gunshots.

The fighting had begun with a gun battle at the Presidential Palace and escalated quickly. International organizations in the Terrain Hotel and elsewhere throughout the city immediately placed their staff on lockdown, and while some were beginning to discuss evacuation, it was still up for debate whether it was preferable to leave or shelter in place until the hostilities died down. As with the last time that combat had broken out in the city, the main worry was that aid workers would become collateral damage if caught in the crossfire, not that they would be deliberately targeted. In any event, flights out of the country were in short supply and soon were to be halted completely. As the nearby gunfire waxed and waned, the people holed up in the Terrain compound, spent a good part of the weekend crowded together in the first-floor entrance area of a two-story residential building in the inner compound. This lobby area was the official "safe room," so designated because it had a bolted steel door and no window exposure. It now had mattresses on the floor and a supply of food and water for the 21 people taking shelter, a group that included the Internews and other NGO staff members and a small number of waitresses and cleaners from the compound.

On Saturday morning, an Internews colleague who was not normally there on weekends suddenly appeared on the compound. John Gatluak Manguet Nhial was a 32-year old South Sudanese journalist and radio station manager who had worked with Internews for years. Elizabeth Jones describes Gatluak as "an incredibly inspiring person." Educated in Kenya as a refugee, Gatluak returned to South Sudan after independence and made his career in what he knew was a high-risk profession in his country. "Being a journalist in South Sudan is risking one's life," Internews quotes him as saying, "But I have dedicated myself to serving my community through radio as a watchdog, informing them about what the politicians are doing once the citizens elect them to power."[2] Gatluak was running the radio station in Leer, Unity State, when the civil war first erupted in South Sudan. He kept the transmissions going, reporting on security conditions and population displacements, all the while facing harassment and death threats—first from rebels, and then from government forces when they took over the town. Eventually, the soldiers sacked and destroyed the radio station as Gatluak escaped into the bush, surviving there for two months in the wild. Accustomed to the dangers inherent in sudden shifts in conflict dynamics, Gatluak had good reason to fear for his safety at this moment in Juba. His forehead bore the faint tribal scars that identified him as a Nuer, the same ethnicity as the leader of the opposition forces, and over the prior few days, he had been harassed and briefly detained by government forces. He had come to Terrain to shelter with his international colleagues, where, like them, he figured he would be out of harm's way.

The Terrain inhabitants were trapped. Major fighting and shifting frontlines and road blocks along the main road made evacuation or extraction impossible, short of a military-style intervention by UN peacekeeping troops. During that long, anxious weekend spent on lockdown, there were periods when the fighting quieted down long enough for the staff to feel safe venturing upstairs or out of the building, returning to their own rooms to sleep or shower and change clothes and then hurrying back to the safe room when they heard the action ramping back up. On Sunday morning, after spending the night in her own bed in a separate cottage on the compound, Jones awoke to the sounds of gunfire very close. Before she made it back to the safe room, she and four colleagues found themselves trapped by crossfire, crouching against the back wall of their building for almost an hour. "You could see bullets whizzing through the compound," she said. "That's how close it was."

By Monday morning, the group had settled into something like a routine. Every so often someone would go up to the second floor to peek out

[2] Internews (2014). "John Gatluak Manguet Nhial, South Sudan." July 25, 2014. https://www.internews.org/updates/john-gatluak-manguet-nhial-south-sudan

the window, keeping low to avoid stray bullets, and observe the military's movements along the road to report back what they saw to the group and to contacts in the UN and other NGOs in the city, as well as worried colleagues back in the Washington, DC headquarters. "Of course, none of us had the full picture either," says Taylor.

The invasion began that afternoon. The group was once again gathered in the building with the safe room, having just finished that day's emergency rations for lunch, and Jones recalls that she had her laptop out and was trying to do some work when she heard the alarmed voice of one of the cleaning ladies saying there were soldiers *right outside the building*. At this, everyone fell quiet. Internews's in-country security manager, who had assumed the role of informal authority figure for the group taking shelter at Terrain, put his finger to his lips and motioned for people to move away from the windows. In Taylor's recollection, she had not become worried immediately when she found out soldiers had breached the perimeter fence and were inside the compound's residential area. She assumed that because Terrain was so close to the fighting, the men were perhaps just using the compound as a shortcut to pass through or possibly scouting around for some food. As they listened to the sounds of soldiers breaking into and looting an adjacent building, however, the situation revealed itself as more ominous. From the amount of noise they were making it was evident that the men, fresh from battle, were in a state of high adrenaline. As Taylor described it, they were not simply rifling through the rooms; they were demolishing them. Moments later, they heard soldiers directly outside the safe room, on the other side of the steel door, banging and shouting, demanding entry. When those inside declined to open the door, the men began shooting at it. "And that's when it was clear," says Taylor, with characteristic understatement, "that things were more serious than what we thought."

As the bullets continued pummeling the metal and the shouting of the men outside swelled in volume and intensity along with the gunfire, those inside began backing away and moving up the stairs to the second floor, just in case the door should give out. Crouched upstairs, Taylor caught some movement in the corner of her eye and looked over through the open door of her apartment to the window. Men in fatigues were climbing over the balcony. In an instant, the strength of the steel door, upon which a second ago everything had depended, became irrelevant; the soldiers were finding other ways in. A few feet away, Jones looked over at the security manager, who was signaling everyone to stay quiet and get low, at which point, she says, everyone scattered, "instinctively crawling into different rooms to hide." Jones and 11 other people, mostly women, crowded into a bathroom in one of the apartments, and locked the door behind them. Two male colleagues remained in the outer apartment, locking that door as well. Taylor had run into another apartment with three other colleagues, two men and a woman. She and the other woman also hid in the bathroom and locked the door, not knowing what else to do. "Knowing that we're findable, that there was no way you could really hide, and worried that even locking the door was not really smart, because it was clear that they were angry and that they were coming in either way," she said. Once the first men whom Taylor had seen climbing over the balcony had broken in through the window, they went downstairs to open the door to let the others in. And within what seemed to her like seconds, the entire building was full of soldiers.

When the soldiers reached their apartment, Taylor heard the voice of her colleague, the security manager, speaking with them and complying with their demands, trying to deescalate the situation. A moment later the soldiers burst into the bathroom, demanded the two women stand up and hand over their phones, and then marched them out of the apartment. It was during this time that Taylor saw John Gatluak suddenly dart out of one of the rooms and look down the hallway toward the exit. He had been hiding alone in one of the rooms and was hoping to make a break for it before the soldiers discovered him. The men reacted to him with instant violence. Amid shouts of "Nuer!" the soldiers threw Gatluak to the ground, and Taylor watched as they beat him with their rifle butts and fists, dragging him away.

Despite the brutal treatment of Gatluak she had just witnessed, Taylor sensed that it was possible to communicate with at least some of the soldiers in this first group and perhaps even negotiate with them. "Their English language skills were really good, and they seemed better dressed and more professional than some of the waves that came in later." When she noticed a soldier with a wound on the back of his hand—a bullet had clipped a vein and it was bleeding heavily—Taylor brought over her med kit and offered to dress the wound properly. He assented and they spoke a little while Taylor swabbed the wound and applied the bandage, advising the soldier to see a doctor for stitches. Compared to the others, this man seemed to Taylor to be relatively calm and reasonable, and she hoped that helping him would win her measure of protection. Unfortunately, he left with his battalion soon after, Taylor said, "and the next round of soldiers that came were much nastier." It was during this second wave that the rapes began.

While Taylor, Gatluak, and other colleagues were in the hands of the first wave of soldiers, Jones and the others were still barricaded in the bathroom in another apartment; they were the last group to be discovered. Jones recalls that it took the soldiers nearly two hours to break down the doors to reach their hiding place, during which time those who had phones with them were placing frantic calls to the UN, the US embassy, and other organizations in Juba, updating them on the invasion in real time, pleading for help. One of the women posted a goodbye message to family and friends on her Facebook timeline. Despite initially receiving some reassuring messages that help was on the way, the rescue operation they were expecting from the nearby UN peacekeeping forces never arrived. "There was so much time [for a rescue]," Jones remembers. "The UN had a lot of time."

From where she was, Taylor could hear the violent banging and shouting at the perimeters of the last holdout apartment. As the din rose, one of the soldiers in the second wave grabbed Taylor and pulled her away from her male colleagues, took her into the bathroom, and raped her. "It was just the one soldier at the beginning," she said, "and then it got a lot worse from there." At one point, she was allowed out of the bathroom and was able to see two of her male fellow captives sitting on the floor a few meters away. This briefly made the terror more bearable. "We were making eye contact, and at least I didn't feel like I was alone-alone." Soon after, however, the soldiers separated the men from the women, and she saw her male colleagues being marched outside. Her ordeal continued for the next couple of hours. "I was trapped in that room and continually raped," Taylor recounts. Older soldiers were forcing the younger ones to get involved, many of whom showed reluctance and fear but complied. As for herself, Taylor had by this point lost hope. "I expected at the end of it I would be killed."

What happened when the male aid workers were taken outside was described in press accounts by an Internews staffer named Gian Libot. The soldiers took the aid workers in front of the building and made them stand in a semicircle while one of the soldiers delivered a tirade in English about the evildoings of foreigners, the UN, and the US government. "You messed up this country. You're helping the rebels," Libot reported them saying. The aid workers were then told "that we would be made an example, that they were going to kill us."[3] Then Libot saw John Gatluak being ushered toward the rest of the group with his arms raised, a very tall soldier walking behind him, holding a rifle to his head. Gatluak remained silent as the soldiers all began shouting at him, no longer using English. The only word Libot could make out was "Nuer"—uttered just before the tall soldier shot two bullets into Gatluak's head. Four more shots entered Gatluak's body after it hit the ground, as his international colleagues looked on, believing they were next.

Jones and the remaining aid workers hiding in the bathroom did not know what was happening outside but could hear the shouting intensifying. The men were shooting at their door now and a bullet came through and hit one of them in the leg. Soon enough, the soldiers broke in. At that point, the shared story of the group hiding in the bathroom shattered into multiple individual nightmares as the women were pulled away in different directions to be sexually assaulted and raped. Different women tried different tactics—some trying to talk the men out of it, some fighting back. "One of the women in our group got a huge black eye from a rifle butt for resisting." Jones says. "And for me, I just, I really wanted to live. I didn't want to make anyone angrier than they already were, so I personally chose not to resist."

For Jones and most of her colleagues, it was another two hours before they were rescued. When the aid workers were rounded up and taken out of the building, however, it was not clear at first that they were being led to safety. It was not UN forces that came to extract them, but rather the South Sudanese National Security Service (NSS). As they were being led across the compound to the parking lot, Jones and her colleagues saw Gatluak's body lying on the ground where he had been executed. It was only once they were inside the NSS building and an Internews staff member was on the phone with Molly Phee, the US ambassador to South Sudan that Jones began to feel they were now safe. What none of them realized at that time was that three of their colleagues, including Jen Taylor, had been left behind in the compound.

Taylor, who had been enduring repeated sexual assaults in the intervening hours, was eventually taken to a downstairs room where another woman was being held. "More assaults happened there to both of us," she

[3] Serafica, R. (2016). "Filipino aid worker remembers ordeal in South Sudan attack." *Rappler*, August 20, 2016. Retrieved 28 May 2019, from https://www.rappler.com/move-ph/143624-filipino-aid-worker-south-sudan-attack

says. By the time those men had left, and the two women were alone, the sun had set and it was getting dark. The power was out because the soldiers had stolen all the diesel fuel from the generators. Accustomed to the constant hum of the generators, the women now found themselves in an eerie silence as well as utter darkness. They crept into a bathroom and pulled the door shut to hide from any remaining looters. They didn't dare venture out, as noises from upstairs let them know that they were not alone in the building. In stifling heat, they spent a sleepless night on the bathroom floor with a shower curtain wrapped around them in an attempt to keep the swarms of mosquitos at bay. With every tiny movement they made, the noise of crackling plastic sparked fear that they would be discovered.

At first light, they emerged from the bathroom, trying in vain to step quietly through the debris of the looted building, and went outside. A dog bounded up to them. Taylor knew the animal well; he was an informal resident of the compound named Kit. They realized then that the noises they heard during the night must have been Kit, searching for his familiar people. He looked terrified.[4] When they came upon the body of their colleague John Gatluak lying on the now deserted grounds, the women went back inside to find a sheet to cover him with.

At the sound of voices in the distance, the two women panicked and hid, bracing for the worst. To their relief, it turned out to be another colleague and a Terrain staff member who had been hiding together in a separate part of the compound. It was from them they heard, to their amazement and horror, that nearly everyone else had been driven away the previous night—they had missed the rescue. The group made a snap decision to grab anything useful they could find in the chaos, and flee into the bush, so they wouldn't be sitting ducks for any soldiers returning to the compound to loot during the daylight hours. Looking back, Taylor chuckles at the things they stuffed into backpacks: some useful, like med kits and mosquito repellent, some decidedly less so, such as a handful of her favorite jewelry and a colleague's jar of gummy vitamins "for hair, skin, and nails." Just as they were about to make a run for it, someone put an old Nokia phone in Taylor's hand, and she heard the voice of an Internews colleague on the other end telling them to sit tight, that someone was

[4] Jen Taylor reports that Kit and the other Terrain compound pets were later rescued and brought to Uganda, where they found adoptive homes, with the exception of one "sausage dog," who caught the fancy of a border agent and was confiscated.

coming to get them. Despite their desperate urge to get away from the compound, where they were sure the attackers would return any minute, they agreed to wait. Forty agonizing minutes later, a span that felt to Taylor like hours, a private security company contracted by Internews arrived to take them out.

Pivot Points and Peak Insecurity Moments

Like all sudden shifts in conditions and "unprecedented" attacks, the raid on the Terrain Hotel was unthinkable just before it happened, yet in hindsight creates the illusion of predictability. In addition to many other factors having to do with the weak command and control of South Sudanese forces, the raid occurred at a moment of peak volatility in the conflict—the conclusion of a ferocious battle in and around the capital city. At such moments, the risk for major violence is highest. Foreseeing, planning for, and managing such pivot points are incredibly challenging.

For the common soldier, as the saying goes, the experience of war consists of long stretches of boredom punctuated by brief episodes of sheer terror. Such is the nature of most human events; periods of seeming stasis eventually, and precipitously, give way to periods of chaotic change, which later settle down again into a new status quo, and on it goes. At the peak points of volatility and flux, things move rapidly, information becomes sketchy and less reliable, previous assumptions must be abandoned, fear and other extreme emotions take over, and predictability is lost. The nineteenth-century military theorist Carl von Clausewitz, who gave us the term "the fog of war," wrote in his treatise *On War* that uncertainty pervades conflict even at the best of times: "[T]hree quarters of the factors on which action in war is based are wrapped in a fog of greater or lesser uncertainty." The fog gets thicker as events take a sudden turn, and just at the point where decisions need to be made exceedingly fast.

New, decisive moves by belligerents in conflict zones create the greatest uncertainty and thus maximize the potential for violence against aid workers. The way that attack numbers track with general insurgent violence in different subnational areas[5] but not with general crime and murder rates (as will be discussed in the next section) lends empirical support to the

[5] Data from the Aid Worker Security Database (www.aidworkersecurity.corg) compared with that of the Global Terrorism Database (https://www.start.umd.edu/gtd/) by province in Afghanistan and Syria 2014–2016.

humanitarians' perception that, as a general rule, it is safer for aid organizations to operate in places where the territory is under the established control of any one party. When another party makes a bid for control or a new set of actors arrives on the scene (for instance, IS in Afghanistan), the landscape of key actors and potential threats has changed in an instant. The information accumulated by the aid organizations becomes obsolete. Things are calm and predictable until suddenly they aren't.

In a related phenomenon, experienced humanitarian field workers and security professionals will often tell you that the most dangerous time for an aid worker is right at the beginning of a new field posting. The Sheik study in the *British Medical Journal* supports this contention, finding that one-third of all aid worker deaths occurred within their first 90 days of an assignment, irrespective of their past experience in other field settings. Seventeen percent died within the first 30 days.[6] Most anyone who has undertaken a field assignment in a foreign country can attest to the plausibility of newcomer status correlating with higher risk. The learning curve is very steep in a new environment, and in the early days of a new posting, you are still trying to orient yourself to the setting. When so much around you is still unfamiliar, your normal security instincts can be easily overwhelmed by the torrent of new information. Only after some time spent acclimating will you again be able to intuit something different or amiss in a situation, or pick up subtly threatening signals. At the same time, you are becoming more of a known quantity to those in the community, and, if you are doing the job correctly, you are actively forging these contacts.

The newcomer's risk does not only apply to international staff and organizations. The majority of aid workers in all humanitarian organizations are host country nationals, but unless they are hired from the immediate vicinity of the project, it is possible for them to be almost as "foreign" to the local environment as their international counterparts. They may have come from another part of the country where conditions, religious identities, ethnicities, and even the language may be different. They may face different, sometimes even greater, risks than their expatriate counterparts owing to their ethnicity or other affiliation with a party to the conflict. The phenomenon also seems to hold true at the level of organizations

[6] "One third of deaths occurred in the first 90 days of service, with 17 percent dying within the first 30 days; the timing of death was unrelated to previous field experience." Sheik, M., et al. (2000). "Deaths among humanitarian workers." *BMJ: British Medical Journal* **321**(7254): 166.

and humanitarian response efforts writ large. When aid organizations first arrive on the scene in a new emergency, they have much work to do getting to know the local communities and cultivating acceptance and support for the projects they intend to run. Before this has happened, they cannot count on locals to provide them with advance warning if armed groups seem likely to strike or to intercede on their behalf.

Before the Terrain raid, none of the NGOs, UN agencies, or private security specialists operating in South Sudan suspected that a large-scale attack against international aid workers in Juba was a significant possibility. In the weeks leading up to it, however, attacks on aid organizations had been on the rise in other parts of the country, primarily in the northern states, where the fighting was most intense. There were also some hints that American aid workers and organizations were coming under the increased scrutiny and disfavor of the South Sudanese government, which had become increasingly resentful of diplomatic pressure by the United States (the new nation's largest benefactor) to settle the conflict. President Kiir had gone so far as to publicly accuse the Americans, and their UN and aid worker allies, of supporting his rival, Machar.[7] Politically motivated security incidents also began occurring in Juba, which had not been seen before. Just days before the Terrain attack, a US diplomatic convoy was fired upon by South Sudanese soldiers, and an unarmored UN vehicle was also shot at, wounding the UNESCO director. Despite these incidents, few assumed it would escalate much further. The implication was that as long as internationals could take shelter and stay out of the line of fire, they would be safe.

As the fighting in Juba progressed, getting and sharing good (verifiable and accurate) information throughout the aid worker community became almost impossible. Jake Trees, the Director of Operational Security for Internews based in Washington DC, described how, as the violence unfolded in Juba over those four days, situational awareness on the part of humanitarian organizations deteriorated and was then made obsolete as the ground shifted under their feet. "Our teams on the ground were equipped for such an attack. They had primary and secondary

[7] Lynch, C. (2016). "Dinner, Drinks, and a Near-Fatal Ambush for U.S. Diplomats" *Foreign Policy* Retrieved 5 November 2018, from https://foreignpolicy.com/2016/09/06/dinner-drinks-and-a-near-fatal-ambush-for-u-s-diplomats/

"Filipino aid worker remembers ordeal in South Sudan attack" (2018). *Rappler*. Retrieved 10 November 2018, from https://www.rappler.com/move-ph/143624-filipino-aid-worker-south-sudan-attack

communications, ample hibernation and medical supplies, and during the peak of the attack, all that equipment was taken. It then became very difficult to get reliable information on what was going down." He added, "And at this point it was becoming clearer to the international community that there had been a total breakdown in the chain of command of the South Sudanese forces engaged in this attack."

The UN Secretary-General's special investigation report on the performance of the peacekeeping mission in South Sudan (UNMISS) revealed how the chaos and confusion of the moment, combined with the mission's dysfunctional command structures, contributed to its failure to intervene during the Terrain attack—despite being stationed less than a mile up the road from the Terrain compound and receiving multiple, pleading requests for help from those trapped inside as the attack was going on[8]:

> On the uniformed side, the Force did not operate under a unified command, resulting in multiple and sometimes conflicting orders to the four troop contingents from China, Ethiopia, Nepal and India, and ultimately underusing the more than 1,800 infantry troops at UN House....
>
> At approximately 15:30, when the soldiers began looting and forcing their way into the accommodations, the residents immediately notified UN Security and UNMISS...The JOC made multiple requests to stand up a quick reaction force to respond but each UNMISS contingent turned down the request, indicating their troops were fully committed. The situation at UN House remained chaotic at this time, with thousands of IDPs in the staff accommodation area, armed men still threatening the perimeter of POC [protection of civilians] site 3, and large numbers of armed Government soldiers still on Yei road in front of UN House's main gate. Even after the Government's highest-ranking general provided a liaison officer to meet an UNMISS quick reaction force at a checkpoint near the main gate to facilitate its movement to Terrain camp, no response team materialized.[9]

Information failures and chaotic responses are common at these pivot points. One dilemma of security management is that it usually takes the

[8] The UN's investigation of the Terrain incident resulted in the firing of Kenyan Lieutenant General Johnson Mogoa Kimani Ondieki from his post as the military head of UNMISS.

[9] United Nations (2016). "Executive Summary of the Independent Special Investigation into the violence which occurred in Juba in 2016 and UNMISS response" *ReliefWeb* 1 November 2016. Retrieved 25 March 2019, from https://reliefweb.int/report/south-sudan/executive-summary-independent-special-investigation-violence-which-occurred-juba

unexpected occurrence of a major incident to revise the general understanding of security conditions. For example, in January 2014, the Lebanese restaurant Taverna du Liban in Kabul was one of the few remaining places designated by the UN's security office as safe places for its personnel to eat out—until a Taliban attack there killed 8 Afghans and 13 internationals (including 2 humanitarian workers). Likewise, Internews' Jake Trees described how the violence in Juba obliterated the previous security consensus:

> We were all still looking at it from the risk lens that we had all agreed on and created over the course of years—that these type of skirmishes were going to take place, but internationals would not be targeted. So the prescription was just to make sure that where you were was as safe as it could be, and if it wasn't, move from it. We did not have a defensive risk stance that expected people to come over the walls to attack you. That would have changed our profile completely; Juba would have looked more like Mogadishu.

As mentioned previously, Médecins sans Frontières (MSF), an NGO that has been more successful than most others at working in violent environments, has nonetheless suffered attacks when it misunderstood the situation on the ground. MSF pulled out all programming from Afghanistan in 2004 after five of its staff members were ambushed and killed in Badghis, and the organization did not return to the country until 2009. In 2013, it did the same in Somalia after a number of attacks against its staff and operations, including a prolonged kidnapping of two of its logisticians. These were two countries in which MSF had been working for decades, and in both cases, the organization had decided it could no longer trust counterparts in armed forces or community interlocutors to provide credible guarantees for the security of its staff; it needed to rethink its entire terms of engagement in each country. A public letter from MSF International's then-president, Unni Karunakara explained the Somalia decision while giving voice to the bitterness and betrayal felt by the organization:

> In some cases, they were actively supporting the criminal acts against our staff. In many other cases, these parties sustained an atmosphere that allowed attacks to take place. Nobody has stood up to say that it is unacceptable to threaten, abduct or kill doctors, nurses and other staff who simply try to bring health care to people who would otherwise have none. Let's be clear. "Parties in Somalia" does not only refer to al-Shebaab, although they have much power and responsibility in many areas where we worked. We are also

> not pointing solely at the government in Mogadishu, which has shown indifference to the 2011 murder of our two colleagues, as the early release of the killer demonstrates. Rather, MSF's conclusion is that acceptance of violence against health workers has permeated Somali society and this acceptance is now shared by many armed groups and many levels of civilian government, from clan elders to district commissioners to the Federal Somali Government.[10]

For a humanitarian organization, abruptly ceasing aid activities and pulling out of a country is a wrenching decision. At the time of their withdrawal from Somalia, an MSF acquaintance of mine described the feelings among members of her organization. "In the end it wasn't that people were actively working against us," she said, "but that they never used their position in the community or clan structure [to help]. They were entirely passive. We know we make a difference there, and so many people won't be served now because we've gone." In both cases, after withdrawing, MSF undertook a lengthy internal planning process to reevaluate its strategy and rebuild a dialogue with contacts in-country, essentially starting over from scratch.

Local and national NGOs don't have the option of pulling out of the country, of course, and many of them continue to work in areas their international counterparts have abandoned for security reasons. Being of the place lends a different perspective on violence and volatility. An Afghan humanitarian worker I spoke with in 2018 belongs to a national NGO that operates in the southern provinces of the country where the Taliban are most active, and over the course of a decade, he has seen more than one international organization pull back from the region after suffering attacks. In his view, there is critical distinction to be made between an environment that is "insecure" (containing continual, imminent threat) and "unstable" (prone to occasional rapid changes and unpredictable threats). Afghanistan is considered to be one of the most insecure operating environments, but this aid worker insists that, "It is more accurate to call it unstable—it could change at any time." He explained that the anti-government forces in the area could "be quiet" for long periods, but when they feel they need to make a strategic advance or put pressure on the government, they can target humanitarians, their assets, and their

[10] Karunakara, U. (2013). "Why MSF Decided to Leave Somalia" *MSF.Org*. *https://www.msf.org/why-msf-decided-leave-somalia*

beneficiaries. The key, he said, was being prepared to stop work and lay low for a while, until the situation settled down again.

Weak States and Their Relationship to Aid Worker Risk

The connection between volatility and insecurity also manifests at the national level. Data on aid worker attacks show, not surprisingly, that humanitarians suffer more major attacks in countries at war than in countries recovering from natural disasters. They also show that it is not merely the existence of armed combat in the environment that makes aid workers more vulnerable, but also the weaknesses of the host state and the widespread disorder that results from this weakness. In many protracted emergencies, the phenomenon of state failure (or fragility) can explain both the need for humanitarian operations and the level of danger that faces them.

A failed state is one whose leadership and institutions are dysfunctional and discredited to the point that it can no longer fulfill its basic responsibilities of governance or exercise sovereign power over its territory.[11] A well-functioning state provides public goods in the form of security (both internal, by maintaining law and order, and external, by dint of national defense); basic utilities and services (such as roads, power, and sanitation); and the institutional infrastructure that allows for civil and economic activity to take place. In their book, *Fixing Failed States*, Ashraf Ghani and Clare Lockhart describe state failure in terms of a "sovereignty gap." The gap is the difference between de facto sovereignty, where the state is accountable to its people for furnishing essential collective goods, and *de jure* sovereignty, which is a case of a state in name only. In the latter instance, state institutions are bereft of both resources and legitimacy,

[11] The US Institute of Peace defines "stable governance an end state where the state provides essential services and serves as a responsible steward of state resources; government officials are held accountable through political and legal processes; and the population can participate in governance through civil society organizations, an independent media, and political parties. Stable governance is the mechanism through which the basic human needs of the population are largely met, respect for minority rights is assured, conflicts are managed peacefully through inclusive political processes, and competition for power occurs nonviolently. National and subnational government institutions may work with a range of non-state partners to provide some of the government functions." *8: Stable Governance*. (2019). *United States Institute of Peace*. Retrieved 1 April 2019, from https://www.usip.org/guiding-principles-stabilization-and-reconstruction-the-web-version/stable-governance

where corruption and patronage decide who receives opportunity and protection, and where "(e)ven when revenues are generated, they generally leave the state rather than remaining at the local level, where they could be reinvested and foster the growth of capital."[12]

Because there is no agreement on a distinct endpoint at which you can say a weak and corrupt state has become a failed state, "state fragility" has become the preferred term to encapsulate the spectrum of nations with weak, unstable, and corrupt governance. States can be fragile to varying degrees, and with increased fragility come political and economic adaptations made by individuals and groups within them. On the economic side, incentives are created to drive the growth of illegal or parallel economies, often around the trade of drugs or weapons. The political response, in the worst case, is the manipulation of fear by "conflict entrepreneurs," a hybrid of political demagogues and war profiteers that benefit from protracted civil conflict.[13] The interplay of power and economic incentives in failed state scenarios favor violence, particularly in a modern age where international markets are easily accessed. Mark Duffield and others have contended that protracted instability and social breakdown are the results of economic adaptation to globalization, driven by expanding international black and gray markets.[14] No matter what force—political or economic—sets in motion the downward spiral of state fragility, vicious circles are at work creating the poverty and conflict traps that characterize protracted "complex emergencies" in countries such as the Democratic Republic of Congo, which has hosted an international humanitarian aid response for more than a decade.

My colleagues and I examined the role of the host state in the security of humanitarian operations in a 2012 report,[15] testing several governance- and conflict-related variables to see if they were correlated to violence against aid workers. The data already told us that countries undergoing

[12] Ghani, A., & Lockhart, C. (2008). *Fixing failed states: A framework for rebuilding a fractured world*. Oxford: Oxford University Press, pp. 29–30.

[13] Discussed in Reno, W. (1997). *Humanitarian Emergencies and Warlord Economies in Liberia and Sierra Leone*. Helsinki, Finland: UNU World Institute for Development Economics Research (UNU/WIDER), and Stoddard, A. (2006). *Humanitarian alert: NGO information and its impact on US foreign policy*: Kumarian Press.

[14] Duffield, M. (1998). "Aid Policy and Post-Modern Conflict: A Critical Review," Occasional Paper 19, School of Public Policy, University of Birmingham.

[15] Stoddard, A., Harmer. A. & Hughes, M. (2012). *Host States and their Impact on Security for Humanitarian Operations*. Humanitarian Outcomes, December.

armed conflict generally also see the most violence against humanitarian aid workers, but we were curious to know if other factors mattered as well. For example, are aid workers safer in a dictatorship or a democracy? Does the degree of corruption or the level of government effectiveness make violence against humanitarian operations more or less probable? Do trends in attacks on aid workers map with the overall crime levels in the country, or are they independent phenomena? To answer these questions, we looked at the countries hosting aid operations in which humanitarian actors experienced the highest number of major attacks over a six-year period from 2006 to 2011—Afghanistan, Sudan, Somalia, Sri Lanka, Pakistan, Democratic Republic of the Congo, Chad, Haiti, Iraq, and the occupied Palestinian territories—and compared their attack data against governance indicators. The variables we tested included whether a major conflict was occurring, the intensity of violence (by number of deaths) in the territory, the type and stability of the government, and various measures of the strength and quality of governance and rule of law.[16] As expected, the presence or absence of armed conflict was found to matter the most. The more intense the conflict, the greater the number of attacks there were on aid workers, including cases of "incidental violence" where aid workers are not the intended target, such as crossfire and air strikes. There were also correlations between attacks against humanitarians and low levels of political stability. Higher numbers of attacks occurred in countries whose governments scored lower on measures of political and economic effectiveness, legitimacy, and general rule of law. Interestingly, the type of political regime in place did not seem to matter, only its strength and stability. As we concluded in the report, "Weak government institutions, whether democratic or autocratic, were more predictive of aid worker attacks than either entrenched dictatorships or strong institutional democracies."[17]

Despite correlations between attacks on aid workers and the intensity of conflict, which would suggest that violence against humanitarians is merely a facet of the overall violence in a setting, the number of aid worker killings did not seem to have any significant correlation to overall criminal homicide rates in host countries. In addition, when we compared them to

[16] The governance variables were sourced from World Bank's World Governance Indicators, and national homicide rates as sourced from the UN Office of Drugs and Crime. All values were averaged for the years 2006–2010, excluding years where no data were available.

[17] Stoddard, Harmer, & Hughes, 2012, p. 5.

crime rates globally, we found that countries in Latin America with the highest murder rates in the world have very low rates of aid worker attacks. This would seem to suggest that violence against aid operations exists as a separate phenomenon from general crime, and one that is more indicative of a state undergoing active political conflict. For that reason, we went so far as to propose in our report that attacks on humanitarians could be used as one of the metrics of state fragility.

If we are correct that attacks on humanitarian workers are a symptom of state failure as well as a byproduct of war, the precarious position of humanitarian organizations and their staff becomes clear. For it is the government of the emergency-affected state that is formally responsible for enabling aid organizations to do their work safely and unimpeded, according to the United Nations Charter and the "host country agreements" that are signed by the governments of countries on the receiving end of an international aid response. Despite these agreements covering all manner of issues—from communications, to transport, to safety and security—what is on paper virtually never translates to meaningful support. The host state's responsibility for the safety and security of aid workers is not articulated in any detail within the agreements, much less operationalized on the ground. In fact, most aid workers and organizations we consulted were unfamiliar with the details of these agreements, or that they even existed. More importantly, the same could be said for the local state security authorities in the more remote areas of the country where aid projects were running.

In conflict-related humanitarian emergencies, the role of host states in providing security for humanitarian operations amounts to a Catch-22. It would not be appropriate or desirable for military forces engaged in the conflict to protect humanitarian operations with weapons. In fact, when some national militaries or police forces have insisted on this in the past, such as requiring the aid convoys to have uniformed armed escorts, humanitarian organizations have found it akin to painting a target on their own staff. What humanitarians want from host governments or military actors is not direct protection, which would compromise neutrality, but rather the creation of a "permissive environment" (sometimes called "ambient security"), which would control the threats to their staff and operations within a sphere of activity. This, of course, demands the capacity to exert force and maintain stability across vast stretches of territory, which such fragile states rarely possess. In other words, if humanitarians can enjoy ambient security in an area, they may not need to be there in the first place. The reality is that in many protracted conflicts, humanitarian organizations are the ones fulfilling the basic service roles—including security—that those governments fail to provide.

When the Attacker Is the State

Not only are many host states fundamentally incapable of extending their power and rule of law to create a credible security umbrella for aid operations, in many cases, they themselves are a direct threat.[18] No case exemplifies a dysfunctional security relationship between humanitarians and the host government more vividly than South Sudan, which currently tops the Fragile States Index,[19] and where, as one UN humanitarian worker put it, "there is a violation of the agreement with the government two to three times a day." Military actors on all sides of the conflict have committed atrocities against civilians, which is a reflection of increasingly weak command and control of (undisciplined, underpaid) forces and the deep, ethnically based animus fueling the power struggle in the country. Although the fighting is no longer as intense as in the early years of the civil war, it has become more fragmented and elusive of resolution. As we observed in our 2017 *Aid Worker Security Report*, as the South Sudanese conflict stretched on, it became "less like an asymmetric battle between a government and an insurgency and more like a war between equally lawless belligerents, growing more chaotic as fracturing between the parties continues."

During the civil war, the efforts of the major donor governments and the United Nations to bring an end to the conflict proved largely ineffectual, despite providing peacekeeping support and humanitarian funding to the tune of over US$1.8 billion.[20] At various times, in response to atrocities, these donor governments leveled targeted sanctions against specific government and military officials[21] without evident effect. In the aftermath of the Terrain raid, in which John Gatluak was killed, other aid workers wounded, and at least 5 women raped, sufficient international pressure was brought to bear that 11 soldiers were made to stand court

[18] Stoddard, Harmer, & Hughes, 2012.

[19] The Fund for Peace (2018). *Fragile States Index 2018*. Washington, DC: The Fund for Peace.

[20] UN Financial Tracking Service.

[21] https://www.treasury.gov/resource-center/sanctions/Programs/Documents/south-sudan.pdf

martial. Ultimately, 10 of them went to prison.[22] (The verdict also ordered the rape victims to be paid US$4000 each and Gatluak's family to receive 51 cattle.) The survivors' feelings on the proceedings are understandably conflicted. On the one hand, the fact that formal charges were brought at all was an achievement of sorts. (Amnesty International proclaimed it "a first step toward fighting impunity in the war-torn country.")[23] But many questioned its legitimacy, not least because out of the scores of men who took part in the violent raid, only 11 stood trial. Jen Taylor describes her own ambivalence regarding the aftermath: "The problem I have with this kind of justice is that the number of people who were arrested and tried is so small. I suspect that the men left in the cells are only there because they don't have connections." Remembering the younger soldiers who were coerced into participating in the rapes, she notes "Some of them were *really* young and clearly not happy doing it. You could see in their faces that they were fucking terrified."

Apart from the actions of the South Sudanese forces, there are unanswered questions and some deep bitterness on the part of survivors regarding the behavior of the UN, particularly the failure of its peacekeeping mission to intervene to help the people at Terrain. Not only did it decline to send in a rescue team in response to pleas for help during the attack, the mission failed to act when it was notified by Internews later that evening that three of its female staff were still unaccounted for. They made no attempt to extract the women, leaving Taylor and the others to spend the night in the ravaged compound until the private security team came to pick them up the next morning. Survivors were disappointed further by the lack of transparency the UN displayed when it released only the Executive Summary of the Secretary-General's report, rather than the full document.

Elizabeth Jones and some of the other American victims also felt let down by their own government. While the Federal Bureau of Investigation (FBI) facilitated the testimony of victims for the trial, and arranged for them to testify remotely and anonymously, the US government had very little else to offer in the way of diplomatic action. The attack occurred just

[22] *"South Sudan soldiers sentenced to jail for murder, rape in 2016 hotel raid"* (2019). *U.S.* Retrieved 26 March 2019, from https://www.reuters.com/article/us-southsudan-security/south-sudan-soldiers-sentenced-to-jail-for-murder-rape-in-2016-hotel-raid-idUSKCN1LM0XK

[23] Ibid.

months before the 2016 election and the subsequent changeover of administrations, and when Jones spoke to government officials in December, in an attempt to advocate for a stronger response, one frankly admitted to her, "Look, the timing is really crazy. All of us who you are talking to now are not going to stay in our positions." A UN Security Council resolution for an arms embargo on South Sudan would not pass for another two years, during which time atrocities against civilians continued.

The relationship between humanitarians and the powerful Western states that fund their organizations is a tricky one at the best of times. While needing to preserve their independence from political actors, humanitarians also look to them for most of their funding and for a degree of political advocacy and diplomatic support. In South Sudan, Jones says, "Donors are giving money for humanitarian aid but not doing anything to protect it." Jones believes that the highly publicized case of the attack on Terrain was a missed opportunity to strengthen protection of humanitarian workers, but at the same time, she is keenly aware that protections are much weaker for South Sudanese civilians, who have faced violence at the hands of armed forces throughout the civil war. Her colleague Jen Taylor echoes the sentiment: "[The trial] only happened because we're expats and because of international pressure," she says. "This kind of thing happens to women in South Sudan every single day," she said. "I can complain as much as I want about the level of justice that I received, but it's still a hell of a lot better than any woman in South Sudan is probably ever going to get."

As shocking as the Terrain compound raid was, it was by no means the first or the deadliest attack committed by forces of a host government on humanitarian workers. In Sri Lanka in 2006, in what is now known as the Muttur Massacre, the French NGO Action Contre la Faim (ACF; Action Against Hunger) lost 17 Sri Lankan workers, mostly ethnic Tamils, all shot at close range, execution style, inside ACF's office in Muttur. While the Sri Lankan government denied their soldiers were responsible, the international consensus brooked little doubt that the Sri Lankan Army was behind it. The murder of 17 staff members in one incident is an inconceivable loss for a single organization, and ACF denounced it in a public statement as a war crime.[24] Despite international outcry, the incident was not

[24] "As civilians, the victims should have been protected under international humanitarian law by the Geneva Conventions and their protocols, as well as by customary rules. These

resolved and no one was brought to justice. A report published by ACF in 2008 read, "After following the three Sri Lankan investigations over more than 18 months, ACF observes bitterly that these investigations set up following the Muttur tragedy have little or no chance of establishing officially the persons criminally responsible for this war crime (direct perpetrators and chain of command)."[25]

In another example, in 2014, US airstrikes destroyed an MSF field hospital in Kunduz, Afghanistan,[26] killing 14 staff members, 24 patients (including three children), and 4 other civilians. An additional 37 people were wounded. As is the standard procedure when it operates in a war zone, MSF had earlier provided the coordinates of its hospital to the armed forces to avoid becoming collateral damage; but the US military's official account of the incident ultimately concluded that the bombing was a "tragic but avoidable accident caused primarily by human error,"[27] saying it had mistaken the hospital for a nearby government building that had been captured by Taliban forces who were firing on Afghan soldiers. However, this explanation is undermined by statements made by the Afghan government that implied, falsely, that Taliban terrorists were using the MSF hospital and its staff and patients as human shields. Suspicions persist that the Afghan military forces deliberately passed on this false information to cause the US forces to strike the hospital, angry that MSF was treating wounded opposition fighters. The US military's investigation resulted in disciplinary action taken against 16 personnel but no criminal charges. MSF's calls for an independent investigation by a neutral international body have gone unheeded.

Since humanitarians cannot count on protection from government actors, any more than they can count on the willingness of armed forces to abide by international humanitarian law, the only way to ensure security in fragile states is to rely on their own institutional protocols. However, this, as we will see in the next chapter, presents its own challenges.

killings constitute therefore a war crime." From Action Contre la Faim (2008). *The Muttur Massacre: a struggle for justice*, ACF, June 2008, p. 8.

[25] Action Contre la Faim (2008). *The Muttur Massacre: a struggle for justice*, ACF, June 2008, p. 5.

[26] https://www.msf.org/kunduz-hospital-attack-depth

[27] *US forces 'punished for hospital attack'*. (2019). *BBC News*. Retrieved 31 March 2019, from https://www.bbc.com/news/world-us-canada-36164595

References

Action Contre la Faim. (2008, June). The Muttur Massacre: A Struggle for Justice. *ACF*.

Duffield, M. (1998). Aid Policy and Post-Modern Conflict: A Critical Review. Occasional Paper 19, School of Public Policy, University of Birmingham.

Filipino aid worker remembers ordeal in South Sudan attack. (2018). *Rappler*. Retrieved November 10, 2018, from https://www.rappler.com/move-ph/143624-filipino-aid-worker-south-sudan-attack

Ghani, A., & Lockhart, C. (2008). *Fixing Failed States: A Framework for Rebuilding a Fractured World* (pp. 29–30). Oxford: Oxford University Press.

Internews. (2014, July 25). John Gatluak Manguet Nhial. *South Sudan*. https://www.internews.org/updates/john-gatluak-manguet-nhial-south-sudan

Karunakara, U. (2013). Why MSF Decided to Leave Somalia. *MSF.Org*. https://www.msf.org/why-msf-decided-leave-somalia

Lynch, C. (2016). Dinner, Drinks, and a Near-Fatal Ambush for U.S. Diplomats. *Foreign Policy*. Retrieved November 5, 2018, from https://foreignpolicy.com/2016/09/06/dinner-drinks-and-a-near-fatal-ambush-for-u-s-diplomats/

Patinkin, J. (2016, August 15). Rampaging South Sudan Troops Raped Foreigners, Killed Local. *AP NEWS*. Retrieved February 2, 2019, from https://apnews.com/52f948f476874cbda6277492a4f8468e

Reno, W. (1997). *Humanitarian Emergencies and Warlord Economies in Liberia and Sierra Leone*. Helsinki: UNU World Institute for Development Economics Research (UNU/WIDER).

Serafica, R. (2016, August 20). Filipino Aid Worker Remembers Ordeal in South Sudan Attack. *Rappler*. Retrieved May 28, 2019, from https://www.rappler.com/move-ph/143624-filipino-aid-worker-south-sudan-attack

Sheik, M., et al. (2000). Deaths among Humanitarian Workers. *BMJ: British Medical Journal, 321*(7254), 166.

South Sudan soldiers sentenced to jail for murder, rape in 2016 hotel raid. (2019). U.S. Retrieved March 26, 2019, from https://www.reuters.com/article/us-southsudan-security/south-sudan-soldiers-sentenced-to-jail-for-murder-rape-in-2016-hotel-raid-idUSKCN1LM0XK

Stoddard, A. (2006). *Humanitarian Alert: NGO Information and Its Impact on US Foreign Policy*. Bloomfield: Kumarian Press.

Stoddard, A., Harmer, A., & Hughes, M. (2012, December). *Host States and Their Impact on Security for Humanitarian Operations*. New York: Humanitarian Outcomes.

The Fund for Peace. (2018). *Fragile States Index 2018*. Washington, DC: The Fund for Peace.

United Nations. (2016, November 1). Executive Summary of the Independent Special Investigation into the Violence which Occurred in Juba in 2016 and UNMISS Response. *ReliefWeb*. Retrieved March 25, 2019, from https://reliefweb.int/report/south-sudan/executive-summary-independent-special-investigation-violence-which-occurred-juba

US forces 'punished for hospital attack'. (2019). *BBC News*. Retrieved March 31, 2019, from https://www.bbc.com/news/world-us-canada-36164595

CHAPTER 5

Organizational Impediments

The International Humanitarian Sector and the Ambivalent Effects of Growth

Along with the character of most armed conflicts now occurring, the organized provision of humanitarian aid has evolved into something quite different from what was envisioned by Henry Dunant and Western European leaders in 1863. Today's international humanitarian sector, with annual resources estimated at roughly US$27 billion in 2018,[1] encompasses not only the International Committee of the Red Cross and the National Red Cross/Red Crescent societies, but also hundreds of significantly sized international non-governmental (private) organizations (NGOs) and thousands of smaller national and local NGOs that work in crisis-affected countries. The way the sector is configured and funded has implications for how its constituent organizations perceive and manage their risks, which in turn affects the extent to which the sector is able to cover the needs of populations in conflict zones.

When it comes to the sector as a whole, three related factors are inhibiting its ability to expand its reach on the ground: (1) the incentives for organizations to grow large in organizational size but not in operational scope; (2) the inevitable loss of agility and appetite for innovative risk that comes with organizational age; and (3) the sector's fragmented sense of

[1] Development Initiatives (2018). Global Humanitarian Assistance Report 2018. http://devinit.org/wp-content/uploads/2018/06/GHA-Report-2018.pdf

A. Stoddard, *Necessary Risks*,
https://doi.org/10.1007/978-3-030-26411-6_5

responsibility for providing humanitarian coverage to populations in crisis. As a consequence, while there are more humanitarian actors today, providing more aid in war zones than at any time in the past, the humanitarian presence falls well short of the need.

Improving humanitarian coverage of needs may require fundamental change. The humanitarian aid sector is often likened to an oligopoly, in that a small number of the largest international organizations command the lion's share of the global resources. These include the three principal United Nations (UN) humanitarian agencies—the United Nations Children's Fund (UNICEF), the UN High Commissioner for Refugees (UNHCR), and the World Food Programme (WFP)—along with the International Movement of the Red Cross and Red Crescent, and the half-dozen or so of the largest international NGOs, among them Médecins sans Frontières (MSF), Save the Children, and the International Rescue Committee. For the UN agencies and many of the largest international NGOs, much of their operational expenditure flows downstream to other international and national NGOs as sub-grants, creating a funding pyramid with the largest organizations at the top. This kind of market concentration is not unusual in the private sector. Many sectors and industries are similarly dominated by a small number of giants, such as the 10 parent corporations that control nearly all of the world's packaged food products, or the 15 largest automotive companies that produce 81 percent of the world's cars.[2] The "Pareto principle," or "law of the vital few," postulates that in most human endeavors, roughly 80 percent of the resources/outputs will derive from or be controlled by roughly 20 percent of the actors/inputs.[3] But the NGO sector also differs from the private sector and other industries in that it is mostly publicly funded; although all the international NGOs seek private donations from individuals, foundations, and corporations, for the majority of them, the greater part of their operating budgets comes from public funding. In any given year, government grants

[2] "These 10 companies control everything you buy." (2019). *Business Insider*. Retrieved 6 April 2019, from https://www.businessinsider.com/10-companies-control-the-food-industry-2016-9; "These are the Biggest Car Companies in the World" https://www.verdict.co.uk/biggest-car-companies/

[3] The Pareto principle is named for the Italian economist Vilfredo Pareto, who observed the phenomenon in his 1896 paper, "*Cours d'économie politique*," in which he showed that 20 percent if Italy's population owned 80 percent of the land.

account for three quarters or more of the billions spent on humanitarian aid response.[4]

If broad-based competition is intrinsically limited in an oligopolistic market, it is stunted even further in one that runs primarily on donor government grant funding. To be sure, among the top tiers of large international NGOs, few rules of the free market apply. Market shares are stickier, there are few new entrants, and mergers and shutdowns are exceedingly rare. Unlike in free market conditions, where customers benefit from having a large number of competitors vying for their business, the customers in this case are the donor governments deciding which organizations to fund. Because government agencies are burdened with limited staffs and operational budgets, it is not necessarily in their interest to have a wide and diverse pool of organizations to choose from. Rather than managing hundreds of smaller grants for every humanitarian emergency they contribute to, it is far preferable to give fewer and bigger grants to a limited number of large, established, and trusted organizational partners. Donor government officials hold their grantees to strict measures of fiduciary responsibility, but they mostly do not evaluate them against each other or against any rigorous, objective standards of effectiveness and performance. In other words, aid organizations are accountable to their donors for spending money appropriately, not for making the biggest dent in the needs of the affected population.

In this environment, which rewards growth in organizational size and administrative capacity but not operational scope or innovation, even the largest NGOs will feel continued pressure to grow lest they be eclipsed by still larger ones that can suck up ever larger grants, presumably providing more economies of scale for the donors. However, they will feel little competitive pressure to radically innovate and improve their programming to serve greater numbers of people more effectively. This is not to argue that humanitarian action ever could or should function like a commercial industry; the aid sector deals in global public goods that appropriately sit outside the domain of market forces. Instead, the drive to get better at assisting people in need is supposed to emanate from the organization's mission and values. The problem with this supposition is that as an organization ages and grows large, its staff members naturally become less personally connected to the original mission and impulse, and the interests

[4] Development Initiatives (2018). *Global Humanitarian Assistance Report 2018.* http://devinit.org/wp-content/uploads/2018/06/GHA-Report-2018.pdf, p. 26.

of protecting and growing the organization can sometimes work counter to its purported values. (We shall return to this tension between organizational interests and values in Chap. 6.)

A popular and long-standing notion in organizational theory posits that organizations exhibit "life cycles" analogous to those of biological organisms.[5] The different variants of this idea have in common that organizations of all types, from commercial corporations to charitable groups, all pass through distinct phases of growth, and at each phase they exhibit specific characteristics as well as susceptibility to specific pitfalls and potential crises that could spell their end. The phases are described roughly as follows:

1. Birth/existence: An organization is established and fueled in its early startup days by the creative energy of a founding leader(s), which must eventually give way to more structured management as it begins to grow larger. If the leader resists change, a leadership crisis can result.
2. Growth/survival: Like young trees struggling upward to get out of the shadow of their taller neighbors, organizations must grow quickly to ensure survival. At this phase, what was once informal and autonomous decision-making is replaced by directorship, and decision-making hierarchies and procedures are developed.
3. Maturity/success: The organization has neared or reached its maximum growth potential and has more moving parts than can be managed effectively in a vertical structure. More horizontal coordination is needed between these parts, which, if not done well, can lead to cumbersome and inefficient processes of what's called a "crisis of red tape."
4. Renewal/streamlining: Organizations that do not succumb to the typical crises of the earlier phases will at this phase seek renewal, trimming back some cumbersome bureaucratic trappings of its earlier growth, proclaiming a time to go "back to basics" and shooting for a second wind.

[5] For example, Lester, D. Parnell, J. & Carraher, S. (2003)."Organizational Life Cycle: A Five-Stage Empirical Scale." International Journal of Organizational Analysis; 2003; 11, 4; ABI/INFORM Global pg. 339.

Lewis, V., and Churchill, N. (1983). "The Five Stages of Small Business Growth." Harvard Business Review, 61(3), pp. 30–50.

5. Decline: At the end of an organization's lifespan, it will see its role and share in the industry diminish until it eventually shuts down or is absorbed by another.

When an organization grows (if it is able to avoid the crises associated with the various stages listed above), it will reliably undergo certain changes—some positive, some negative. Growth will often make possible economies of scale, allowing the organization to do more and to do it more efficiently. As it grows, an organization may institutionalize its way of working so that desired outputs and organizational values do not have to depend upon specific individuals and personalities. It acquires the capacity to better regulate itself and abide by more stringent standards of performance. On the negative side, large organizations are typically less nimble, less likely to innovate, and more risk averse.

Among the 50 most prominent international organizations operating in humanitarian response (i.e., those that would be located squarely in the "maturity/success" stage of evolution), the median year of founding is 1973. A few, such as Save the Children, were founded in the early twentieth century in response to needs in countries affected by World War I, a few others in the interwar and World War II period, among them the International Rescue Committee (1933) and Cooperative for Assistance and Relief Everywhere (CARE) (1945), but most of the major humanitarian international non-governmental organization (INGO)s operating today came into being in the 1970s and 1980s. Apart from Médecins sans Frontières, which was established in 1971, the top five giants in the sector all have birthdates before 1966. As with most any organizational entity, when a humanitarian aid group reaches a certain size and maturity, organizational interests—the need to grow, to guard its assets, to protect its reputation, and to keep the largest clients happy—naturally become more prominent in decision-making, inevitably trending toward caution and away from bold moves and radical innovation. The fact that the sector is dominated by mature organizations affects how well it succeeds in gaining access to needy populations in high-risk situations or, alternatively, devising alternatives for when access by traditional humanitarian actors is simply impossible.

From the perspective of meeting the needs of populations most harmed by conflict, the current organizational landscape is not encouraging. When my colleagues and I set out to measure humanitarian presence and coverage of need in the most violent environments, we found that in Afghanistan, south-central Somalia, South Sudan, and Syria, most humanitarian organizations were clustered in the areas that were safer and easier to access, which often happened to be the areas controlled by parties the Western donor governments favored. By contrast, places that were contested or under the control of opposition forces, which often had higher and more severe needs, were chronically under-covered by the humanitarian response.

This skewed coverage clearly raises problems of humanitarian ethics as well as overall effectiveness. In part, it is a problem of diffuse and fragmented responsibility—the humanitarian sector's version of the tragedy of the commons. For nearly every emergency, there are far more needs than any single organization can hope to meet on their own. Moreover, there is no common leadership across the numerous humanitarian organizations operating in each emergency—only voluntary and time-consuming efforts at coordination—and therefore no collective accountability or sense of responsibility for covering all of the needs. As I described in a blog post called "The View from the Foxhole," the atomized nature of humanitarian response leads to a myopia of sorts on the part of each organization. "While each actor may be justly satisfied that they are programming as well and as impartially as they can within their limited area of operation, they do not feel individually responsible for the larger picture. The result is large segments of the population whose needs go unmet."[6] In other words, even every organization working impartially in their area can add up to a highly partial overall response.

The lack of collective responsibility for coverage can help explain the "access inertia" of many humanitarian organizations in insecure areas, but a more immediate cause is the security risk itself. Organizations are obliged to uphold a "duty of care" to their staff members, and to not expose them to undue risks, and the definition of acceptable versus unacceptable risks varies from one organization to another. If you are managing a humanitarian organization in a country in conflict and have finite resources of staff and funding, it only makes sense to consolidate operations within an operational area where you feel you can work safely; you will be less inclined to negotiate your way into new territory. As we have seen, NGOs face little pressure from international donors and coordinating bodies to act any differently in this regard. A 2016 study we conducted on risk management at

[6] Stoddard, A. (2016) "The View from the Foxhole: How risk and the fragmented perspective of agencies limits the reach of humanitarian aid." Guest blog for the Advanced Training Program on Humanitarian Action (ATHA), atha.se: December, 2016.

major international NGOs revealed that leadership perceived intensifying risks to their organizations across the board, but particularly in the most extreme conflict environments, which at that time included Afghanistan, Central African Republic, Iraq/Syria region, Somalia, South Sudan, and Yemen. In our survey, a majority of international NGO respondents also agreed that the sector as a whole was responding to the intensifying risk environment by becoming more risk averse and shrinking its operational presence in the most insecure places without devising alternatives for aiding the populations trapped there.

To better understand the insecurity access dynamics at the level of individual organizations, we must look at how risk management has evolved in the humanitarian sector, and how the major donor governments have made working in conflict zones more rather than less risky for them.

Managing Risk and Practicing Duty of Care

In the days before NGOs had anything resembling security risk management systems, aid workers like Michael O'Neill were often left to their own devices when things went pear shaped in the field. Having joined the Peace Corps after college, O'Neill spent most of the 1980s doing rural development in what was then a poor but peaceful Sierra Leone, traveling most places by motorbike, developing a strong affinity for the West African country and its people. He would return again in 1990, after completing a master's degree in Canada, but by this time, Sierra Leone was on the brink of a disastrous civil war.

O'Neill was employed by a US-based INGO assigned to lead the Sierra Leone Red Cross relief effort. With his years of experience in the country and fluency in Krio, he often accompanied International Committee of the Red Cross (ICRC) delegates to the field. One day, while on a field mission to the eastern city of Koidu, O'Neill found himself trapped amid active hostilities as rebel forces of the Revolutionary United Front (RUF) attacked and took control of the city. Assuming that the victorious RUF fighters would eventually find their way to the compound where he was lodged and having no avenue for escape, O'Neill knew his best chance for staying alive in rebel hands would be to highlight his position in the organization universally known to provide relief in war zones. He painted the Red Cross emblem on the compound gates and with the help of the compound's owner, they scrounged up pieces of red and white cloth, fashioning a Red Cross banner on to spread across the roof to ward off potential aerial attacks. The men then put word out among local contacts that injured combatants and civilians could be brought there for treatment. The gambit briefly worked; people came in with gunshot wounds and O'Neill made use of his Red Cross training to treat them. What's more, when the RUF fighters showed up at the compound, O'Neill remembers listening from inside as they debated with each other over whether or not they should enter the building with their weapons, this being a Red Cross facility. The rebels eventually took O'Neill and the Red Cross driver, Ali Bangura, prisoner and held them for 35 days. While a hostage, the RUF used O'Neill as a propaganda tool, parading him around and photographing him being interrogated by the rebel leader, Foday Sankoh. They hoped to use him as leverage to get international relief aid into rebel-held areas. Throughout this time, O'Neill continued to invoke the Red Cross mantle, arguing that hostage-taking was not an acceptable way to achieve their objective and managed to win small victories of principle along the way, such as getting the soldiers to keep their weapons outside of the Red Cross vehicles while they were using them to transport the hostages.

The experience left O'Neill with a renewed respect for the potential influence of the international humanitarian principles, as well as their limits. What left an even deeper impression, however, was how casually he and his organization had approached the issue of his physical security in the midst of an intense and volatile conflict. When he and Bangura eventually negotiated their release from RUF captivity and returned to the Red Cross office in Freetown, it was to everyone's general amazement—they had assumed that he and Bangura were dead. Back then, NGO staff were not issued radios or required to make regular check-ins, and often there was no means of communication from remote locations at all. Nor were there any standard arrangements for traveling in convoys of at least two vehicles when in high-risk areas. NGO staff members working in the "deep field," were effectively on their own. "It revealed to me that neither donors nor organizations paid much attention to their duty of care," O'Neill says, marking the stark difference between today's approach to operational security risk management and what the norm was in the early 1990s. "How could you set up a project in a conflict zone with no prior assessment, no training, and no security procedures?"

Once back in the United States and now employed as the Coordinator of Volunteer Safety and Overseas Security for the Peace Corps, O'Neill set about gathering field-based examples of good practice and lessons learned in minimizing risk to personnel without preventing them from going to risky environments where the needs were most severe. Some staffers in other international NGOs had begun this process as well. Harrowing incidents like O'Neill's had begun to stack up, convincing some NGO managers that the time was ripe to get their security act together, and a couple of major pivotal events also helped to propel the process forward. One of them was the execution-style murder of the ICRC workers in the field hospital in Chechnya in 1996, mentioned in the beginning of this book. A rise in targeted attacks was not the only impetus, however. In 1993, 31-year old American project officer named Ken Rutherford was working for the International Rescue Committee (IRC) when his vehicle hit a landmine on a road in Somalia. Rutherford survived the explosion, but his injuries were so severe that he required amputations of both legs below the knee. While arranging for their employee's medical evacuation and treatment, IRC made the unhappy discovery that their insurance would not be paying for his considerable medical expenses, as they had no "war risk" rider attached to their insurance policy for field staff. Had his injury been caused by a traffic accident, it would have been covered; "acts of war," as the landmine represented, were not. Clearly, if NGOs were to continue being active in situations where they could become either targets or collateral damage, they would need to build the organizational knowhow and capacities to better manage the risks to their staff.

In 1998, with funding from the Office of U.S. Foreign Disaster Assistance (USAID) and coordination by the NGO consortia InterAction and RedR, a group of humanitarian practitioners and researchers came together to develop the first global interagency security trainings. Two of them were Philippe Dind of ICRC and Robert MacPherson of CARE, who at the time were among the very few people who held the position of security manager, as a dedicated, singular function, for their respective organizations. Michael O'Neill, who held a similar security role at the Peace Corps and who had begun developing protocols based on his lessons-learned research, joined the group, bringing his templates with him.[7] The

[7] Other members of the NGO Security Training Team and early participants of the training who went on to become experts in humanitarian operational security were Jan Davis and Rob Lowe of RedR, Lucy Brown (American Red Cross), George Devendorf (Mercy Corps), Jonathan Dworken (Center for Naval Analysis), David Dyck (Eastern Mennonite University), Heather Hughes (Oxfam), Randy Martin (International Rescue Committee and later Mercy

five-day trainings, held in the United States and the United Kingdom, covered principles of security management and in-depth practical guidance such as facilities protection, convoy management, proper radio usage, and security risk assessment. O'Neill recalls that it was an organic humanitarian initiative, with few members of the group having backgrounds in military- or police-based security expertise. Rather, the members were mainly aid programming practitioners, well versed in the objectives and the particular vulnerabilities of fieldwork. The elements of the course slowly spread throughout the sector, forming the cornerstone of a great many INGOs' security plans hence forward. One participant, Koenraad Van Brabant, collected the core principles and best practices into the first edition of the Humanitarian Practice Network's *Good Practice Review 8: Operational Security Management in Violent Environments* (referred to as GPR 8, for short). The GPR 8 remains among the most downloaded and widely used of HPN's research products.

By the time the training sessions began in the late 1990s, the UN system was somewhat further along in development of a security risk management system. The UN Security Coordination office (UNSECOORD—the predecessor of the UN Department for Safety and Security) had been established back in 1982, after rioters in Saigon targeted UN offices and burned them down, marking first time the UN as an entity was directly attacked, but security awareness and training were still rudimentary across the organization. Later that decade, when Robert Painter was working on Operation Lifeline Sudan (OLS), he saw firsthand the dangerous gaps in security among most humanitarian NGOs operating in the region. With the leadership of colleagues who had experience in UNSECOORD, such as Alan Burkle, Graham Emory, and Steve Gluning, the UN group developed a training program for aid workers participating in OLS to better cope with threats and hazards in the environment. Painter recalls that a lot of the training was in basic survival tactics, such as what to do if you get lost in the bush, as well as basic first aid and hand signaling for when verbal communication was impossible or dangerous. As rudimentary as it was, this training course, like the course later developed by the NGOs, also proved to be a seminal initiative and eventually formed the basis of the UN's security risk assessment and the broader risk management model.

Corps), Toby Porter (Oxfam and later Save the Children), Charles Rogers (World Vision), Jane Swan (Interaction), and Lisa Schirch (Eastern Mennonite University).

First Principles in Humanitarian Operational Security: The Enabling Approach, Acceptance, and Residual Risk

The security principles and procedures that humanitarians developed as a matter of necessity at the end of the twentieth century borrowed from traditional military security ideas but with an important difference. By making the humanitarian program central to the security risk assessment, the model proceeds from the assumption that the aid operations would necessarily involve some exposure and vulnerability. Security measures must therefore be designed to minimize the risk as much as possible while allowing the program to go forward. This "enabling approach" to security represents a change from the traditional restrictive security mindset, in which the easiest and most effective way to safeguard staff is to circumscribe their movements. It has not always been easy for field security managers to live up to this enabling approach concept, however. The difficulty was especially pronounced within the UN security services, where the majority of staff came from police or military backgrounds and viewed having a security incident occur on their watch as a potentially career-ending event.

In addition to the enabling approach, three concepts that grew out of the early NGO security training initiative are central to understanding operational security management for humanitarian organizations: protection, deterrence, and acceptance. The first two draw from a more traditional view of security. Protection is when you harden the target—building blast barriers, installing gates and window bars, riding in armored vehicles, and the like. Deterrence involves posing a counter-threat to make those who might attack you think twice, such as employing armed guards or traveling with armed escorts. The third, acceptance, seeks to neutralize the threat by fostering relationships of trust with local communities and entering negotiations with belligerents. Together, the three concepts form what is known in the humanitarian sector as the "security triangle."[8] While most humanitarian organizations will employ elements of all three strategies in different situations, they traditionally eschew deterrent measures and weapons in all but the most extreme cases,[9] and place great store on acceptance.

[8] Various authors (2010). *Operational Security Management in Violent Environments (Revised Edition)*: Humanitarian Practice Network, ODI.

[9] Somalia in the early 1990s is one such example where nearly every aid group on the ground was relying on armed protection to operate. UN humanitarian actors and for-profit

A problem with any appealing visual model, though, is that some might take it too literally—in this case, as three distinct and self-contained options for security strategies. The 2011 updated version of *GPR 8* tried to correct this misperception:

> The triangle model was not meant to imply that an aid agency simply decides, at an institutional level, which approach is preferable (or where the agency sits on the triangle) and conducts its operations accordingly. The reality is much more fluid. First, a particular approach only has a chance of being effective if it is adapted to its environment, and if the organisation has the capacities and competencies to handle that approach. Second, in any given operating environment an organisation will probably choose a mix of approaches. As risks evolve, the organisation will have to adapt by altering the balance of approaches. Notably, shifting to a protection approach usually will not mean abandoning an acceptance approach; rather, the two components will be combined. Hardening the target may require more outreach in order to build trust and gain acceptance. Third, the effectiveness of any approach will be influenced by what other aid agencies are doing.[10]

Defining the acceptance approach by virtue of the absence of the others is another common mistake. Some organizations have assumed that, simply by rejecting armed guards and heavy protection measures, they are, by default, following an "acceptance" approach. As has been made clear in many conflict settings, however, this is not how acceptance works; it needs to be pursued actively, through continual outreach to community members and negotiated access with belligerents. Defining acceptance in the negative was the error made by those who argued for removing the rocket launcher from in front of the Canal Hotel in Baghdad, in hopes that what Robert Painter called "emblematic protection" would prevent attack. Finally, because acceptance is not static, but rather a constant process, it cannot be treated as merely an approach to security. It must be baked into everything the organization does, from programming to administration to hiring.

The updated GPR 8 included another important caveat on the security triangle: "Finally, no approach, by itself or in combination, will reduce the

government contractors that provide large-scale reconstruction aid services in war zones more commonly opt for heavy protective and deterrent measures.

[10] Various authors (2010). *Operational Security Management in Violent Environments (Revised Edition)*: Humanitarian Practice Network, ODI, p. 55.

risk to zero."[11] This speaks to ***residual risk,*** a critical concept that was not yet fully formed, or at least not sufficiently emphasized, in previous decades. A risk of any kind is composed of two components: probability and impact. It is a measure of the probability that you will encounter a specific threat (potential for harm) in the environment and the severity of consequences that would result (on individuals, the program, and the organization) if you do. Some threats, such as the detonation of a nuclear or biological weapon, would have enormous impact if realized, but are unlikely enough that the risk would be considered low. The threat of a staff member being mugged on the street may be far more likely, but the limited impact means that this risk would still be low enough for an organization to comfortably manage. Residual risk is what remains after all measures have been taken to reduce the probability and to mitigate the potential impact of adverse events. At this point, what is important is for those who may be affected to understand, acknowledge, and explicitly accept this risk.

In the case of kidnapping (which for some female victims has been known to entail repeated sexual violence), informed consent is challenged by the difficulty for people to mentally integrate the potentiality of high-impact events.

> It is almost impossible to conceive of the consequences fully—made harder by the fact that, understandably, victims of kidnappings generally tend not to share their often highly traumatic experiences in the public realm. Taking the decision to work in a high-risk environment is therefore often done with an incomplete picture of what a kidnapping incident might entail and how the individual would cope if it happened.

In the Islamic State (IS)-controlled areas of northern Syria in 2014, kidnappings of international staff were becoming increasingly likely, and with the devastating impact this has for both the victim and the organization, proved too high a risk for most international organizations to continue operations there.

Accepting the residual risk and remaining in high-risk areas can be a difficult pill to swallow for most organizations, as it requires the blunt recognition, as Michael O'Neill put it, that "it is not the security manager's job to keep people safe." Rather, an organization's duty of care ends at the responsibility to reduce risks to an acceptable level and ensure that staff has given their informed consent to work in the knowledge of the residual risks they face.

[11] Ibid.

More Recent Developments and Pieces Still Missing

Humanitarian organizations have advanced considerably in their approach to security in the past two decades. Whereas in the 1990s there were only a few organizations that had professional positions dedicated to security risk management, there are over 200 such professionals now at both the country and field office levels. Some of the larger NGOs maintain regional security personnel providing analysis and support to country offices as well. Strong risk management capacity doesn't come cheap, though, and many small and some medium-size NGOs continue to struggle to make these organizational investments in the face of ever more challenging and complex environments.

In the 2010s, humanitarian organizations found themselves responding to the humanitarian needs created by major new conflicts in South Sudan, Syria, Yemen, northern Nigeria, Mali, and Central African Republic, along with continued violence in Afghanistan, Democratic Republic of Congo, and Iraq. All of these non-international conflicts involve multiple non-state armed forces—insurgent groups operating at both the national and international levels—posing multiple and overlapping risks. Western donor governments, just as prominent as they have always been in funding the humanitarian response, have added to the risks faced by NGOs by giving them reason to fear heavy punitive repercussions if any of their relief aid should ever end up in the hands of one of these sanctioned groups. In a study my organization conducted with the NGO consortium InterAction, I asked some senior managers of large international NGOs what sort of imagined risk scenario kept them up at night, and their answers frequently involved a front-page scandal in which their organization's resources ended up in the hands of a terrorist group.

Humanitarians' recognition of separate but intertwining risk areas—security, legal, financial, and reputational risks, for example—represents the latest major development in their approach to risk management. The largest international NGOs have begun to adopt holistic integrated systems, or what is known as enterprise risk management (ERM), which, as its name suggests, has its roots in the private sector. ERM requires managers to identify and assess all kinds of risks that may affect the organization and its people, allowing them to prioritize where to focus their mitigation efforts. To do this, the system gathers information from the bottom-up, with the participation of every department and field office to build an annual "risk register" to help managers keep track of the risks and the efforts to address them. The more highly developed ERM systems also have procedures for regular audits to ensure the proper follow-up. The idea, while valid and promising, has flaws. One problem is that if it is not well designed, the process can be cumbersome, bureaucratic, and slow to adjust to changing conditions. Another, more significant, issue is that these systems generally fail to integrate the work done with or through local organizations. Operational partnerships between international and local humanitarian actors, ranging from the standard sub-grants to more egalitarian arrangements, are central to humanitarian response. And with the intensifying risk environment in conflict-affected countries like Syria, local operational partnerships have become increasingly critical as international organizations withdraw for security reasons. In addition to being necessary for humanitarian access, partnering is now the stated goal of many international organizations, which pledged in 2016 to work toward empowering national organizations and increasing their share in humanitarian funding resources for the sake of more effective aid programming and more sustainable outcomes. Unfortunately, most international organizations' risk management systems don't fully incorporate the partnership, and the risks to their partners, as an extension of the organization and its work. Rather, they view the partner and partnerships as risks in themselves. To protect themselves against fiduciary risk (corruption, theft, and fraud), most organizations institute tight financial controls on their partners and vet them for previous questionable practices, but they spend much less time and resources on security risk management.[12] This is despite wide agreement that insecurity is the biggest threat facing humanitarian actors in conflict settings, and that international organizations have at least an "ethical" duty of care to their partners. Like so much else, in the humanitarian sector, it is a donor-driven phenomenon and has created some moral dissonance among practitioners.

In truth, many international NGOs still do not do right by their own national staff when it comes to security. It is not as bad as it once was, but there are still wide discrepancies between the level of security training and inputs (e.g., off-hours transportation, communications equipment, and site security at home) that is offered to expatriate aid workers as opposed to those hired in country. For example, arrangements for emergency evacuation in the case of deteriorating security conditions are extremely rare,

[12] Stoddard, A., Czwarno, M. & Hamsik, L. (2019). *NGOs and Risk: Managing uncertainty in local-international partnerships. Global Report*. Washington, DC: InterAction.

as the cost of moving national staff members and their families is prohibitive. It is also uncommon to offer additional protective measures for national staffers at their homes or for their safe transit between home and work. This is unfortunate, because their status as an employee of an international organization makes them vulnerable to targeting for political or economic reasons. In hundreds of interviews with security professionals, I came across only one security manager who took the step of going to each national staff member's home to get the geographical coordinates for emergency planning and assessing each residence for security needs. This is not the norm, but it should be.

Humanitarian organizations that have been successful at maintaining aid operations in highly insecure and volatile areas have done so by embedding deeply in local communities and investing in building their situational awareness. In many cases the international NGOs have managed to do so by emulating national NGOs and local Red Cross/Red Crescent societies—keeping their international identity low profile, localizing their activities and personnel hires to the immediate vicinity, and minimizing senior staff visits. For those international organizations like ICRC and MSF that negotiate their way into conflict zones as openly international, neutral actors, it is even more important that they have a precise understanding of the armed actors and their objectives.

The problematic ethics of providing greater security support for international staff vis-a-vis their national staff and national partner organizations brings up another underdeveloped area in risk management. At the time of this writing, humanitarian organizations are only beginning to consider "ethical risk" as another risk area to be managed, along with security, fiduciary, information, and the like. In addition to the equal treatment of nationals, ethical risk would encompass the risk of violating humanitarian principles or failing to safeguard aid recipients and local community members from exploitation and abuse by predatory staff members.

Lastly, the concept of "program criticality" is essential to the enabling approach, but it is still fuzzy within most NGOs' security risk management systems. As the name suggests, program criticality is a measure of how critical the program is for the people it is serving, and how big a hole it would leave if it were withdrawn. Is it life-saving? Does it provide necessary human services not available elsewhere? Or is it non-urgent and appropriate to put aside temporarily while waiting for conditions to stabilize? The more critical the programming, the higher the level of residual risk the organization should be willing to accept to keep it running. Although this feels intuitive to humanitarians, and the NGO representatives I have spoken with say they generally have it in mind when they are making security decisions, most have not yet incorporated it into their formal risk assessment processes.

The Access Dilemma: Donor Governments and Their Relationship to Aid Worker Risk

Donor governments can add to the security risk of the humanitarian organizations they fund in a number of ways. By taking a hard line on fiduciary controls while not insisting on equally stringent security risk management measures, they create conditions where organizations direct more effort and attention to securing their monetary and material assets rather than the safety of their staff members and partners. This fiduciary risk focus has even come to be reflected in the organizational architecture of humanitarian NGOs, where "partnership coordinator" positions are located within financial or legal compliance departments as opposed to in programming departments or as a crosscutting role. At the whiff of financial mismanagement or wrongdoing, it is common for donors to cease all grant disbursement payments pending investigation. Not only does this potentially disrupt a vital aid program, it can also expose the NGO to risks that come from not being able to pay field staff or provide what was promised in the community. One former director of a Syrian NGO described to me in tears how she attempted to keep her organization running and to pay her staff while being investigated for accounting irregularities. Rather than sending technical support to help her straighten out the problems, the donor and the international NGO that had provided the sub-grant took a hard line and blocked all disbursements and most communications for months until she could rectify the situation. By that time, it was too late—the organization had been forced to close down.

The focus on combatting fraud also tends to squeeze resources at the ground level. The principal humanitarian donors rarely object to including extra funding for requested security costs, but they also do not require that their grantees provide the same level of support for their sub-grantees. National organizations, which rely on these sub-grants from international organizations for most of their funding, have strong incentives to keep their operational costs as low as possible to win these contracts. This very often translates into cutting corners on security. For example, they may send their staff into high-risk areas on public transport or put them up in insecure accommodations.[13] This is commonplace, and since international organizations typically do not discuss security plans with their national partners, it often goes unnoticed.

Donor governments can also create risks for humanitarian actors through policies that are intended as risk mitigation, but paradoxically result in new hazards and obstacles to humanitarian access. The practice of "de-risking" by banks is an indirect example of this. Governments have come down hard on banks for instances in which sanctioned groups used them to move cash, sometimes under the guise of phony charitable organizations. In turn, banks have sought to avoid future penalties by closing the accounts of legitimate NGOs (especially from the Muslim world) and restricting transfers to countries where these groups are active. Humanitarian organizations, suddenly unable to move money to fund their projects via the formal banking system, have had to resort to informal systems like *hawala* networks (an informal system of cash transfers common in Muslim countries) which are more costly, or physically carrying cash, which is dangerous. An overriding concern of governments is to prevent sanctioned (i.e., "terrorist") groups from diverting or otherwise benefitting from humanitarian contributions. Compounding the problem, after 9/11, many donor governments issued a number of new and increasingly stringent regulations for humanitarian organizations to prevent "terrorist" groups from diverting humanitarian contributions to their operations. In 2018, the US government passed new rules and regulations to this effect for organizations working in the Lake Chad basin, Syria, and the occupied territories of the West Bank and Gaza. The next largest donor government, the United Kingdom, followed suit, proposing similarly purposed restrictions of their own.[14] The ambiguous language in these rules has prompted well-founded fears of potential prosecution should the organizations inadvertently find themselves on the wrong side of the law. In 2018, the NGO Norwegian People's Aid paid a US$2 million settlement

[13] Hamsik, L. (2019). *NGOs and Risk: Managing Uncertainty in Local-International Partnerships – Case Studies: Northeast Nigeria & South Sudan*. Washington, DC: InterAction.

[14] Adamczyck, S. (2018). "UK counterterrorism travel ban could criminalise humanitarian assistance" ODI: 30 November 2018. Retrieved from https://www.odi.org/comment/10709-uk-counterterrorism-travel-ban-could-criminalise-humanitarian-assistance

for violating US counter-terror regulations in its Gaza program, even though the program in question was not funded by the US government.[15]

By adopting a formal stance of "zero tolerance" on corruption and diversion, and "no-contact" rules regarding sanctioned groups, the donors create a moral hazard for the organizations they fund. Aid groups are forced to choose either to leave areas where insurgent groups are active, and thus abandon needy civilians, or to quietly continue the necessary negotiating that their staff must do with these armed groups or their interlocutors. This latter choice often results in the organization's leadership adopting a willful blindness and culture of silence, which prevents NGOs from speaking of these practices even to each other, much less their donors. At the same time, they are pushing this hugely important and potentially dangerous responsibility onto the shoulders of local staff members. The idea of a blanket humanitarian exemption or waiver to these laws and regulations has been raised, but it has not yet been seriously considered by the major donor governments.

It bears mention that donor governments can add to insecurity for humanitarian actors in more direct ways as well. When my colleagues and I analyzed the data on aid worker attacks by the various perpetrator groups responsible, we were surprised to find that, "When measured by body count alone, it is states that are responsible for the most lethal attacks" meaning that when a state was behind the violence, intentional or not, more aid workers died. "In 2015 and 2016, 54 aid workers were killed by state actors mostly by air strikes by Russia and the US in Syria and Afghanistan, and by an upsurge in the state-sponsored violence in South Sudan."[16]

More generally, as discussed in the preceding chapters, the inescapable association of the most prominent humanitarian organizations with powerful Western states can inspire violence against them. With the exception of the Bangladesh-based mega-NGO, Bangladesh Rural Advancement Committee (BRAC), which is focused on development and not yet a major actor in conflict-driven humanitarian emergencies, each one of the largest international NGOs is Western in origin. Most also receive the

[15] Charity and Security Network (2018). "Norwegian People's Aid Settles Enforcement Case Over Democracy Building and Mine Removal Projects US Says Were Material Support" Retrieved from https://www.charityandsecurity.org/News_NPA-_US_Settle_Case

[16] Stoddard, A., Harmer, A., & Czwarno, M. (2017). *Aid Worker Security Report 2017: Behind the Attacks: a look at the perpetrators of violence against aid workers.* Humanitarian Outcomes.

majority of their funding from their home governments.[17] Only MSF has been able to garner most of its resources for humanitarian response from public donations, but even these are sourced overwhelmingly from Western Europe and North America, as is the small percentage of public funding they do receive from donor governments.[18] Diversifying the donor base for coordinated international humanitarian response receives rhetorical support, but it is not clear how much, if at all, the current major donor governments have pressed other nations to climb aboard. These donors have an interest in maintaining the status and visibility of their generosity, and the soft power they may see it as bringing, as attested to by the ubiquitous national branding of the aid. Every bag of grain or rice delivered with USAID funding, for example, proclaims its origin as "from the American people" in a tagline next to the logo. And in June 2018, an image making the rounds on social media (to wide derision) showed a row of newly built latrines with the donor's logo "UKAID" largely printed on the door of each privy.

All of these donor-driven risks have had a "chilling effect" on humanitarian access[19] in certain conflicts, converging with the sector's other security challenges and ethical gaps to drive down the humanitarian presence where it is most needed. Looking back on the developments made in security risk management in the sector since his experience in Sierra Leone, Michael O'Neill (who went on to serve for 14 years as the Global Safety and Security Coordinator for Save the Children, and now has his own consultancy for NGO risk management) sees where there is much more work to be done. When assessing the effectiveness of security risk management, he says, "Access is the ultimate measure of success." Ultimately, no system is worthwhile if it does not serve to extend the reach of relief aid to civilians. "This was always the objective," says O'Neill. "It took us INGOs a while to find our way back to that."

[17] Although the Gulf states have begun to contribute significant sums to the formal humanitarian system, the other non-Western largest economies such as China and Brazil do not yet meaningfully participate in the international humanitarian regime and contribute much less to global humanitarian emergency response efforts relative to their wealth.

[18] Public donors to MSF in 2017 were Belgium, Canada, Denmark, Germany, Ireland, Luxembourg, Netherlands, Norway, Spain, Sweden, and Switzerland (Médecins sans Frontières, 2018).

[19] Mackintosh, K. & Duplat, P. (2013), *Study of the Impact of Donor Counter-Terrorism Measures on Principled Humanitarian Action*. Geneva: Norwegian Refugee Council and UN OCHA.

Surely, part of the solution to the access problem has to be adopting new ways of working when the old ways are made impossible. As seen in parts of Syria and Afghanistan, security risks can make it effectively impossible for Western international organizations to work. In the case of Syria, hybrid international-national NGOs began springing up with founders from Syrian diaspora communities around the world mobilizing funding. These "diaspora NGOs" operated essentially as local Syrian entities and helped to fill some of the presence gaps, but humanitarian coverage of Syrian needs remained sparse, as it is in the parts of Afghanistan where fighting is most prevalent and where the Taliban are powerful.

I brought up the problem of humanitarian access with Fatima Gailani, President of the Afghan Red Crescent Society, when we met in her Kabul office in 2014. Gailani is the daughter of Pir Sayed Ahmed Gailani, who led the National Islamic Front of Afghanistan in opposition to the Soviet occupation in the 1980s, and she received her higher education as an exile in Iran and in the United Kingdom. After the Taliban were removed from power in 2002, she took part in the drafting of Afghanistan's new constitution. Over tea and a generous spread of sweets and dried apricots, she described to me the successes and as yet unmet potential of her organization.

The Afghan Red Crescent is over 80 years old and well known to Afghans across the country. As is the risk with the Red Cross/Crescent societies in politically unstable countries, the Afghan Red Crescent went through periods when it was too closely linked to the current parties in power, which appointed its leadership. Since starting her tenure in 2004, Gailani successfully revitalized the organization and restored its credibility as a neutral aid entity working for all Afghans. By the time we spoke, the organization had access to "95 percent of the country," Gailani noted with pride, and maintained offices or some sort of operational presence in every province. This is far better coverage than even the largest international NGOs and UN agencies had achieved. If this was the case, and internationals were restricted to places where they determined they could operate safely, I asked, "Why didn't the international community not seek to partner with, and channel aid through, the Afghan Red Crescent?"

"This is my question too," she said. "Internationals only remember we are here when they suddenly can't move due to insecurity." But even then, despite the ARCS's wide presence with ready-made platforms for aid deliveries and eagerness to collaborate, she claimed she had not received much interest from internationals. "I say to them, 'We are in these provinces and can monitor your aid with our volunteers. What we have underway already you can improve, and what we don't have you can hire us to do it,'" just as the international organizations do in other implementing partner arrangements.

"However," she stipulated, "we do insist on no emblems on the sacks."

References

Adamczyck, S. (2018, November 30). *UK Counterterrorism Travel Ban Could Criminalise Humanitarian Assistance*. ODI. Retrieved from https://www.odi.org/comment/10709-uk-counterterrorism-travel-ban-could-criminalise-humanitarian-assistance

Charity and Security Network. (2018). *Norwegian People's Aid Settles Enforcement Case over Democracy Building and Mine Removal Projects US Says Were Material Support*. Retrieved from https://www.charityandsecurity.org/News_NPA-_US_Settle_Case

Development Initiatives. (2018). *Global Humanitarian Assistance Report 2018*. http://devinit.org/wp-content/uploads/2018/06/GHA-Report-2018.pdf

Hamsik, L. (2019). *NGOs and Risk: Managing Uncertainty in Local-International Partnerships – Case Studies: Northeast Nigeria & South Sudan*. Washington, DC: InterAction.

Lester, D., Parnell, J., & Carraher, S. (2003). Organizational Life Cycle: A Five-Stage Empirical Scale. *International Journal of Organizational Analysis, 11*, 4. ABI/INFORM Global p. 339.

Lewis, V., & Churchill, N. (1983). The Five Stages of Small Business Growth. *Harvard Business Review, 61*(3), 30–50.

Mackintosh, K., & Duplat, P. (2013). *Study of the Impact of Donor Counter-Terrorism Measures on Principled Humanitarian Action*. Geneva: Norwegian Refugee Council and UN OCHA.

Stoddard, A. (2016, December). The View from the Foxhole: How Risk and the Fragmented Perspective of Agencies Limits the Reach of Humanitarian Aid. Guest Blog for the Advanced Training Program on Humanitarian Action (ATHA). *atha.se*.

Stoddard, A., Harmer, A., & Czwarno, M. (2017). *Aid Worker Security Report 2017: Behind the Attacks: A Look at the Perpetrators of Violence Against Aid Workers*. New York: Humanitarian Outcomes.

Stoddard, A., Czwarno, M., & Hamsik, L. (2019). *NGOs and Risk: Managing Uncertainty in Local-International Partnerships. Global Report*. Washington, DC: InterAction.

Various Authors. (2010). *Operational Security Management in Violent Environments* (Revised ed.). London: Humanitarian Practice Network, ODI.

CHAPTER 6

It's Not About Us: Addressing the Security Dilemma with the Ethics of Professionalism

An Airstrike in Idlib

Before Syria descended into a bloody and protracted civil war, Mustafa Haj Yousef was enjoying a successful career importing electrical and plumbing appliances. The then 38-year-old married father of four had spent his life in his hometown of Khan Sheikhan, a small city in the northwestern governorate of Idlib, and had learned the trade working with his brothers. He had recently embarked on a new business venture, forming a partnership with a friend to produce copper sanitary tools in their own plant. It was just at the time that the popular uprisings that came to be known as the Arab Spring were spreading from North Africa to the Middle East and beginning to capture the imagination of much of the Syrian population, which had lived under the authoritarian rule of the Assad dynasty for 40 years. Haj Yousef found himself swept up in the tidal wave popular revolution as well, as all his previous business interests fell away. When the anti-government protests began in Syria, he says, "I left all this and began to participate in the peaceful uprising; and that occupied my life."

The civil uprising in Syria met with a violent response by the government, and by the summer of 2011 had developed into full-blown warfare. Over the next few years, the opposition fractured and the multiple warring parties began to carve up the country. The southern and western parts were still mostly controlled by the Assad government, while the Islamic State held much of the west, spanning the Syria-Iraq border.

A. Stoddard, *Necessary Risks*,
https://doi.org/10.1007/978-3-030-26411-6_6

Kurdish forces controlled a large swath of the north, and various other rebel groups had territory in parts of the southwest and northeast. Humanitarian needs were enormous, as bombing campaigns displaced millions of people and destroyed vital infrastructure. The ferocity of the fighting and the complicated international politics surrounding the crisis conspired to make Syria the hardest to access and least well-covered emergency by the humanitarian system in recent history. For the international humanitarian agencies that were officially allowed by the government to work inside Syria, their operations were tightly circumscribed by the government, which effectively controlled which areas received assistance. International aid organizations also set up cross-border operations from Turkey, Lebanon, and Jordan, but compared to the vastness of the needs, the international response was minuscule and relied heavily on local groups and newly formed Syrian NGOs to serve as primary responders.

Having jettisoned his pre-war life and business pursuits, Haj Yousef joined the local coordinating committee of Khan Sheikhan. These coordinating committees sprang up around Syria as centers for public information, human rights monitoring, and reporting about revolutionary activities, and many soon became organizing bodies for humanitarian relief distributions in their local areas. He was glad to be engaged in this important work but wanted a more direct role in saving the lives of his fellow Syrians trapped amid the war. When the opportunity arose, he joined the relief organization called Syria Civil Defence (SCD), commonly known by their nickname, the White Helmets. SCD began as local groups of volunteers that came together in late 2012 in many non-government-controlled areas to rescue people from the rubble left by the barrel bombs and to provide them with emergency medical care and transportation to safety. The groups quickly organized and professionalized, developing training courses for emergency trauma care and search and rescue and establishing command-and-control centers for each locality. Less than two years later, the groups had formed a national organization operating across eight governorates, coordinating the work of thousands of volunteers.

In 2013, Haj Yousef traveled to Turkey for his SCD training in search and rescue techniques and came back home to start work as a rescue volunteer. He and his colleagues would respond in the immediate aftermath of air strikes, with little protective gear other than their white helmets and dig wounded civilians out of the rubble. These missions were physically grueling and emotionally intense; the rescuers were often surrounded by the family and neighbors of the victims, and the outcomes would resolve in immense shared sorrow or joy. It was also incredibly dangerous work. As previously mentioned, in one of the more barbarous aspects of the Syrian conflict, the Russian and Syrian armed forces have deliberately targeted SCD operations in double tap strikes, where a second bombardment is explicitly timed to take out the rescuers of the victims of the first.

One memory that won't leave him occurred on 20 December 2015. Haj Yousef was coordinating a team responding to an airstrike site in Khan Sheikhan when the second round of shells began to fall and a colleague, a man named Abdul Aziz Talawi, was hit. He raced to where other team members were struggling to rescue their wounded colleague while the shelling continued all around them. "We felt that we were in the last moments of our lives," Has Yousef says. "Thankfully," he adds, "we were able to protect the body of Abdul Aziz Talawi."

As the war in Syria ground on, Haj Yousef undertook additional training, and in turn, he trained up other volunteers to form a larger response team for his area. From rescue volunteer, he rose to be the center manager and later the sector leader for all of Khan Sheikhan. Many other of Haj Yousef's colleagues have been killed in these strikes, and he says the awareness that death could come at any moment is pervasive among all his co-workers. As of May 2019, he quoted a figure of 262 White Helmets killed and 769 wounded on the job. His family members are also keenly aware of the danger, and their fears for him have been the subject of ongoing "discussions," as he diplomatically puts it. To date, their efforts to persuade him to leave this work, even for a short rest, have been unsuccessful. "Syria Civil Defence means to me all my life," he says, and for it, "I have given up all my business and my life and my friends."

Eight years have passed since the civil war began, and Mustafa Haj Yousef now has five children: Asma, Mohammed, Yahya, Hamdo, and Mona, the youngest being five years old. He notes with pride that his eldest daughter is studying pharmaceutical science. He now directs the entire Idlib section of the White Helmets and with no less fierce commitment than when he first joined. "I dedicated my life to save our injured and displaced people." For him and his colleagues, he says, it is much more than an occupation: "It has become a duty."

The Need to Professionalize

> Would it not be possible, in time of peace and quiet, to form relief societies for the purpose of having care given to the wounded in wartime by zealous, devoted and thoroughly qualified volunteers? (Henry Dunant, *A Memory of Solferino*)

The aid workers profiled in the preceding pages, and the many hundreds of others like them who have experienced violence while doing their work, belong to an inherently dangerous occupation whose risks have been compounded by the nature of current civil conflicts and the global political environment in which they occur. Despite significant advancements in aid organizations' security risk management thinking and systems, not to mention over a century of advocacy and diplomatic efforts aimed at promoting adherence to international humanitarian law (IHL), aid workers are persistently and increasingly the targets of attack by armed forces. The incentives of non-state armed actors to target humanitarians, the inability or unwillingness of host governments to provide protective environments, and the underinvestment in critical negotiating skills have resulted in a sparse humanitarian presence in conflict-driven emergencies, where aid is needed most. Powerful donor governments have added to the risks, and in the process have further diminished humanitarian access, by adopting a punitive approach toward humanitarian organizations that they perceive as "assisting" these non-state actors.

Today, there are fewer voices from the humanitarian sector arguing that the numbers of violent attacks on aid workers do not represent a significant and intrinsic problem. The International Committee of the Red Cross (ICRC) now leads the chorus in proclaiming that these attacks constitute a crisis, which political leaders must address. Speaking to the UN Security Council in March 2019, ICRC's president, Peter Mauer, said, "The taboo that warring parties would not attack aid workers has been trashed. We need strong leadership, political will and determined action to restore this taboo." The norms of civilization have always been trampled by warfare, of course, but Maurer's point speaks to the extent to which today's non-international conflicts seem to have rendered them practically irrelevant. He is also, unfortunately, preaching to the choir. State actors need less convincing that it is a matter of mutual interest to support the rules of war, as the notion reinforces the system and their place within it. Armed opposition groups not yet in control of a state apparatus, however, or global jihadist movements seeking to overturn the international order, would be foolish to abide by these constraints. In its public advocacy, the ICRC often inadvertently reveals this dilemma. In June 2018, the organization tweeted, "Is everyone obliged to observe the rules of war? Yes, International Humanitarian Law is universal. The Geneva Conventions, which are central to #IHL, have been ratified by 196 States."[1] The tweet omits the fact that the majority of warring parties today are non-state entities. International humanitarian law, with its rules of war, is an example of what historian Yuval Noah Harari would call a social fiction. Like the value of currency or national borders, these shared ideas have no objective reality, but they are necessary for nearly all of human cooperation. However, it is only "as long as this communal belief persists, the imagined reality exerts force in the world."[2] In other words, like Tinker Bell, IHL relies on all of us actively believing in it to survive. These legal norms and principles, forged in the context of international wars of a different age, remain just as morally valid, but their fragility is showing. And for humanitarian workers, they are less helpful as tools.

In the absence of political solutions and will required to put an end to the conflicts, few possible solutions present themselves to the problem of how to enhance secure access for humanitarian operations to reach civilian populations suffering amid war. Two strands of thinking have seemed to form within the discourse—neither of which, I argue, are ultimately persuasive. The first proposes to augment or reform international law and principles, an idea tentatively floated by government actors; the second is a call for the sector to reform itself, bringing the humanitarian enterprise "back to basics."

As regards the first idea, governments are now witnessing the weakness of international humanitarian law to protect the humanitarian operations they fund and exploring potential ways to shore it up. No longer as willing as they were in the 1990s to extend their military power in the name of "humanitarian intervention," the Western powers continue to funnel humanitarian contributions as one of their primary means of engagement with these imploding states, but the problems of insecurity for aid workers and obstacles to humanitarian access continue to stymie these efforts. To probe this issue, the UK government's humanitarian office commissioned

[1] @ICRC 4 June 2018, https://twitter.com/ICRC/status/1004188528438210560

[2] Harari, Y. N. (2015). *Sapiens: A brief history of humankind* (First U.S. edition. ed.). New York: Harper, p. 63.

my research group, Humanitarian Outcomes, to conduct a scoping study on the idea of creating a new set of international principles for secure humanitarian access.[3] What we found was that humanitarians, particularly those doing the frontline negotiations with armed actors, did not imagine that a new set of international principles on access would make any real difference in how they go about doing their work and staying safe.

> Stakeholders expressed a range of concerns, including the risk that a new set of 'principles' will confuse or undermine the current frameworks that inform principled humanitarian action. Many also were sceptical of the feasibility of states agreeing to new principles, given that they have not even shown interest in taking forward recent legal guidance on the access issue. Finally, some fear that the process, inevitably involving the UN, would result in further politicisation of humanitarian action, resulting in even less access. They called instead for greater political pressure on affected states and other parties to the conflict to meet their responsibilities to protect and assist the local population, rather than focusing on creating more space for international responders.[4]

The second strand of thought, endorsing a "back to basics" approach for the humanitarian sector, has been around longer and incorporates much of the criticism and debates in humanitarianism that were touched on in Chap. 5. Since the end of the 1990s, a growing number of humanitarians have contended that aid organizations have grown too large, too rigid, and too corporatist, all of which diminishes their effectiveness by dampening their intrepid spirit and value-driven ethos. In addition, as organizations grew, many of them expanded their remits into antipoverty and social justice arenas that diluted the mission of neutral, apolitical humanitarian assistance to people in need. A version of this argument can be found in David Rieff's 2002 book *A Bed for the Night: Humanitarianism in Crisis.* Looking back on the conflicts of the 1990s, such as Bosnia and Kosovo, Rieff paints a picture of a morally confused humanitarian sector that was punching above its weight. By seeking political outcomes, he argues, the humanitarian organizations effectively colluded with their donor governments in a fantasy that framed the conflicts as straightforward

[3] Harmer, A., Stoddard, A. & Sarazen, A. (2018). *Humanitarian access in armed conflict: A need for new principles?* Humanitarian Outcomes, December, p. 1.

[4] Harmer, A., Stoddard, A. & Sarazen, A. (2018). *Humanitarian access in armed conflict: A need for new principles?* Humanitarian Outcomes, December, p. 1.

contests of good and evil. In doing so, he argues, they sacrificed their neutrality and independence, losing the unique value they once added. Rieff therefore entreats humanitarians to stay in their lane, to do less:

> Let humanitarian be humanitarianism. Let it save some lives, whatever the compromises it has to make along the way, and let it tend to the victims and remind that corner of the world that it is lucky enough not to be in agony of the incalculable suffering, misery, and grief that literally billions of people feel every day of their lives. Is that really so little?[5]

A few years after *A Bed for the Night* was published, the ICRC's Director-General, Angelo Gnaedinger, sounded a similar note in a speech with the title, "Humanitarian Action: Today's new security environment has forced us back to basics."[6] The speech was in response to recent attacks against aid workers in Afghanistan and Iraq, and Gnaedinger was appealing for a return to the core humanitarian principles as a means to protect aid workers who had become targets in conflicts and who had become too closely associated with state military actors:

> We at the ICRC believe that our security can only be fostered through the rigorous preservation of space for independent and neutral humanitarian action…These four principles [neutrality, impartiality independence and non-militarisation of aid] are our way of doing things and are central to our vision of humanitarianism in the XXIst century. We will defend that vision tenaciously because we believe not only will it be an effective bulwark against injustice and inhumanity but also because it allows us to reach and protect those who too often bear the brunt of armed conflict.

Today, the back-to-basics argument is perhaps most forcefully articulated by Mark Dubois, a former MSF staffer and thought-leader on issues in humanitarianism. The Western political phenomenon of military "humanitarian intervention" that Rieff was originally concerned with has long since been replaced by "the global war on terror," but Dubois and

[5] Rieff, D. (2002). *A Bed for the Night: Humanitarianism in Crisis*. New York: Simon & Schuster, p. 333.

[6] ICRC (2004). *Humanitarian action: "Today's new security environment has forced us back to basics." ICRC.org*. 27-02-2004 Statement Retrieved 4 May 2019, from https://www.icrc.org/en/doc/resources/documents/statement/5x6e5t.htm

others still find ample cause to lament the mission creep of humanitarian organizations into areas where their foundational principles lose their meaning and come to be associated with statist projects. Specifically, he asserts, humanitarian actors do this by stepping in for absentee states to provide basic services in protracted crises. Dubois argues that humanitarians ought not to attempt to end all need. Instead, their objective should be limited to triaging and then meeting the most urgent needs of people experiencing true (i.e., temporary) humanitarian crises.[7] In a 2016 article for *The Guardian*, Dubois writes,

> Why is this humanitarian specificity so important? Because the overwhelming majority of humanitarian needs are generated by war (the UN secretary general's report puts the figure at over 80%) and war makes access tricky. To reach people in conflict, humanitarians have but one power, the power of trust. The people with the guns and bombs must be convinced that you seek to fix humans full stop. Distrust will flare if you come with an agenda to address the causes of their suffering, reinforce national authorities or stabilise fragile states.[8]

While the back-to-basics line of argument may resonate with many in the sector, it is difficult to see how it suggests any specific actions that would directly address the twin problems of preventing attacks on aid workers and obtaining better access to populations in crisis. It assumes that hewing more closely to the original mission and principles would instill trust, which would in turn confer protection. As I have tried to illustrate in the previous chapters, this assumption is faulty. The humanitarian sector is inextricably enmeshed with the Western-dominated nation-state system, and even the most principled and independent humanitarian actors will still be attacked when it serves the interests of armed insurgencies, which, in asymmetric conflicts, is much of the time. Attempting to draw brighter lines between your organization and the major donor governments, or between short-term humanitarian crises and protracted complex emergencies, holds little promise.

There is a deeper problem with the back-to-basics argument, however. Its premise, that there was once a time when brave and skilled humanitarians

[7] Dubois, M. (2018). *The New Humanitarian Basics.* HPG Working Paper. London: ODI, p. 23.

[8] Dubois, M. (2016). "Don't blur the lines between development and humanitarian work." *The Guardian*, 12 May 2016. Retrieved 3 May 2019, from https://www.theguardian.com/global-development-professionals-network/2016/may/12/dont-blur-the-lines-between-development-and-humanitarian-work

sallied forth into the most dangerous places to bring relief to the most vulnerable people, just isn't true—at least not at any significant scale. Like all examples of false nostalgia, the myth of a lost humanitarian golden age thrives in the absence of empirical evidence. When one looks back at the funding, staffing, and operational data of previous years, however, it is evident that in decades past, the humanitarian operational footprint was much smaller, meaning many fewer people were being helped. Take Médecins Sans Frontières (MSF), now the world's largest international humanitarian NGO, as a case in point: in 2017, MSF employed 37,900 locally hired staff members in 72 countries and deployed roughly 8000 international professionals on field assignments.[9] In 1999, the year it won the Nobel Peace Prize, it was a third of its current size, with 15,000 local employees and 2500 internationals.[10] And for most of its first two decades of existence, the 1970s and 1980s, the organization focused on sending small volunteer medical missions to a handful of countries each year, with total worldwide personnel numbering only in the hundreds. Others of the world's largest international NGOs show similar, if less compressed, growth trajectories. Recall also that only 20 or so of these organizations typically respond to the most volatile conflict contexts to begin with. The majority of NGOs have neither the resources nor the risk appetite to operate in such areas. I do not doubt that the aid workers who worked in field operations 20 years ago or more remember a very different sort of humanitarian response. They may indeed recall a time of greater boldness, of a more intrepid humanitarian spirit, but overall, there was also much less aid work being done. So, while it is true that humanitarian access in conflict zones and coverage of the most severe needs are insufficient,[11] the answer is probably not to be found by going *back* to anything.

[9] Figures for combined field staff of all MSF sections sourced from MSF (2018). "International Financial Report 2017": "In 2017, near 8000 health professionals, logistics specialists and administrative staff of all nationalities left on field assignments to join more than 37,900 locally hired staff working in medical programmes in over 72 countries."

[10] "Médecins Sans Frontières – Facts." 1999 NobelPrize.org. Nobel Media AB 2019. Sat. 4 May 2019. https://www.nobelprize.org/prizes/peace/1999/msf/facts/

[11] See Healy, S. & Tiller, S. (2014). Where is Everyone? Responding to Emergencies in the Most Difficult Places. MSF, 2014, and Stoddard, A., Jillani, S., Caccavale, J., Cooke, P., Guillemois, D., & Klimentov, V. (2017). Out of Reach: How Insecurity Prevents Humanitarian Aid from Accessing the Neediest. *Stability: International Journal of Security and Development*, *6*(1). doi:https://doi.org/10.5334/sta.506

Where, then, should humanitarians focus their efforts? I confess that if the accumulated knowledge of humanitarian operational security of the past few decades suggests any definitive solutions, I have failed to discern them. There are no easy answers to the problem of aid worker violence, and it is naïve to believe that understanding the causes and conditions of a human problem will always yield a corresponding course of action to solve it. War is violent and dangerous and poses risks to humanitarians, just as it does to journalists and human rights monitors and every other human being within its radius. Situations entailing hard choices and uncertain outcomes often demand that we select the least-worst of bad options.

Accepting, therefore, that there is no such thing as a no-risk environment, experience can offer some lessons on what the minimum basic requirements are for humanitarians seeking to access the areas of greatest needs while minimizing the danger:

Assess, understand, and acknowledge the risk. The essentials of security risk management should be part of every organization's toolkit. These include threat assessment and actor mapping, assigning scores to risks based on the probability of encountering the threat and the impact it will have if you do. These tools are necessary and useful not because they replace human experience and intuition but because they augment them. Data and procedure can help guard against the cognitive biases and errors of omission that are omnipresent in decision-making even in non-stressful situations. Once the risks are assessed and weighted, resources can be allocated to mitigate them accordingly.

Treat security risk management as an area of expertise and staff it accordingly. Organizations should dedicate positions at all levels—headquarters, country offices, and (if resources allow) subnational locations—in which, appropriately trained individuals focus on the security of staff as their sole remit. The scope of work should not be tacked on to an existing position, nor should it be siloed and separate from other functions. Security risk managers should work in harmony with program staffers to ensure an enabling, rather than restrictive, approach to security.

Once you have assessed the risks to the best of your ability, implement all appropriate mitigating measures using an acceptance-based approach. Mitigation strategies will likely include elements of protection and, occasionally, deterrence, but no matter the extent of protective and deterrent measures adopted, organizations must continuously reach out to the communities, local power holders, and potential threat actors in an ongoing dialogue to gain and maintain familiarity, acceptance, and tolerance of the organization and its activities. All risk mitigation entails cost, and organizations unable to devote the resources needed to adequately secure their staff and the staff of their partner organizations should not attempt to operate in high-risk areas.

Explicitly accept the residual risk using program criticality as the guiding principle. After all risk mitigation measures are applied, it is important to explicitly accept the remaining "residual" risk of working in this area. The level of risk that is assumed by the individual and organization should be commensurate with the criticality of the program to the people in need. By the same token, there will be certain times and threat environments in which the risk to humanitarian staff will be unacceptably high (e.g., inside some IS-controlled territories). It is equally important to recognize when this is the case.

Invest in negotiation skills and capacities. Identifying the armed actors who may pose a threat, and understanding their interests and their values, requires dedicated staffing resources beyond those of general security risk management. Train staff in transactional, "win-win" techniques and strategies and employ lessons learned from past negotiation cases. Understand that communications with armed groups will be more effective if they do not focus on educating them on, or promoting adherence to, international humanitarian principles, but rather appealing to their interests and finding points of mutual benefit. As experienced humanitarian negotiators advise, the principles can be used as a calling card, but they should not be the focus of the negotiation. When appealing to values, localize them within the context that is nearest and most meaningful to your counterparts—be it religious, cultural, or ideological. Develop procedural and operational principles for the relationship, for instance, when and how to reopen discussions and raise problems and concerns. Foresee the disputes that may arise around the agreement and plan in advance for a resolution mechanism.

Equalize duty of care for national staff and extend it to national partners. Duty of care must be promoted as an ethical and moral value within the organizational culture and not be simply a requirement to safeguard against liability. As such, duty of care to national staff should be on a par with that of international staff and extended as far as possible to national partner organizations, which typically have the least amount of resources allocated for security. To do this, organizations must approach risk management as something wider than self-protection—it must encompass the partnership as well. When risks are not shared between partners, they are transferred from the stronger partner to the weaker one, and this is not only unethical but also self-defeating. "Risk mitigation policies that do not acknowledge and co-own residual risk, but rather seek to transfer it to the subsidiary partner, result in perverse outcomes,"[12] ultimately increasing the risk to all.

Ethical Critiques and Debates in Humanitarianism

If there is a common thread running through all of the above, it is an ethic of professionalism as regards security risk management for humanitarian action in war. I do not mean "professionalism" in the sense that is often attached to the word in humanitarian debates—that is, as a synonym for corporatism and a distancing from the fundamental altruistic values of humanitarianism. What I am referring to instead is a branch of ethics that encompasses both personal and organizational values while at the same time transcending the parochial interests of both. As I will attempt to argue in the remaining pages, an ethics of professionalism can best serve the ultimate goal of humanitarian action.

At its core, humanitarianism is about people helping other people in need. As Hugo Slim observes, despite the intuition that this should be "the simplest thing in the world," there is no single, clear set of what could be called humanitarian ethics. "In fact," authors Barnett and Weiss agree, "multiple ethics run through humanitarian action, and not all of them are necessarily compatible."[13] Because ethics is concerned with questions of the rightness or wrongness of actions, it should not be surprising that the multifaceted humanitarian sector encompasses numerous different, and at times conflicting, ethical considerations. There are ethical debates having to do with the quality and effectiveness of the aid work, the respect and dignity afforded to aid recipients, the extent of collaboration with national aid organizations and governments, and many others—not to mention the applied ethics embodied in the conflict-related principles

[12] Stoddard, A., Czwarno, M. & Hamsik, L. (2019). NGOs & Risk: Managing uncertainty in local-international partnerships: Global report. Washington, D.C.: InterAction, p. 5.

[13] Barnett, M. N., & Weiss, T. G. (2011). *Humanitarianism Contested: Where angels fear to tread.* Milton Park, Abingdon, Oxon, England; New York: Routledge, p. 112.

of impartiality, neutrality, independence, and humanity. Slim's book, *Humanitarian Ethics: A Guide to Morality of Aid in War and Disaster*, provides a thoroughgoing historical and comparative review of the various ethical precepts that interweave within humanitarian action. I will not attempt anything so comprehensive here. Instead, I take a rough-grained approach to what I see as the key ethical issues at play, starting with the ethical arguments that have been used to find fault with the sector and its personnel.

One strain of ethical critique of humanitarian action is rooted in post-structuralist political theory, drawing on the ideas of theorists such as Foucault and Derrida, in which the humanitarian sector is viewed as an extension of power relationships between strong and weak states. Much of Mark Duffield's writing on humanitarianism, for example, concerns "the use of aid as a tool of global liberal governance."[14] Humanitarian academics take a universally negative view of the instrumentalization of aid for political and economic ends, which they trace back to imperialism and colonialism. The charge is not groundless. As Slim writes, "[M]any of the world's large modern agencies that make up the formal humanitarian system emerged in the context of Western languages and neocolonial interest, thought patterns and operational practices."[15] Even the terminology used by aid workers, Slim points out, takes on this "expeditionary" flavor, with phrases like "going on missions" and "out into the field."[16] That foreign aid is a component of the soft power of Western governments cannot be disputed. "For decades," writes Antonio Donini, "humanitarian action represented the smiley face of globalisation."[17]

The neocolonialist paradigm connects to another, more personalized critique, which depicts Western aid workers as paternalistic and self-serving, perpetuating the sanctimonious conceit of "whites in shining

[14] Duffield, M. (2002). Social Reconstruction and the Radicalization of Development: Aid as a Relation of Global Liberal Governance. *Development and Change*, *33*(5), 1049–1071. doi:https://doi.org/10.1111/1467-7660.t01-1-00260

[15] Slim, H. (2015). *Humanitarian Ethics: A Guide to the Morality of Aid in War and Disaster.* Oxford University Press, p. 10.

[16] Ibid., p. 11.

[17] Donini, A. (2016). "The crisis of multilateralism and the future of humanitarian action." *The New Humanitarian*. Retrieved 13 May 2019, from http://www.thenewhumanitarian.org/opinion/2016/11/30/crisis-multilateralism-and-future-humanitarian-action

armor."[18] Nowhere do these accusations ring more fervently than within the humanitarian sector itself. In a blog post entitled "A New Humanitarian Ethics?", Marc Dubois confesses to occasionally falling prey to the feelings of superiority and "coolness," that his "MSF-ness" confers upon his self-image, and the troubling questions it raises generally about the motives of those who choose to make their careers in the humanitarian sector:

> Among other traits, this is my self-curated individuality and selflessness—my 'sacrificing' a more common career that would have brought far greater financial reward. But how can it be selfless if it goes so far to defining myself? …What happens if this changing of the guard exposes the sector's ugly secret, the danger that my work has always been (ponderously) about me, then multiplied by the number of humanitarians?[19]

The cognitive dissonance described by Dubois rings a bell; I recognize it in my own experience as a former practitioner and have heard similar thoughts expressed by other aid workers. It is feeling at once the pride of working in a noble and self-sacrificing endeavor and the shame that you are ultimately not making a lick of difference and engaged in some sort of moral fraud. In the introduction to *Humanitarian Ethics: A Guide to the Morality of Aid in War and Disaster*, Hugo Slim recounts the mixed feelings he had when people used to congratulate him on the "wonderful work" he and his colleagues were doing. "[O]ur work did not always feel wonderful but rather difficult, contested, confusing and prone to failure of various kinds. Indeed, I have never worked in or visited any humanitarian operation that people have described in purely positive terms."[20]

There is perhaps no other field of work that appears as simultaneously self-congratulatory and self-flagellating as humanitarianism. It could be a vestige of religion (which, predating the modern humanitarian sector,

[18] Schimmelpfennig, S. (2010). "Whites in Shining Armor." Huffpost.com. Retrieved 8 May 2019, from https://www.huffpost.com/entry/whites-in-shining-armor_b_708882?guccounter=1&guce_referrer=aHR0cHM6Ly93d3cuZ29vZ2xlLmNvbS8&guce_referrer_sig=AQAAAGk_FRDdbJHFVi36fXvjDcQYwq1_Nb3WvEhHFXEl-C-yQCPZnJO2IFL9RF2dWYhM7M15vQ7bLEFAlBA_jERIxxY1_JX-GTSzIwI0y4VB0NZVoG8OSe2Va-P_f5yl-c5Fpyuvez-NfDtz3ZnqrCzfV2e-WSySdVw9w167WFh31Gu3d

[19] Dubois, M. (2019). "A New Humanitarian Ethics?" *The Humanicontrarian*, Blog 3, February 10, 2019. Retrieved 28 May 2019 from: https://humanicontrarian.com

[20] Slim, H. (2015). *Humanitarian Ethics: A Guide to the Morality of Aid in War and Disaster*. Oxford University Press, p. 6.

makes up a strong strand of humanitarianism's DNA) expressing itself—oscillating between sanctimony and doubt. For the purposes of constructing a useful ethical framework for assessing and guiding humanitarian action, however, concerns of personal purity are beside the point.

Doing Good or Being Good

Ethical discourse on humanitarian action, and on charitable acts more broadly, is cleaved by two opposing instincts about what it means to be good, a philosophical argument that goes back centuries. The various ethical questions and debates that arise in the humanitarian sector reduce into those that are primarily concerned with *doing* good (performing effectively against appropriate objectives and delivering quality results) and those that place more stock in *being* good (having the right motives, morals, and values behind all actions). The former is known as consequentialism (or utilitarianism) and the latter as deontology. Consequentialists emphasize results and outcomes, holding that the ethical act is one which produces, in the words of its founding philosopher, Jeremy Bentham, "the greatest good for the greatest number," Deontology, on the other hand, rooted in the philosophy of Immanuel Kant, puts greater emphasis on rules of morality and behavior. For deontologists, the action itself can be moral or immoral regardless of the outcome; the means are no less important than the ends.

The ethical critiques that focus on humanitarians' motives, on the power relationships implied, are deontological in nature. These have recently gained a great deal more fodder by sexual abuse and exploitation scandals that came to light within the humanitarian sector, involving major organizational players such as Oxfam and Save the Children. The #Aidtoo movement, which followed in the wake of the #Metoo movement, added to the negative stereotype of hypocritical and self-serving opportunists betraying the values they purport to espouse while being shielded and enabled by their organizations and passed around like bad pennies throughout the sector. Such critiques are wholly legitimate, but they do not often illuminate the path forward.

The other types of humanitarian critiques, which focus on effectiveness and outcomes (such as the lack of sufficient access in conflict zones and inadequate coverage of humanitarian needs that this book describes), reflect a consequentialist ethic. By taking the attributes of the individual aid providers out of the equation, this line of ethics allows the focus to be trained on the affected population and how well the sector does (or does not) serve them. Highly critical reviews of the sector's performance in the Rwandan refugee camps in Goma in the 1990s led to the Sphere Standards, a set of technical best practices codified "to improve the quality and accountability of humanitarian action across all sectors"[21] and the Humanitarian Charter, a shared commitment by signatory organizations "to make humanitarian aid accountable to affected populations."[22] These result-oriented critiques thus usually contain the seeds of the solutions within them.

The Problem of Prioritizing and Predicting Consequences

Before arguing that the consequentialist ethic is generally the more appropriate tack for approaching humanitarian action, I must digress for a moment to discuss the ways in which it can fail to be helpful.

The effective altruism movement (EA) embodies consequentialism as a guide to individual philanthropic giving. Based on concepts articulated by the philosopher Peter Singer and operationalized by the philosopher and altruism entrepreneur Will McCaskill, EA promotes an ethic of charitable donorship that strives to optimize the impact of each donation measured by the results it yields for the well-being of the largest number of people. Singer posited that failing to act to help another in need is just as bad, from a moral calculus, as committing a harmful act itself, since the results are the same. Practitioners of EA therefore strive to give as much as they feasibly can, and in the most efficient way possible, to maximize the extent to which it helps others.

One can find little to criticize in a movement that encourages millionaires to spread rather than hoard their wealth, but the elegant abstractions of EA are a poor guide to addressing the messy totality of human suffering. Malaria sickens hundreds of millions of people each year and kills close to half a million, mostly young children, placing it among the world's severest public health problems. Yet, transmission of the mosquito-borne disease can be effectively prevented with simple, low-cost interventions. Consequently, McCaskill's EA-based organization, Give Well, lists the Malaria Consortium

[21] "Humanitarian Standards Partnership" sphere.org. Retrieved from: https://www.spherestandards.org/humanitarian-standards/standards-partnership/

[22] "Humanitarian Charter" Retrieved from: https://www.spherestandards.org/humanitarian-standards/humanitarian-charter/

as its top recommended charity, based on the number of deaths averted per donated dollar it receives.[23] Adopting a cost-efficiency principle for maximizing lives-saved is a brilliant way of encouraging philanthropy among a certain cohort of wealthy individuals (EA is especially popular within the tech sector), but to follow its cost efficiency logic would be to arrive at the reductio ad absurdum where the best course of action would be for everyone in the world to turn their disposable income into bed nets. Lives saved is an important metric but so is reducing suffering, both chronic and acute. Unfortunately, suffering is subjective and far harder to measure. In this example, who's to say where the suffering is greater: Is it people dying from malaria and their communities being decimated from the disease? Or might the suffering be worse for people suddenly forced to flee from conflict and atrocities, in need of shelter, food, and protection?

Consequentialist ethics also cannot answer the question of how wide or narrow a focus to take when suffering and dying occur in incalculable different ways and places, yet resources are finite. Some years ago, while visiting the East Kivu region of the Democratic Republic of Congo, I learned that a Western international organization was working in the area on behalf of the local gorilla populations that had lost their habitats and become endangered by the conflict. I was immediately offended. How insufferably privileged and effete these people were to devote such time, effort, and money to this cause, I thought, when there were actual human beings displaced by the conflict and in dire need of aid. My initial indignation was later tempered as I reflected that, after all, there was plenty of suffering to go around, the gorillas needed help too, and ultimately there was room enough in the world for some people to address themselves to this particular problem. This may be the heart of the matter: humanitarian crises and human needs are so vast that they demand collective responses, above and irrespective of individual acts of charity. Humanitarian analyst Paul Currion, writing about EA, has made this point: "There's a political problem, too: this is charity for the age of neoliberalism, a technocratic exercise that privileges individual over collective action, and reduces that action to money spent on the basis of cost-effectiveness."[24]

[23] Give Well (n.d.) "Top Charities" givewell.org. Retrieved from: https://www.givewell.org/charities/top-charities

[24] Currion, P. (2016). "Too true to be good." *The New Humanitarian*. Retrieved 8 May 2019, from http://www.thenewhumanitarian.org/opinion/2016/09/14/too-true-be-good

Consequentialist ethics also do not provide much guidance on the question of how to balance short-term versus long-term consequences. The 2016 Battle of Mosul can serve as an example. In October of that year, Iraqi armed forces, supported by the US and other coalition allies, launched a military campaign to retake the city of Mosul from the Islamic State, which had controlled it for two years. As is typical of urban warfare, civilian casualties were heavy, with an estimated 10,000–11,000 killed and thousands more wounded. In the lead-up to the military campaign, it became clear that the Iraqi army was not prepared to provide the necessary emergency medical care, which is the responsibility of armed forces under international humanitarian law. Instead, in an unusual collaborative arrangement, the coalition turned to the United Nations humanitarian country team, and in particular the World Health Organization (WHO), to organize the medical trauma response. WHO oversaw the creation of a coordinated "trauma referral pathway" following US military guidelines, wherein field medics would stabilize wounded civilians and combatants and then transfer them to hospitals, all of which would be embedded within the military's frontline operations.

When WHO turned to its usual NGO partners to collaborate in implementing this plan, they found few takers. The largest medical humanitarian organization, MSF, refused to participate on the grounds that it would violate the principle of neutrality for humanitarians to serve as an arm of the invading force. This would seem at first a purely deontological argument—placing abstract principles above the human lives at stake—but MSF was worried about the consequences as well. Not only would it set a terrible precedent in allowing the warring parties to abdicate the responsibility to provide care to the wounded, they argued, but it would also decrease the humanitarian actors' future effectiveness in the region. How would they be able to negotiate neutral access in insurgent-held areas if they were to attach themselves to one side of the conflict? It was no trivial dilemma: the humanitarians may have been correct on the negative long-term consequences of participating, but in the meantime, what of the wounded Iraqi civilians sure to die without this intervention? In the end, WHO put together a trauma response and referral pathway using an assortment of non-traditional partners, including private and volunteer groups, many of which had never before worked in a war zone. In a case study of this episode led by my colleague Hosanna Fox,[25] we concluded

[25] Fox, H., Stoddard, A. & Davidoff, J. (2018). *Emergency trauma response to the Mosul offensive, 2016–2017: A review of issues and challenges*. Humanitarian Outcomes, March.

that while the embedded humanitarian trauma response unquestionably saved lives (an estimated 1500–1800 people),[26] it should not have been necessary in the first place. The government of Iraq and the allied forces should have taken greater steps to meet their responsibilities under international humanitarian law, and the humanitarian community should have pushed harder to make this to happen. Besides, Fox notes, "At least a small number of Iraqis [likely including those who had been associated with IS, or IS families] were scared off by the militarized care. Our survey of people who were in Mosul during the battle found 11 percent of those with urgent medical needs avoided the facilities, citing fears for their safety as the primary reason." Even so, it is unclear what the ethical response should have been. One of the medical teams that participated in the response was led by a young ER (emergency room) doctor from New York City. In an interview he gave to Fox on his experience, he laid out the dilemma: "If you [humanitarians] want to be close to the front lines, you have to accept military presence, there's just no way around it. So, the question is: are the lives saved worth the price? We think so."[27]

The Mosul case illustrates the problem of applying a strict consequentialist frame in cases where there are unavoidable trade-offs between short- and long-term consequences, and it is impossible to predict which course of action will ultimately yield the greatest benefit. This is not an argument against consequentialist ethics in humanitarian action, only a caution that predicting consequences is complex and ethical trade-offs are inevitable. On the other hand, the deontological critiques provide even less of a guide for evaluation of humanitarian action and tend instead toward more unhelpful navel-gazing. Some of these have suggested that humanitarians should seek to deconstruct the unjust power relations that currently characterize the system, reconceptualizing what now operates along a model of "compassion," with powerful givers and lowly receivers, to something more akin to an exchange or transaction between equals. Aside from failing to clarify just what an egalitarian exchange model would look like practice, this approach continues to be focused, unhelpfully, on the individual morality of aid providers as opposed to where it should be focused:

[26] Spiegel, P., Garber, K. Kushner, A. & Wise, P. (2018). The Mosul Trauma Response: A Case Study. John Hopkins Centre for Humanitarian Health. February, 2018, pp. 36–37. http://www.hopkinshumanitarianhealth.org/empower/resources/reports/

[27] Stoddard, A. (2018). "Mosul: Lives saved, credibility lost?" *The New Humanitarian*. Retrieved 8 May 2019, from https://www.thenewhumanitarian.org/opinion/2018/03/21/mosul-lives-saved-credibility-lost

on a collective rationality geared to improving results for aid *receivers*. Many would agree that the current charitable model needs replacing, but the goals of humanitarianism are likely best served, I would argue, by a system modeled on collective goods and an ethics of professionalism.

In his book, *Against Empathy*, Paul Bloom argues that the human emotion of empathy (feeling another's pain) is in most cases a poor basis for addressing human need and suffering at scale. "Empathy is biased," he writes, "pushing us in the direction of parochialism and racism" and making us blind to the long-term consequences of our actions. Noting the well-established psychological phenomenon of people feeling stronger emotional urges to help a single starving child than a faceless mass of starving children, he illustrates how empathy is also "innumerate, favoring the one over the many."[28] Society fares better, Bloom argues, when we respond with "rational compassion"—in other words, when we care about others' suffering and use disinterested and deliberative moral reasoning to address it without being guided by our emotions. Daniel Kahneman takes a similar view, observing that emotional morality, an intuitive response triggered by vivid personal stories (such as the one starving child), leads to different responses than does "cognitive morality." While your emotional response will naturally become diluted as the number of affected people goes up, cognitive morality allows for correct moral weighting and actions to respond. As Kahneman put it, "You *know* that it's better to save 500,000 than 5,000 even if you don't feel better." This realm of cognitive morality, he adds, is the appropriate domain of policymakers.[29]

Empathy and altruism surely rank among the best features of human nature, but they are not what we should be basing aid policies and systems on. The motivation and "humanitarian spirit" as experienced by individuals may be necessary to initiate movement, but they do not work well at scale. This is also true in security risk management; when it comes to matters of life and limb, it would be irresponsible and unethical to place our faith in human intuitions and voluntaristic ways of working. Professionalism, in the sense I intend it, sits neither within the personal nor the organizational domain but is inclusive and transcendent of both.

[28] Bloom, P. (2016). *Against Empathy: The Case for Rational Compassion*. New York, NY: Ecco, an imprint of HarperCollins Publishers, p. 9.

[29] Daniel Kahneman quoted in Harris, S. (2019). "Making Sense with Sam Harris #150 – The Map of Misunderstanding (with Daniel Kahneman)." *YouTube*, YouTube, 13 Mar. 2019. www.youtube.com/watch?v=iKLE3TmtFhY

The Professional Humanitarian

What kind of person becomes a humanitarian aid worker? Presumably, some altruistic tendencies play a part in steering individuals to this sector, but undoubtedly there can be other motivators as well. For the international aid worker, there may be some escapism or adventure-seeking involved, or at least an interest in traveling the world and experiencing different ways of life. Many national aid workers find themselves in the profession out of a desire to help their neighbors or fellow nationals affected by crisis, but aid work could also be attractive to them for economic reasons. In some contexts, jobs in the aid sector offer salaries far higher than the local norm, especially for nationals with advanced education and multiple languages. For some, there is also the appeal of the image; the humanitarian cachet that Marc Dubois wrote about is very real in some circles. Many years ago, shortly after MSF won the Nobel Peace Prize, a college administration officer I knew shared an anecdote: a survey of the graduating class revealed the number one most admired occupation cited by the students was working for MSF.

It is therefore unlikely that Hugo Slim is speaking for all aid workers when he writes, "Entry into humanitarian aid work is primarily vocational, impulsive and urgent. It is a voluntary response to a moral call that we feel and share, as immediate neighbors and global neighbors. In this sense, humanitarian help is the great domain of the amateur: literally, the lover of something, which in this case is our fellow human beings."[30] A good number of aid workers, particularly those with a secular bent, would stop well short of considering their choice of occupation a moral calling. But as Slim observes in the same chapter, "Humanitarian ethics has long been torn between the passion of voluntarism and the importance of professional qualifications."[31] For those who view these two things as being in conflict, the passion element is critically important. It is the energy that drives humanitarian action forward and hopefully keeps it on the correct moral path. To this way of thinking, humanitarianism stripped of the personal emotional drivers is bloodless and bureaucratic, obsessed with metrics, and when push comes to shove, will inevitably favor organizational interests over the core mission of helping people. But this is where they get it

[30] Slim, H. (2015). *Humanitarian Ethics: A Guide to the Morality of Aid in War and Disaster.* Oxford University Press, p. 11.

[31] Slim, H. (2015). *Humanitarian Ethics: A Guide to the Morality of Aid in War and Disaster.* Oxford University Press, p. 12.

wrong. Granted, as described in Chap. 5, organizational interests often do come to trump personal motivations as a natural byproduct of organizational growth. However, working for the good of a specific organization is not what I mean by an ethos of professionalism.

The definition of a profession is "a paid occupation, especially one that involves prolonged training and a formal qualification." As such, it is different from a job, or even a career, which is the succession of jobs that make up the individual path of one's working life. Nor is it identified with the place of employment; its locus is in the individual. Being a doctor, for instance, is a profession, and this identity typically supersedes the affiliation with any particular hospital or medical practice. This also is why an ethics of professionalism in humanitarian action would not serve as an argument for expanding the use of commercial entities to provide relief aid. Corporate interests to maximize the bottom line are a different matter altogether, and it is not hard to see how they could conflict with humanitarian values. The most salient part of the definition of professionalism from an ethical standpoint, I would argue, is the idea of valuable skills acquired through training and careful application. People generally do not wish to become professionals out of any romantic ideas of heroism or self-sacrifice, and the personal pride and satisfaction of belonging to a profession do not derive from identifying as a morally good person; they come instead from identifying as a *skilled* person. A professional earns respect from applying his or her expertise to worthwhile work. The paycheck isn't the point, but it may be a signifier of the length of their training and the value of their skills. Does the question of compensation somehow sully the humanitarian act? Make it less purely good or moral? In my general observation, North American humanitarian actors may be more comfortable with the blending of altruistic and economic objectives than their European counterparts. One of my earliest jobs in the humanitarian sector was as a junior-level program assistant to Cooperative for Assistance and Relief Everywhere (CARE) US's Regional Director for Asia, a dynamic woman named Shelly Kessler, who, in her mid-30's seemed impossibly advanced and professional in her work compared with my just-out-of-grad-school naiveté. In our introductory conversation, she spoke about her work history at CARE and other NGOs. She mentioned that she found the field of relief and development to be rewarding work, "But I definitely think of it as my career," she added. "It's not a calling or anything." Similarly, in response to an article that recapitulated the whites-in-shining-armor criticism, the former Director of the U.S. Office of Foreign Disaster Assistance, tweeted, "No aid worker I know (and I know many) thinks they are synonymous with virtue. They consider themselves professionals, not heroes or saints."[32]

Professionalism, as a subset of ethics, inhabits the space in a Venn diagram where the spheres of personal and collective ethics overlap. *Personal* professional ethics entail upholding such values as honesty, integrity, and competence and the pursuit of mastery. *Collective* professional ethics—which, for our purposes, can exist at the level of a humanitarian organization or a larger international body—would include things like a commitment to effectiveness, quality, and sufficiency of aid; practicing duty of care to staff and partners; and being accountable to donors and recipients. An organization's professional ethics are not equivalent to its interests (meaning things like solvency, growth, good reputation, and so forth), though in the best case, they can be adjacent. In some sense, the humanitarian sector has already embraced a set of professionalist ethics as reflected in the Sphere Humanitarian Charter and Minimum Standards in Humanitarian Response. The Sphere project was launched in the aftermath of the shambolic and widely criticized humanitarian response to the Rwandan refugees in Goma after the genocide. The ensuing sector-wide soul-searching exercise resulted in a set of codified technical standards, the Sphere Handbook, in an attempt to prevent a repeat of the amateurish, even harmful, practices that were observed in Goma by some well-meaning but unqualified charitable groups. The Sphere standards cover the technical performance minima across the major functional areas of humanitarian assistance, including food, water, health, and shelter programing. The technical standards are overlain by nine commitments that make up the "Core Humanitarian Standard," such as "humanitarian response is effective and timely" (Commitment 2), "humanitarian response strengthens local capacities and avoids negative effects" (Commitment 3), and "humanitarian actors continuously learn and improve" (Commitment 7).[33]

I first became interested in the subject of humanitarian professionalism reading the results of a research program led by Peter Walker, who at the time directed the Feinstein International Center at Tufts University and who was one of the "fathers" of Sphere. In their 2009–2010 study, Walker and colleagues "explored the case for professionalizing humanitarian

[32] @JeremyKonyndyk (16 February 2018). [Twitter post]. Retrieved from: https://twitter.com/JeremyKonyndyk/status/964536453983277056

[33] Spherestandards.org

action through an international professional association, the development of core competencies, and the creation of a universal certification system for aid workers."[34] Although the study focused mainly on concrete, technical issues of international standards and skillsets, the authors also invoked the notion of professionalism as "an ideal that transcends national boundaries"[35] and proposed a new conceptual framework for humanitarian action; one evolved from an "ad hoc, emotive-based, largely Western-driven system to a more global system of defined service delivery, which is increasingly pressured to define and regulate its competence, coverage, and purpose."[36] The same idea has long been championed by humanitarian practitioners such as Ronald Waldman, an MD and public health expert who has played leading technical roles in just about every major humanitarian emergency since the late 1970s. The humanitarian sector's transition from good intentions and best impressions of what's needed into what Waldman calls a "competence-based model" still has some way to go. In an article for *The Lancet* co-authored by Michael Toole, another humanitarian veteran, they write:

> [O]ur work can only be accomplished if the evidence-based principles that are so fundamental to medicine and public health are given the greatest possible consideration in determining what gets done. In the practice of humanitarianism, however it might be defined, science is clearly not sufficient but is, more than ever, necessary.[37]

A professionalist ethical frame for humanitarianism recognizes that the endeavor is important and that it is an ethical duty not just to do it, but to do it well. It acknowledges that there are specific practical and technical skills that must be trained and existing bodies of knowledge on best practice to be learned. It respects the practitioners and organizations that emphasize expertise and proven effectiveness. As such, it would favor the well-trained but emotionally indifferent practitioner over the passionately

[34] Walker, P. et al. (2010). "A Blueprint For Professionalizing Humanitarian Assistance." *Health Affairs* 29, 12 (2010): 2223–2230, p. 2223.

[35] Ibid., p. 2224.

[36] Walker, P. & Russ, C. (2011). "Fit for Purpose: The role of modern professionalism in evolving the humanitarian endeavour" *International Review of the Red Cross,* 93, 884. December 2011, p. 1195.

[37] Waldman, R., & Toole, M. (2017). "Where is the science in humanitarian health?" *The Lancet, 390*(10109), 2224–2226. doi:https://doi.org/10.1016/s0140-6736(17)31275-8

altruistic amateur in terms of achieving the best possible outcome—much as you would prefer your surgeon to be good at his job rather than warm and caring, if you had to choose. Professionalism in humanitarian security risk management likewise holds the most promise for achieving the critical objectives, enabling critical aid to get through while protecting the lives of the people who provide it.

Given the examples presented in this book, the preceding may seem so self-evident as to be hardly worth stating. Yet, there are still some influential voices in the humanitarian sector who argue against the professionalization of security. A 2016 book edited by Michaël Neuman and Fabrice Weissman of the MSF think tank *Centre de Reflexion sur l'Action et les Savoirs Humanitaire* (CRASH) makes the case that professionalization has weakened, rather than strengthened the capacities of humanitarians to cope with security risks.[38]

> [M]anuals such as the GPR 8 contribute to the discrediting of individual judgment and initiative. Whereas the awareness approach of the mid-1990s valued the individual and their capacity to adapt to new environments, the 'management approach' tries to eliminate or minimise the role of the individual through the modelisation of security and risk.[39]

In the book's authors' view, the systems, procedures, and manuals created under a professionalized approach to security risk management do not augment managers' decision-making—they replace them, with the end result being disempowered aid workers and increasingly risk-averse organizations. They take an equally cynical view of organizations' practice of duty of care to their staff, which they believe has more to do with a fear of being sued than with any sense of ethical obligation. Throughout the book, the word "professional" is conflated with "bureaucratic," and the authors betray a very superficial knowledge of how security risk management actually works in practice.[40] What my colleagues have found over

[38] Neuman, M. and Weissman, F. (Eds.) (2016) *Saving Lives and Staying Alive. Humanitarian Security in the Age of Risk Management. London:* Hurst, 2016.

[39] Beerli, M.J. & Weissman, F. (2016). "Humanitarian Security Manuals: Neutralising the human factor in humanitarian action" in Neuman, M. and Weissman, F. (Eds.) (2016.) *Saving Lives and Staying Alive. Humanitarian Security in the Age of Risk Management. London:* Hurst, 2016, p. 139.

[40] For rebuttals to the arguments in *Neuman and Weissman's book*, see Cunningham, A. & Lockyear, C. (2016). "A response to Saving Lives and Staying Alive." 2 May 2016,

years of field-based research, hundreds of interviews and thousands of survey responses,[41] however, is that aid workers need, use, and appreciate security risk management practices. Without discounting their own intuitions and experience, they can use the systems and knowledge as a step-by-step method for systematically thinking through multiple variables, ensuring they have covered the bases and checked their biases. As Walker and Russ underscore in their research, experiential learning is integral to professionalism. "All professions recognize that experience, as well as knowledge and skills, is an essential part of being a professional."[42] A good security risk management system does not replace personal judgment, detailed contextual knowledge, and well-honed intuitions from experience; on the contrary, they rely upon them to work. As Walker and Russ underscore in their research, experiential learning is integral to professionalism. "All professions recognize that experience, as well as knowledge and skills, is an essential part of being a professional."[43] A good security risk management system does not replace personal judgment, detailed contextual knowledge, and well-honed intuitions from experience; on the contrary, they rely upon them to work.

In highly complex and high-stakes situations that demand extensive knowledge and quick decision-making, human brains need systems and guidelines to ease the cognitive load and give them more space to devote to higher-level functions. Physician and author Atul Gawande effectively distills this idea into the simple exemplar of a checklist:

> You want people to make sure to get the stupid stuff right. Yet you also want to leave room for craft and judgment and the ability to respond to unexpected difficulties that arise along the way…The checklist doesn't tell him what to do, he explained. It is not a formula. But the checklist helps him be

URL:https://www.msf-crash.org/en/blog/war-and-humanitarianism/response-saving-lives-and-staying-alive; and Stoddard, A., Harmer, A. & Haver, K (2016). "Data are not Dangerous: A response to recent MSF CRASH critiques." *Overseas Development Institute Humanitarian Practice Network (HPN).* Retrieved 13 May 2019, from https://odihpn.org/blog/data-are-not-dangerous-a-response-to-recent-msf-crash-critiques/

[41] For all of Humanitarian Outcomes' published research products on humanitarian operational security and secure access, go to: https://www.humanitarianoutcomes.org/publications?work_area=3

[42] Walker, P. & Russ, C. (2011). "Fit for Purpose: The role of modern professionalism in evolving the humanitarian endeavour" *International Review of the Red Cross,* 93, 884. December 2011, p. 1201.

[43] Ibid.

> as smart as possible every step of the way, ensuring that he's got the critical information he needs when he needs it, that he's systematic about decision making, that he's talked to everyone he should.[44]

While diametrically opposed, the MSF CRASH critique of professionalism makes the same ethical error as the stereotypical self-interested organization they inveigh against. The error is in not concerning itself solely with what would achieve the best outcome for the recipients of aid but rather dwelling on the aid providers, and whether they are properly engaging in the act of humanitarian assistance, as they define it. The biggest problem with professionalism, as they see it, is that it is killing off humanitarianism's "chivalrous spirit." This isn't to claim there are no problems or weaknesses in organizations' security risk management, or that risk-aversion isn't a real concern. A UN-commissioned report written for Humanitarian Outcomes by Ashley Jackson and Steven A. Zyck found that organizations' efforts at promoting an enabling approach to security "...has not always led to maintained or increased presence and proximity"[45] to affected populations in high risk areas, noting also that "Many humanitarian organizations were still found to approach risk and key decisions surrounding evacuations, returns, and the use of remote management based on relatively weak analyses and vague perceptions rooted in media coverage of particular crises."[46] But no evidence exists to show that risk management systems, where applied, have caused a decrease in humanitarian operational presence. Michael O'Neill, whose career began at a time when there was zero systematic security management and has participated in every major phase of its evolution, sees no excuse for humanitarian organization not to have basic practices in place. He recommends that any aid worker about to embark on an assignment first ask this question of the organization: "Can you describe for me your security risk management system?" If they can't answer that, he warns, you should consider very seriously whether you want this deployment.

[44] Gawande, A. (2009). *The Checklist Manifesto*. Henry Holt and Co., p. 51 and 167.

[45] Jackson, A., & Zyck, S.A. (2017). *Presence & Proximity: To Stay and Deliver, Five Years On*. UN OCHA, June 22, p. 13.

[46] Ibid.

The Core Elements of a Professional Approach to Humanitarianism in Conflict Zones

In the preceding chapters of this book, I have illustrated what I believe are the major causes and consequences of attacks against aid workers, which continue to increase in the most violent operational settings. Against the backdrop of non-international, asymmetric conflicts, we have seen how humanitarian organizations lack the presumption of neutrality, how insurgent groups find justification in and advance their interests by targeting them, and how their risk is further heightened by conditions of volatility and impunity in fragile states and by strong states' actions related to the global war on terror. This state of elevated risk has combined with the fragmented, shortsighted interests of organizations in the humanitarian sector to hinder the extent to which it can achieve secure access to affected populations, leaving millions of people in need of aid unreached. Again, while not pretending there are any clear or easy answers, below I submit how a professionalist ethos and approach, rather than one emphasizing personal motives or organizational advantages, is the most promising path forward.

A professional approach to security risk management demands a situational awareness and deep contextual understanding, derived from a detailed mapping of potential threat sources, which leaves little doubt that the humanitarian actors are constituent parts of this ecosystem, viewed in various ways by the other actors. As such, there is no danger of falling prey to the belief that they are exempt from the contestation or relying on "emblematic protection" or abstract legal principles. This particular tendency is displayed more by headquarters staff than aid workers on the ground. When you are based in an international capital headquarters office, field operations can begin to seem abstract, and hence you're more comfortable in dealing with other abstractions such as the rarefied ideal of "humanitarian space."

Contending with Non-state Actors As humanitarians working to negotiate access in conflict have increasingly learned and begun to apply in practice, communicating and negotiating with armed groups is an essential skill to enable relief aid in war zones. The organizations that have developed significant skillsets and knowledge bases in this area have begun to share it with others in training courses and written guidance. In such negotiations, most experts in this area agree that the experiential element is critical, and thus entities like the Geneva-based Centre of Competence on Humanitarian Negotiation (CCHN) have conducted interviews and compiled case examples to be used as teaching tools. Referring to this practical experience in specific cases is viewed as a key component of a professionalized approach to negotiating, not its opposite.

Operating Amid Volatility and Impunity in Failing States Humanitarian organizations often work in environments where the host state lacks the capacity to provide the necessary law and order to create a protective environment for humanitarians' work. Moreover, the state is typically a party to the conflict and may be corrupt or malign in ways that pose direct threats to the aid workers. Security management in these environments requires deft handling of the relationship with the government and an alert eye to sudden shifts in conflict conditions where the risk can suddenly spike. Security managers will face peak moments of volatility where information is scarce and options are unclear. No manual or procedure can guarantee reaching the right decisions in such moments and acknowledgment of this too is a component of professionalism. Remember, the objective of security risk management is not to guarantee everyone's ultimate safety but to reduce and mitigate the risks as far as possible.

Institutional Obstacles and the Challenge of Access By being fragmented among numerous autonomous organizations, each with their own interests leading them to pursue growth in size but not necessarily in operational scope in war zones, the humanitarian sector has largely failed to assume collective responsibility for improving humanitarian access in high-risk contexts. A professionalist ethic, detached from the interests of whatever organization one happens to work for, would arguably lend incentive to solving this problem. Rather than overstating access to make the organization look good to donors, the more professional approach would be to collaborate with other organizations and non-traditional actors to problem-solve and innovate new approaches to this problem. Under this approach, it would be highly unethical to be protective of an organization's turf or mandates or to be complacent about the small amount of coverage each organization is achieving. This would naturally lead to a more robust effort to support and strengthen the capacity of local and national organizations, devolving more responsibility to them where they are able to make greater impact.

Navigating Ethical Issues The ethics of humanitarian action are complex and involve numerous, often conflicting, values and principles. There will seldom be cases of clear right and wrong answers but instead a continuing need to balance contradictory principles and conflicting motives if an effort to maximize benefit and minimize possible harm. As Haver and Carter wrote, "The humanitarian mission—living up to the principle of humanity—is all about the art of finding acceptable compromises."

Doing Good, Better Finally, humanitarian aid workers in insecure environments understand that providing quality assistance is one of their best means of achieving the acceptance of local communities and the tolerance of armed groups. Conversely, shoddy work can and has been used as an excuse to attack them. Professionalism in the provision of aid will thus also enhance the security of its providers.

Henry Dunant may be known as the founder of a worldwide network of volunteer societies, but his movement was at bottom a recognition of the need to professionalize humanitarian response. The ad hoc volunteer efforts by altruistic amateurs that he witnessed after the Battle of Solferino were wholly inadequate to the needs; they lacked the skills, equipment, preparation, and organization to do the job properly. Paid or unpaid, Dunant's call for a corps of "thoroughly qualified" aid providers envisioned an effective, *professional* humanitarian response.

References

Barnett, M. N., & Weiss, T. G. (2011). *Humanitarianism Contested: Where Angels Fear to Tread*. Oxon: Routledge.

Beerli, M. J., & Weissman, F. (2016). Humanitarian Security Manuals: Neutralising the Human Factor in Humanitarian Action. In M. Neuman & F. Weissman (Eds.), *Saving Lives and Staying Alive. Humanitarian Security in the Age of Risk Management*. London: Hurst.

Bloom, P. (2016). *Against Empathy: The Case for Rational Compassion*. New York: Ecco, an imprint of HarperCollins Publishers.

Cunningham, A., & Lockyear, C. (2016, May 2). A Response to Saving Lives and Staying Alive. Retrieved from https://www.msf-crash.org/en/blog/war-and-humanitarianism/response-saving-lives-and-staying-alive

Currion, P. (2016). Too True to Be Good. *The New Humanitarian*. Retrieved May 8, 2019, from http://www.thenewhumanitarian.org/opinion/2016/09/14/too-true-be-good

Donini, A. (2016). The Crisis of Multilateralism and the Future of Humanitarian Action. *The New Humanitarian*. Retrieved May 13, 2019, from http://www.thenewhumanitarian.org/opinion/2016/11/30/crisis-multilateralism-and-future-humanitarian-action

Dubois, M. (2016, May 12). Don't Blur the Lines Between Development and Humanitarian Work. *The Guardian*. Retrieved May 3, 2019, from https://www.theguardian.com/global-development-professionals-network/2016/may/12/dont-blur-the-lines-between-development-and-humanitarian-work

Dubois, M. (2018). *The New Humanitarian Basics*. HPG Working Paper. London: ODI.

Dubois, M. (2019, February 10). A New Humanitarian Ethics? *The Humanicontrarian*, Blog 3. Retrieved May 28, 2019, from https://humanicontrarian.com

Duffield, M. (2002). Social Reconstruction and the Radicalization of Development: Aid as a Relation of Global Liberal Governance. *Development and Change*, *33*(5), 1049–1071. https://doi.org/10.1111/1467-7660.t01-1-00260.

Fox, H., Stoddard, A., & Davidoff, J. (2018, March). *Emergency Trauma Response to the Mosul Offensive, 2016–2017: A Review of Issues and Challenges*. New York: Humanitarian Outcomes.

Gawande, A. (2009). *The Checklist Manifesto*. New York: Metropolitan Books/Henry Holt.

Harari, Y. N. (2015). *Sapiens: A Brief History of Humankind* (First U.S. Edition. ed.). New York: Harper.

Harmer, A., Stoddard, A., & Sarazen, A. (2018, December). *Humanitarian Access in Armed Conflict: A Need for New Principles?* New York: Humanitarian Outcomes.

Healy, S., & Tiller, S. (2014). *Where Is Everyone? Responding to Emergencies in the Most Difficult Places*. MSF. London: Médecins Sans Frontières.

International Committee of the Red Cross. (2004, March 27). *Humanitarian Action: "Today's New Security Environment Has Forced us Back to Basics."* ICRC.org. 27-02-2004 Statement Retrieved May 4, 2019, from https://www.icrc.org/en/doc/resources/documents/statement/5x6e5t.htm

Jackson, A., & Zyck, S. A. (2017, June 22). *Presence & Proximity: To Stay and Deliver, Five Years On*. UN OCHA. New York: Humanitarian Outcomes.

Médecins Sans Frontières – Facts. (1999). NobelPrize.org. *Nobel Media AB 2019*. Sat. 4 May 2019. https://www.nobelprize.org/prizes/peace/1999/msf/facts/

Neuman, M., & Weissman, F. (Eds.). (2016). *Saving Lives and Staying Alive. Humanitarian Security in the Age of Risk Management*. London: Hurst.

Overseas Development Institute Humanitarian Practice Network (HPN). (2019). Retrieved May 13, 2019, from https://odihpn.org/blog/data-are-not-dangerous-a-response-to-recent-msf-crash-critiques/

Rieff, D. (2002). *A Bed for the Night: Humanitarianism in Crisis.* New York: Simon & Schuster.

Schimmelpfennig, S. (2010). *Whites in Shining Armor.* Huffpost.com. Retrieved May 8, 2019, from https://www.huffpost.com/entry/whites-in-shining-armor_b_708882?guccounter=1&guce_referrer=aHR0cHM6Ly93d3cuZ29vZ2xlLmNvbS8&guce_referrer_sig=AQAAAGk_FRDdbJHFVi36fXvjDcQYwq1_Nb3WvEhHFXEl-C-yQCPZnJO2IFL9RF2dWYhM7M15vQ7bLEFAlBA_jERIxxY1_JX-GTSzIwI0y4VB0NZVoG8OSe2Va-P_f5ylc5Fpyuvez-NfDtz3ZnqrC-zfV2e-WSySdVw9w167WFh31Gu3d

Slim, H. (2015). *Humanitarian Ethics: A Guide to the Morality of Aid in War and Disaster.* Oxford: Oxford University Press.

Spiegel, P., Garber, K., Kushner, A., & Wise, P. (2018, February). *The Mosul Trauma Response: A Case Study. John Hopkins Centre for Humanitarian Health* (pp. 36–37). http://www.hopkinshumanitarianhealth.org/empower/resources/reports/

Stoddard, A. (2018). Mosul: Lives Saved, Credibility Lost? *The New Humanitarian.* Retrieved May 8, 2019, from https://www.thenewhumanitarian.org/opinion/2018/03/21/mosul-lives-saved-credibility-lost

Stoddard, A., Harmer, A., & Haver, K. (2016). *Data Are Not Dangerous: A Response to Recent MSF CRASH Critiques.* Humanitarian Practice Network. Retrieved from https://odihpn.org/blog/data-are-not-dangerous-a-response-to-recent-msf-crash-critiques/

Stoddard, A., Jillani, S., Caccavale, J., Cooke, P., Guillemois, D., & Klimentov, V. (2017). Out of Reach: How Insecurity Prevents Humanitarian Aid from Accessing the Neediest. *Stability: International Journal of Security and Development, 6*(1). https://doi.org/10.5334/sta.506.

Stoddard, A., Czwarno, M., & Hamsik, L. (2019). *NGOs & Risk: Managing Uncertainty in Local-International Partnerships: Global Report.* Washington, DC: InterAction.

Waldman, R., & Toole, M. (2017). Where Is the Science in Humanitarian Health? *The Lancet, 390*(10109), 2224–2226. https://doi.org/10.1016/s0140-6736(17)31275-8.

Walker, P., & Russ, C. (2011). Fit for Purpose: The Role of Modern Professionalism in Evolving the Humanitarian Endeavour. *International Review of the Red Cross, 93,* 884, 1195.

Walker, P., et al. (2010). A Blueprint For Professionalizing Humanitarian Assistance. *Health Affairs, 29*(12), 2223–2230.

Epilogue

The Ebola Doctor

Craig Spencer is a 37-year-old doctor who lives in New York City. At age 11, upon making the disappointing discovery that there was no such profession as "sharkologist," Spencer set his sights instead on a career in medicine. Specifically, he planned to become a cardiothoracic surgeon, having read that they pulled down the unimaginable fortune of US$130,000 per year, and he spent the next several years happily pursuing this new obsession. "I was the only 14-year old who could tell you what a T wave was on an EKG," he recalls. In 2005, while still in medical school in his home city of Detroit, Spencer took a student volunteer assignment to work in a hospital in the Dominican Republic, which proved transformative. The trip opened his eyes to conditions outside the US, and he was struck both by the disparities in medical care and by the way it felt to make a real impact on the lives of people in need of help. He also noticed how working without the high-tech medical equipment that Western physicians take for granted helped hone his skills and instincts as a doctor.

Before finishing medical school, Spencer took a year off to work on public health projects in China, which further deepened his fascination with international humanitarian work. No longer on the path of cardiothoracic surgery, Spencer had decided to specialize in emergency medicine, which translated best to a range of different contexts and would be of value to the humanitarian missions he now knew he wanted to pursue.

A. Stoddard, *Necessary Risks*,
https://doi.org/10.1007/978-3-030-26411-6

Knowing French was also an asset, and between 2008 and 2014, Spencer took assignments with various NGOs, working in Burundi, Democratic Republic of Congo, Rwanda, and elsewhere. He looked forward to eventually working with Médecins Sans Frontières (MSF), which required its volunteer doctors to be two years past their residency before they go on international deployments. When his first position with MSF eventually came, it would bring with it tabloid notoriety and a brush with death.

In December 2013, an Ebola epidemic broke out in the West African nation of Guinea. Over the following months, the deadly virus spread to the neighboring countries of Liberia and Sierra Leone, creating a region-wide public health emergency that threatened to become a global pandemic. Volunteers were desperately needed to treat patients and stem transmission, and Craig Spencer put in for an assignment with MSF. His friends and family were worried for him, naturally, but supportive. Spencer recalls his fiancée saying, "If you are not the person to do this—with your experience in pandemics and international emergency contexts—then who is?" Even with the strict protocols they were using in the field, the risks to medical staff were not negligible. Shortly before Spencer began his pre-deployment training and orientation, an American doctor named Kent Brantley contracted the disease while working in Liberia and was flown back to the United States for treatment. Then, while Spencer was in the middle of his training, word came down that the first MSF staffer, a Norwegian doctor named Silje Lehne Michalsen, was infected as well. MSF announced this news to the trainees, admitting that they did not know how the infection happened, but they still believed that the teams would be safe if they followed the protocols. Still, they said, everyone was free to reconsider their deployment given this new development. A handful of trainees decided not to take the risk and went home. Spencer considered his odds and weighed them against the critical importance of this work. He reasoned that with hundreds of people working in Ebola responses over the years and so few becoming infected, the risk was worth taking.

He spent his six-week deployment working in an Ebola treatment center in Guinea, where he remembers extremely long days, continually surrounded by death, sadness, and fear. At that point in the 2014 Ebola emergency, things looked particularly bleak. "There was no reason for optimism, no indication that things were getting better," Spencer says, "In fact, quite the opposite." The most difficult part of the assignment for him was witnessing the suffering of his national staff colleagues, so many of whom had lost family members. "*They* didn't get to leave after six weeks," he notes. Returning home at the end of his assignment, Spencer was exhausted and depressed.

At the time of his return, US airports were still struggling to implement the cautionary procedures for travelers arriving from Ebola-affected areas. When Spencer got off the plane in New York and went through customs and immigration, no one flagged him for screening despite his appearance, which almost comically announced where he had been (he was wearing an MSF t-shirt and carrying a *kora*—an enormous West African string instrument). He took it upon himself to inform the airport staff, "You're supposed to do something special with me." The screening and interview with officials from the Centers for Disease Control and Prevention (CDC) took about 30 minutes. They spoke to him about the work he had been doing in Guinea, took his temperature, assessed his risk, and told him how to access their resources if he needed them, before clearing him to proceed home.

The Ebola virus spreads through direct contact, and an infected person is not contagious until they develop symptoms of the disease. The incubation period from exposure to the onset of illness is between 2 and 21 days. The procedure for returning MSF medical staff members, therefore, was to monitor themselves for 21 days, take their temperature twice per day, and immediately report any symptoms. Until such time, they were not recommended to change their regular activities. It is tough enough to reintegrate back into normal life after such a grueling and traumatic assignment, so these professionals are advised to keep their routines, see friends, and take it easy on themselves for a while. Spencer took this advice, all the while anxiously counting the days until he could consider himself safe. It was on the morning of his 4th or 5th day back, and 11 or 12 days since he last treated an Ebola patient, when Spencer noticed a slight fever. In an article for the *New England Journal of Medicine* about his experience, Spencer wrote, "[I]n some bizarre way I felt almost relieved. Although my worst fear had been realized, having the disease briefly seemed easier than constantly fearing it."[1]

As per the protocol, he notified MSF, which informed the appropriate public health authorities. Things quickly began to spin out after that, when the New York Department of Health held an open conference call about Spencer's case, which required no press credentials to join. As a result, Spencer was still in the ambulance on his way to the hospital, when he began to get calls from reporters, as did his parents, whom he had not had time to tell. A public panic, stirred up by exaggerated media reports,

[1] Spencer, C. (2015). Having and Fighting Ebola—Public Health Lessons from a Clinician Turned Patient | NEJM. (2019). *New England Journal of Medicine*. Retrieved 23 May 2019, from https://www.nejm.org/doi/full/10.1056/NEJMp1501355

swirled through New York and caught national attention. People were angry at him. They lambasted him for moving about the city while symptomatic (which he hadn't been) and questioned his motives for going overseas in the first place. While some publicly praised the young man for risking his life to save others and help stem the tide of a potentially global outbreak, these voices were initially drowned out by the vitriol of others who demanded to know how dare he ride the subway and go bowling. The cover of the *New York Post* shrieked, "EBOLA HERE!"[2] Not-yet-candidate Donald Trump tweeted, "The Ebola doctor who just flew to N.Y. from West Africa and went on the subway, bowling and dining is a very SELFISH man—should have known!"[3] The anxiety reached truly irrational proportions as my former organization, Médecins du Monde USA, was asked by their New York landlords to find new office space immediately, despite the fact that they had not sent any doctors to the Ebola response.

During his stay in isolation at Bellevue Hospital, Spencer became very ill and lost 20 pounds but remained conscious throughout. He doesn't remember reflecting on the high likelihood that he would not survive (at that time, the virus had a 59 percent fatality rate), but he was worried about his fiancée, who was in quarantine at home. His fever finally broke on November 4, 13 days after he was admitted, and the following week, after two negative tests 20 hours apart, he was allowed to go home. The press reports on the day of his release took a very different tone; photos show a smiling Spencer being hugged by Mayor Bill de Blasio and surrounded by cheering hospital staff. Mercifully, his 15 minutes of fame as the Ebola doctor were ending, but Spencer also noticed with dismay that the ongoing epidemic in Africa, and the conditions and international missteps that helped it to spread, had also disappeared from public consciousness once people no longer sensed an imminent local threat. A few months later, fully recovered and newly armed with Ebola antibodies, Spencer returned to West Africa on another deployment.

Although he faced a different sort of lethal risk than the targeted violence this book has described, I chose to include Craig Spencer's experience as a case example of the particular combination of altruism, high-level technical skill, and calculated risk-taking that embodies the professional humanitarian model. He is also a testament to how the benefits of professionalism in humanitarian action flow in both directions. Spencer, who

[2] New York Post cover, 24 October 2014. Retrieved from: https://nypost.com/cover/covers-for-october-24-2014/

[3] @realdonaldtrump (2014, October 24). [Twitter post]. Retrieved from: https://twitter.com/realdonaldtrump/status/525635174877630464?lang=en

continues to volunteer for MSF and teaches at the Columbia University Mailman School of Public Health where he is the Director of Global Health in Emergency Medicine, speaks passionately about how his humanitarian work has made him a better physician. "There are so many things that [as emergency doctors] we are meant to do well, that we never do here in the US," he says. "There's a huge difference between drilling and training and actual first-person experience," he says. "For example, I'm expected to be good at triaging multiple casualties; it's one of our core responsibilities. I've done that zero times in the US, but in Burundi I did it on a daily basis. I'm really good at that stuff."

There is a limit to how effective and responsive a system can be when it continues to run on a charity model, dependent on voluntary contributions from wealthy governments and the empathy of their publics. We saw the limits of public empathy reached abruptly in the fear and hostility that met with Craig Spencer's infection. Unless and until international humanitarian assistance is reorganized and resourced as a global public good, perhaps funded through assessed international contributions like the UN peacekeeping forces, it will continue to depend on a patchwork of autonomous organizations and altruistic individuals with all of the collective shortcomings and lack of accountability that brings. Today, more than 20 years after the Rwanda attack that shook my organization and shifted my career path, attacks on humanitarian aid operations are more numerous and commonplace. As we have seen, governments have not only failed to meaningfully decrease the risk to aid workers, but in some cases they have contributed to them. Humanitarian aid work will not be getting safer any time soon. However, as more aid workers increasingly consider and develop themselves as professionals, rather than as merely employees of an organization or as amateur do-gooders, the more they can reduce their risk and improve outcomes for the people they serve.

Reference

Spencer, C. (2015). Having and Fighting Ebola—Public Health Lessons from a Clinician Turned Patient. *New England Journal of Medicine*. Retrieved May 23, 2019, from https://www.nejm.org/doi/full/10.1056/NEJMp1501355

Index[1]

[1] Note: Page numbers followed by 'n' refer to notes.

A. Stoddard, *Necessary Risks*,
https://doi.org/10.1007/978-3-030-26411-6

The manufacturer's authorised representative in the EU is Springer Nature Customer Service Centre GmbH, Europaplatz 3, 69115 Heidelberg, Germany. If you have any concerns regarding our products, please contact ProductSafety@springernature.com

Printed and bound by CPI Group (UK) Ltd, Croydon, CR0 4YY
05/10/2026
02228123-0001